At a time in actor training institutions when the pressure is on to make vocational training more efficient/economical/expedient, it is refreshing and challenging to encounter a work of deep philosophical reflection and critical examination about what it is we think we are doing to, or for, those who want to become professional actors. This is not yet another book on acting techniques or systems – rather, more importantly, Matthews calls upon teachers and students alike to look 'beneath the skin' as it were and 'make strange' our valuing of, approaches to and experiences of, training. His lyrical meditations on various anatomical 'parts' of the embodied, human experience stretch us to consider afresh what is natural and 'un-natural' such that this polarity is no longer what it seems. One comes away from reading this book with many new insights and questions that hopefully will evoke new conversations for healthily sustainable training practices.

Dr Mark Seton, Honorary Research Associate at the Department of Performance Studies, University of Sydney, Australia

Shamelessly eclectic and enduringly thought provoking, John Matthews' latest intervention into performance training criticism is a highly engaging study. Using an innovative structure of training-as-anatomy – *HAND, FOOT, MOUTH, HEART, EAR* – Matthews treats us to a delicately layered discussion of the 'nascent ideology of training', navigating confidently between evocative vignettes of training experiences to an applied critique of western philosophical thought. Throughout, it is simply and beautifully illustrated, interwoven with a discussion of the craft of woodcutting and printing, prompting us to think productively about the parallel tracks of competence, expertise and mastery.

Prof. Jonathan Pitches, Professor of Theatre and Performance, School of Performance and Cultural Industries, University of Leeds, UK

John Matthews returns to ground he would never call 'his own', but a terroir marked 'training' that has provided the fertile soil for his recent work. On this occasion, in collaboration with woodcut artist Andy Park, an uncertain kind of 'know how' begins to emerge from meditations that allow him to make neighbours of Tom Daley and John the Baptist. While eminent philosophical figureheads such as Peter

Sloterdijk are just getting around to relations between personal training and the self-help generation, *Anatomy of Performance Training* insists such historical processes of preparation for work are ontological and critical to the evolution of human being.

Prof. Alan Read, Professor of Theatre and Director of Performance Foundation, King's College London, UK

In this brilliantly conceived and imaginatively structured book, Matthews opens up the field of training for performance in new and unexpected ways. His erudite yet accessible style is sure to appeal to students and general readers keen to discover why training (and resistance to training) has become so important to the practice of theatre-making.

Prof. Adrian Kear, Professor of Theatre and Performance at Aberystwyth University, UK

A thoughtful, stimulating and wide-ranging text that moves seamlessly across disparate fields of performance and reflects both on their specificities and their similarities.

Prof. Franc Chamberlain, Professor of Drama, Department of Drama, University of Huddersfield, UK

Anatomy of Performance Training provides the student of performance with a wonderful opportunity to delve into the profound physical and philosophical world of the body. Filled with exciting insights and stimulating provocations and challenges, it deepens their theoretical understanding as well as their practice.

Anatomy of Performance Training proposes original innovative insights on the link between theory and practice in performance training; contributes new experiential perspectives to a growing body of writing about practice; provides detailed analysis of the use of the hand, foot, ear, mouth and heart in performance training; and discusses the symbolic and practical significance of that body part in training and in a wider artistic and commercial context.

Niamh Dowling, Head of School of Performance, Rose Bruford College of Theatre and Performance, UK

ANATOMY OF PERFORMANCE TRAINING

ANATOMY OF PERFORMANCE TRAINING

JOHN MATTHEWS

ILLUSTRATIONS BY ANDY PARK

Bloomsbury Methuen Drama
An imprint of Bloomsbury Publishing Plc

B L O O M S B U R Y
LONDON · NEW DELHI · NEW YORK · SYDNEY

Bloomsbury Methuen Drama
An imprint of Bloomsbury Publishing Plc

50 Bedford Square   1385 Broadway
London   New York
WC1B 3DP   NY 10018
UK   USA

www.bloomsbury.com

**BLOOMSBURY, METHUEN DRAMA and the Diana logo are
trademarks of Bloomsbury Publishing Plc**

First published 2014
Copyright © John Matthews, 2014
Illustration copyright © Andy Irvine Park, 2014

British Library Cataloguing-in-Publication Data
A catalogue record for this book is available from the British Library.

ISBN: HB: 978-1-4081-8410-3
PB: 978-1-4081-8405-9
ePDF: 978-1-4081-8505-6
ePub: 978-1-4081-8595-7

Library of Congress Cataloging-in-Publication Data
Matthews, John, 1983-
Anatomy of performance training / by John Matthews.
pages cm
ISBN 978-1-4081-8410-3 (hardback) – ISBN 978-1-4081-8405-9 (paperback)
1. Acting. 2. Performing arts. 3. Movement (Acting) I. Title.
PN2061.M287 2011
792.02'8–dc23
2014009035

Typeset by Integra Software Services Pvt. Ltd
Printed and bound in Great Britain

For our beloved daughter, Gwen

CONTENTS

ACKNOWLEDGEMENTS

Thank you, Faith. Your support and the happy, peaceful space you have made in our lives for me to work made this book, and makes everything, possible. I love you.

Special thanks also to my family, my mother, Mal, my father, Ian, to Jef and Jan, Dave and Alexa, Max and Lorna and Gwen's great-grandparents and cousins. Your love, and good company have inspired me to think, to work and to write.

Thanks to my friends Lee and Victor, who helped me to conceive of the book; Roberta, who has helped me to bring this book to fruition; Adam, Prarthana and Ruth, who have given me new ways to think about, to see and to be a body; and to Jenny and John at Methuen Drama for your generous and creative support throughout.

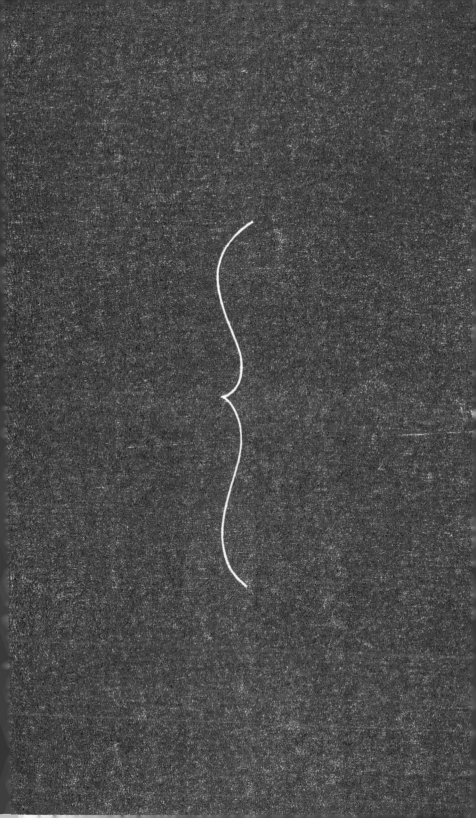

1
FIRST CUT

This book looks a little bit different to most theatre books. It is illustrated throughout with original woodcut prints, by Andy Park, an illustrator who lives and works on the South East Coast of England and who trained at Camberwell College of Art.

Woodcutting is what we might call a traditional or artisan craft and the techniques used have survived, if not thrived, over time. Woodcutting involves cutting an image into a block of wood, or rather cutting an image out of a block of wood by removing the surrounding areas, leaving the image in relief. The work is done by hand with sharp gouges and it is painstaking and precise. The image must be made in lateral inverse form so that when the block is inked and a paper is pressed onto the block with a paper press, contacting the ink on the relief, it leaves the imprint of the cuts, now the right way around on the page. Finally, in this case, these images are digitized for publication under Andy's watchful eye, which is all the time seeking to preserve something of his first cuts in the final image.

The principle of woodcutting is simple, but the practice of producing blocks, and prints from blocks, is anything but. Woodcutting involves sharp tools and careful hands, and acquiring the skills that Andy possesses results not only from tuition but also long periods of experimentation, trial and error, ruined wood blocks and hand wounds.

Woodcutting, like many traditional crafts, draws its appeal from the sense of its continuity through time but I wasn't being nostalgic when I asked Andy to illustrate this book; I asked Andy to illustrate the book in order to know, and to show, more about how skilled practitioners work.

Over the course of working with Andy on the illustrations, I have learnt that when carving wood Andy follows the example of others, his tuition and his intuition, and his imagination as well as the wood itself.

He must find the *right* cuts to make, working with the limitations of the wood, the grain and textures, its depth and imperfections. He *knows* the right cuts to make, from experience, expertise, imagination and his sense of taste but he only *finds* the right cuts in concert with the wood. For Andy, the wood is a summons to his intellect, imagination and skill and in this way the act of his illustrating is characteristic of all practitioners engaged in performance of their practice. These illustrations exemplify Andy's training and they are the residue of the encounter between his expertise and the world and its things.

The hands that Andy uses to carve embody his expertise, as is so for practitioners of all handicrafts but Andy's feet, ears, mouth and heart have also played a very particular part in the accumulation of this know-how. In the chapters that follow I work anatomically by cutting one part from another, much as Andy works on the wood, to describe how hands, feet, mouths, ears and hearts, such as his, are used practically and metaphorically by and in training.

Through training, people obtain competency and expertise, and some attain mastery. The handiwork of experts bears the hallmarks of this process, sometimes quite literally as is the case of jewellers and meta-workers, but more importantly within their practice and its products. Through training, practitioners learn the right way to use tools, exercise judgement, move and rely on their bodies and intellect in the performance of given tasks. The development of talent, the transfer of knowledge and the continuation of practices are all accomplished through training but, for individuals, training may also meet a particular need and lead towards a sense of a more perfect or correct version of self.

Andy is an illustrator because he can make beautiful woodcuts but, seemingly paradoxically and as I will show in this book, he is also an illustrator because he can also choose to *not* cut wood.

For Andy, to learn to be an illustrator is to become something that he already felt himself to be. Some people would say this differently – that Andy has recognized an ambition, but he would say that illustrating is not what he does, but is an aspect of what he is. This personal and deeply felt attraction to the task of making wood cut prints tells us something about Andy, and about the human condition that we all share in. How these primary desires relate to the accumulation of expertise, the stabilization of professional roles and identities and the continuation of practice through time is a matter of training.

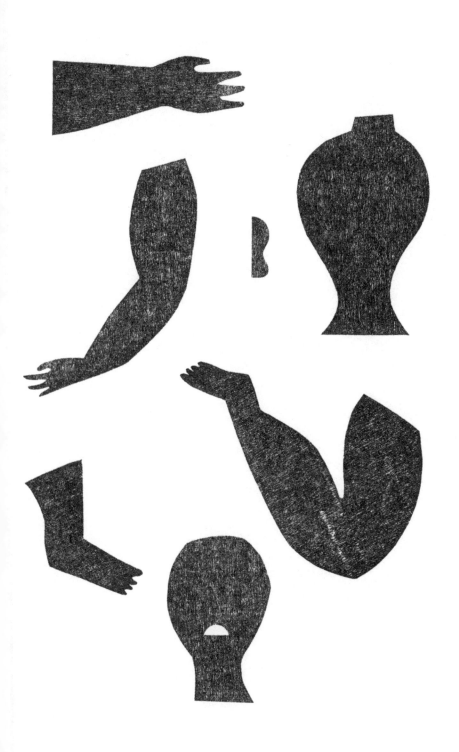

2
ANATOMY

This book makes a set of simple but challenging claims: training is and always has been a response to the problems experienced as a result of having a body and being in the world; training is not something that some of us do, it is something that we all do, although some of us do it and talk about doing it in a particularly self-conscious and organized way; seemingly paradoxically, training arises because of our humanness but training also exists to produce and reproduce specific values about humanness; because of the specific problems posed by being a body-in-the-world today, training has achieved a new currency as a global ideology.

Each of these claims results from contrasting the relationship between training and the human condition with the relationship between training and the socially constructed determinants of being human. *The Human Condition* is the seminal philosophical work by Hannah Arendt (1958), in which she describes the fundamental categories of human life in modernity. The book, and the concept, defines the shared or common features of being human and living amongst other humans, as we did through modernity, and still do after more-or-less surviving what Lyotard not coincidentally called *The Postmodern Condition*.[1] Indeed, for Arendt, being amongst others is one given condition of humanity (which she calls 'plurality') and one that determines facets of our private sense of identity as well as our actions and responsibilities, irrespective of the epochs of theory and cultural production that we humans move through.[2]

My understanding of the human condition comes from Arendt and it is an idea that has taken hold in the collective consciousness today as one aspect of what Roland Robertson, a leading scholar of globalization, has called the 'thematization of humankind'[3] throughout the twentieth century. Consciousness of the world as one place and of humans as one thing within it has, according to Robertson, intensified from the mid-1960s to the present.[4] If we are now living *after postmodernism,* as many, including the sociologist José López and the anthropologist Garry Potter, have suggested, then our new epoch may be characterized by a reappraisal of the significance of a priori concepts, such as the human condition, so thoroughly battered by the epistemological assault of postmodernity.[5] Professors of English and Politics, respectively, Philip Tew and Bertell Ollman both refer to the idea of a 'human condition' in their essays on political and literary life after postmodernism.[6] For them, and for Garry Potter, aspects of the human condition include pain, needs, wants, time, space and, in concord with Arendt, social life.[7]

Following the efforts of this group to understand human life during postmodernism, and during its decline,[8] I am inspired to juxtapose the shared and common features of the human condition, as defined by Arendt and others, with the social constructs of humanness that still, despite the postmodern attack on them, predominate in theory and in social life at the turn of the twenty first century. In this book and through this set of simple claims I am interested to know, and to show, not only how training arises from given human conditions but also how it relates to the conditions that societies have constructed for human living.

Each claim derives from my research into a broad range of training practices. This participatory research has involved learning techniques of performance and teaching actors, observing physiotherapeutic rehabilitation, investigating elite high diving and deep diving training, partaking weekly in yoga classes and living daily in a Benedictine monastery.

Surprising, as it may seem, these diverse practices intersect historically as well as technically. Yoga, for example, is associated with the leisure paradigm also encompassing sport, as well as with spirituality and religious training and more specifically in this context, with twentieth-century European approaches to actor preparation, which is where my own disciplinary expertise lies. The iconic twentieth-century actor-trainers Konstantin Stanislavski[9] and Jerzy Grotowski[10] each considered the uses and suitability of yoga in the preparation of actors and, in my own experience of making theatre with different companies, yoga has provided a physical basis for ensemble relations in rehearsal. In my researches for this book, I have come to yoga through friends and colleagues in dance and theatre at Plymouth, and especially through Lee Miller, who has trained as a yoga teacher and undertook to practise his teaching on me during his formal training.

My interest in deep diving, or rather the breath holding (apnea) required in order to dive to depths, is specifically to do with the phenomenon of bradycardia, or reduced heart rate, and with humans' aquatic history. We live in water before we live on land and, as anthropological research has shown, humans have taken to the depths for survival for millennia.[11] This means that although apnea is associated with an elite group of athletes undertaking exclusive training in specific relaxation, breathing and swimming techniques, it is also an activity intimately linked to our biological existence and our human history. I write about breath holding in light of my interests in this book with the human condition and the historicizing of moments of training practice.

Deep diving, made possible by breath holding, sits alongside high diving as an example of a training context in this book. I have researched a facet of diver Tom Daley's training in the run-up to the 2012 Olympics through interview and correspondence with Ben Dunks, a choreographer employed by Daley's team, but I am most interested in this example here because, as with the heart under water, the ear plays a very specific role in relation to bodies per se, especially in relation to their environments. The human condition entails not only history but also locality, and the training practices associated with Daley's Olympic preparation enable a meditation on the relations between bodies, spaces and the things in the world.

In this book I also draw vignettes of expert practice in art and science – from the life stories of Galileo Galilee and Oscar Wilde. Art and science represent twin pillars of training discourse historically, which links the individual human condition to the social condition of humans. As John Dewey pointed out in his seminal work, *Democracy and Education*, teaching is a means of the 'social continuity of life'.[12] The 'primary ineluctable facts of the birth and death of each one of the constituent members in a social group' make teaching a necessity because as individuals die, 'the life of the group goes on',[13] and the continuity through time of technical expertise in art and science represents this fact.

In addition to these practices and contexts, I have an ongoing research interest in acting and dancing, religious (and more specifically monastic) and rehabilitation training techniques. My interest in acting began when I was cast in a film drama as a schoolboy. I hadn't attended an audition; in fact, I didn't even realize I was being auditioned when I, along with a group of similarly blonde-haired and blue-eyed boys, was invited to the school library to read some scenes with two affable men who turned up at our classroom one day. The production company were visiting schools in South Wales, where the drama was filmed and where I grew up, searching for an untrained boy – apparently they did not want one of the many thousands of professional child actors – to complete the cast. That chance event began a career, which finds me writing this book now and has left me to meditate as to whether I was cast because of a perceived talent or simply because I looked like the blonde-haired and blue-eyed actress already cast in the role of my mother. If the former, what are the determinants of such 'talent', and if the latter, does aptitude always boil down to equations as simple as this? I consider such questions around talent and professional induction in my analyses of training in institutional contexts throughout the chapters that follow.

My interest in rehabilitative medicine as a training context arose during observations of physiotherapy on stroke rehabilitation wards and residential care homes in South Wales. I became interested in rehabilitation as training after recognizing that much of the practice of acting technique that I had encountered since this boyhood experience of performance seemed to be corrective, concerned with fixing problems and rectifying mistakes – for example, counteracting stage fright, involuntary laughter and the forgetting of lines. The notion that training is as much remedial as it is idealizing is tested in this book.

In the summer of 2006, I lived in a Benedictine monastery in West Sussex after becoming absorbed in understanding the historical antecedents of the ascetical demands of the actor training regimes and systems dominating my experience of professional theatre in the twentieth century. Taking what I had read about the 'holy actor'[14] quite literally, I started to wonder where the rigours of acting technique that I was learning originated. Understanding and describing the development, transferral and hybridization of ideas and ideals about training over time is something that I aim to do here in order to show how the common activity of training structurates specific disciplinary examples.

I began conducting research into this broad spectrum of disciplines of training in preparation for my first book, *Training for Performance,* which set out to describe an ontological category of activity, called 'training', manifest in each discipline. *Anatomy of Performance Training* is, in one sense at least, a sequel, or rather the next episode in my continuing project to better understand and better describe the genus of training.

Training for Performance concluded by suggesting that the model of embodiment therein might open up some different ways of thinking about the phenomena that have preoccupied theatre and performance studies in the early twenty-first century and, in this sense, this book picks up where the first left off and builds on the conclusions of *Training for Performance* to show how the general category of training derives from and is co-constitutive of the human condition. *Anatomy of Performance Training* goes into new territory to show how training produces and determines through the body a nascent ideology of training that is asserting itself today.

It is not necessary to have read *Training for Performance* in order to understand the claims made in this book but it might help any readers who haven't if I summarize what the 'training' in *Anatomy of Performance Training* denotes. In an effort to define the meanings of training, generically, when used in a specific disciplinary context, I described training philosophically, as a category of experience composed of at least four processes – vocation, obedience, formation and automatization. These processes feature in all instances where the word 'training' is used in its commonly understood meaning.

Two of the processes defined, vocation and obedience, are recapitulated here in *MOUTH* and *EAR* and these refer to a private aspect of the training experience – one's sense of a very personal summons by and within a given task or activity and the form of practical response entailed by this. The conceptualization of these processes as integral to training, and to its differentiation from discipline, was influenced by the deontological philosophy of the imperative.[15]

In philosophy, the imperative is the ontological force that commands human minds to thought and to action. As Alphonso Lingis describes it, the imperative 'is not a concept...is not a principle, or a law or an order', but rather it is a 'given, a fact'; it is 'the first fact'.[16] The imperative 'is a command that there be principles and that our thought represent order – or that we represent the unprincipled and the chaotic correctly'[17] and it is met with at once in our encounter with the world and its things.

The philosophy of the imperative has a long history – the Stoics found the imperative in the order of the cosmos, while early Christians found the imperative in the creative nature of God and of Man. More recently, Immanuel Kant found the imperative in thinking itself, and in the command to think and to think rightly.[18] For Kant this command possessed a moral dimension – act in such a way that you would be content for your actions to be the law – and the imperfect moral behaviour of humankind, in essence, our failure to treat others as we would ourselves wish to be treated, could be understood in relation to conformity, or contrariety, with the imperative.[19]

Although my theorization of training is influenced by this philosophy, I don't think readers of this book need to dwell within it too formally. I am more interested to describe training in relation to personal and individual experiences of being human. Personally, I have the strong sense that some things that I do are *right* – morally, technically, aesthetically and so on – and some are not, and that my sense of the rightness of my actions is not only to do with the conventions that I have absorbed because of my particular cultural position.[20] I also have the sense that some of my actions do not meet requirements, and that these requirements are not only my own enculturated expectations but rather that my actions fall short of a categorical obligation. The world poses so many problems, and in relation to some of these, I am up to the task and in others I am conscious of my own inadequacy. Addressing this disparity would seem to be a key concern for training.

Raymond Carver expressed his very personal sense of the imperative, and of his response to the command it lays down in his poem *Radio Waves:* 'there is in the soul a desire for not thinking. For being still. Coupled with this a desire to be strict, yes, and rigorous. But the soul is also a smooth son of a bitch, not always trustworthy. And I forgot that.'[21] If you can relate to this feeling, then let these words be a guiding light through the more formally philosophical sections of this book; this is, in essence, what we are talking about when we talk about the imperative.

The other two processes of training that I described in my first book, formation – the process of change experienced through the accumulation of expertise – and automatization – the capacity towards action entailed in expertise – emerge implicitly throughout this book, and specifically in *HEART*, in a discourse on self-representation, and in *HAND*, in an account of the skill of prehension. These more apparent and, in one sense, superficial aspects of training have dominated discourse on training in theatre and performance but the philosophical account of vocation and obedience and a foregrounding of the desire, as Carver has it, to *do things right* unifies the different disciplines and discourses of training you will encounter herein.

The new commentary on these meta-disciplinary aspects of training offered here shows how these processes derive from the human condition and constitute body concepts, and our sense of humanness. The philosophy of the imperative influenced my account of each of these aspects of the training experience, but in this book I move my account on to connect with discourses and philosophies of the body and the ideological and epistemological conditions of training.

My books sit within a field of work that sees aesthetic performances as one subspecies of performance per se, and there are many excellent models for bringing together different forms of performance activity within this field. Jon Mckenzie's *Perform or Else: From Discipline to Performance*[22] draws upon space travel engineering, workplace productivity and management theory and experimental art to demonstrate how all three operate together under a broad-spectrum paradigm of performance. I build on McKenzie's research to show how this paradigm is embedded and reasserted culturally through a nascent ideology of training, that can be conceptualized as an emergent form of a more general class of human activity (of training). By demonstrating how training methodologies and values oscillate between aesthetic and social and cultural fields, both historically and in current practice, this book describes the ideological resurgence of the generalized class of activity that I defined in *Training for Performance*.

In addition to participation in a catholic range of activities of training, my research has involved historical study of training practices and their associated ideologies and theories, particularly of the body. Having, or being, a body is, as social theory has made clear, both a physical and propositional fact. When we talk about the body, we talk not only about the physical envelop for our experiences of the world but also about the constructs and concepts determining the experiences of our bodies, each other's bodies and the world. This latter, propositional concern is what theorists tend to be talking about when they refer to embodiment. The embodiment of this or that social position, cultural value, sexual or gender identity means the way in which the different aspects of my experience of myself in the world – social, cultural and so on – are represented, or experienced, by my physical being.

Self-evidently, the physical body has primacy in our personal histories; we discover and live with it before we get to grips with concepts about it. It probably also has primacy in the evolutionary narrative of human civilization, which has ultimately given rise to the propositional body.[23] This subsequent interest in the propositional body has assumed a privileged place in discourse in the mid-to-late twentieth century.

The sociologist Arthur Frank wrote an overview of literature on the body and concluded that the mid-1990s interest in this area was emerging in social history, clinical psychiatry, anthropology and philosophy simultaneously, and that this interest was arising out of and because of modernism, postmodernism and feminism. In his book *Theatre, Body and Pleasure* (2013), Simon Shepherd points out that this is a bit like saying that the interest in the body in late twentieth-century Western culture arose because of the concerns of late twentieth-century Western culture, but Frank's conceptualization of the relation between body and culture is more nuanced than this.

Frank saw a different relation between body and culture proposed by modernism, postmodernism and feminism. Modernism saw the body as both a constant in a changing world and as a driver and subject of that change, while, for postmodernism, both high theory and low culture dispute the body, what it means and what it does, socially. Through feminism, politics takes over all other representative functions of bodies and Shepherd claims that this – feminism – has provided most impetus to performance and theatre studies.

Shepherd's analysis of the role of theatre in modelling the relation between bodies and culture restates the impact of feminist body art on society in general and theatre specifically in the 1960s and 1970s. The 1960s counterculture revalued the body for its naturalness, and thus its resistance to undesirable social values, forces and positions. This countercultural movement picked up and renovated the theories of F.M. Alexander, Moshe Feldenkrais and others, who in the decades before had advanced a minority position that society was responsible tout court for physical and psychological damage to bodies and that a state of naturalness had to be recuperated through the body, by forms of play and against the organization imposed by culture.

Taking this mass of mid-to-late twentieth-century theorizing together, as part of a broad, Western cultural narrative about the body, Shepherd utilizes the performance studies technique for interrogating social and cultural performances – everyday and ritualized performances of cultural values and identities – through the dramaturgy of the playing of aesthetic roles, and vice versa. He takes the familiar position that 'when a body is prepared for the theatre, this is a specific instance, and operates within the context, of the general process whereby a culture produces the body'.[24]

Performance studies has since its earliest anthropological interests tended to see theatre as a specific instance of cultural performances more generally, or, to see cultural performances as exemplified by theatrical ones. Indeed, Erving Goffman's sociological analysis of *The Presentation of Self in Everyday Life,* which as Shepherd rightly says has proved paradigmatic to performance studies, used a dramaturgical metaphor to describe cultural performance per se, or as Shepherd has it, 'used a vocabulary of dramatic terms to describe human behaviour in everyday life'.[25]

Theatre is, as Victor Turner and Richard Schechner argued, 'an emergent form of a more general class of human activity'[26] and collapsing the distinctions between everyday and aesthetic performances in order to better understand the general class of activity is a central, and arguably definitive methodological approach of performance studies.

Amidst the theorizing of performance studies, theatrical presentations and preparations have emerged as one form amongst other forms of cultural performance, and also as the one form capable of representing and explaining all the others; the logic of naturalistic characterization, and of *playing a role* more generically speaking, reveals and typifies the structures and process of all social role-playing and modelling and renders these open to analysis.

Subsequently, analysis, such as Shepherd's has tended to have a cultural materialist dimension and to consider the operation of political forces on and through bodies in the project of larger movements and interests. For Shepherd, political forces are imbricated with corporeal experience through and by principles, such as pleasure. This imbrication binds together the personal and the cultural and perpetuates certain material values – ethical, economical, political and aesthetical – and extirpates others. The particular patternation of values – the mosaic of totems and taboos – varies from culture to culture and age to age but the means of patternation and its rights and wrongs continue in perpetuity.

All of this twentieth-century theorizing of performance – synthesizing of anthropological and sociological techniques with theatrical-dramaturgical methods and post-structuralist philosophy – has in effect sought to explore how mimesis is embedded within cultures, and the possibilities and dangers that this poses.

Given that theatre is one form of a more general activity, the dramaturgical metaphor may not properly belong to theatre. Imitation and role modelling, which is the definitive activity of theatre in this form of theorizing, certainly doesn't because, as Aristotle wrote, 'imitation is a distinctive feature of man from his childhood: imitation separates him from the animals and it is through imitation that he acquires his earliest knowledge'.[27] In this light, imitation might be reasonably seen as an aspect of the human condition, as essential to humans as plurality or pain; even though Plato famously assaulted theatre in book X of *The Republic* – a fact that has brought perverse satisfaction to practitioners and theorists of theatre alike – he really only does so because theatrical mimesis is the tip of the iceberg; is setting a bad example; is the thin end of the wedge.[28] The real worry is mimesis at large and it is most worrisome to stable society when it occurs in social relations and not representations of these relations.

So, although theatre does not own mimesis, theatre, and performances and rituals more generally, can be understood as a cultural repository for mimetic activity and so we might use theatre and the dramaturgical metaphor as shorthand for the mimetic faculty. This faculty is associated with the broader paradigm of performance which, as Jon Mckenzie has shown, may be concerned with attainment first and foremost and not representation – to perform on stage is really to attain representation and not merely to represent, which happens all the time and anyway (and this is the problem with it). These two aspects of performance theory – mimetic faculty and attainment, measured subjectively – relate to the ideological determinants of humanness that I will come to describe as reliant upon training activity.

With all this in mind, in writing about training for performance I am concerned with the preparation and execution of social roles, subject and identity positions by means of the mimetic faculty but also with the specific requirements to perform (to attain) germane to each discipline.

Much productive thinking in sociology and anthropology has arisen as a consequence of seeing all performances – social, cultural, everyday and so on – as *a bit like theatre*. This has enabled theatre studies to step off the stage and to encounter a range of ritualized performances occurring across culture, and cultures. Theatrical performances and their traditions and techniques of preparation can give insight onto other techniques of preparation for other performances but in defining the generalized category of training, it is vital to maintain a sense of history and specificity. Historically, techniques of training may have transferred to the performance field from other fields, and vice versa. In writing about performance training from a philosophical or historical perspective theatre does not have a special monopoly on the discussion but I do hope that within the discussions that follow something new is learnt for and about theatre.

Rather than asking *what theatre can do for you,* as you and I live our social, cultural, ethical, religious, economic, sexual and political lives, and theorize about these, I am more concerned to show what these lives and theories have done for, to and with theatre; to show how viewing theatre training through the prism of religious training, athletic training or rehabilitation might allow for the kind of self-reflection that occurs when we see ourselves mirrored in the practices and creations of others; and to situate training for theatrical performance amongst – and not above, before or beneath – training for other forms of performance, and to do so in order to better understand the category of training and its role in human civilizations today.

The theoretical position, wherein theatre enables us to understand every other form of performance better, is a recent locus of thought, which in the canonical theatre history runs a through-line between the 'body art' that interests Shepherd, naturalism and the various 'isms' of the 1900s, Restoration and Renaissance drama, medieval and mystery plays and to a constructed point of origin on the ancient Greek stage.[29] At this point of origin sits drama, and much of the theorizing about it, which is still in circulation today. The formal concerns about character, plot and action first expressed in relation to the Greek stage were accompanied by a discourse on ethics – through which the mimetic question was introduced – and also training, state-based as well as the activities associated with personal self-realization.[30]

At this point, which is of course not the Ur-performance but simply *a* performance, well documented, European and at the origins of recorded history, the body emerges at the centre of discourse on representation and training. Training here referred to the proper preparation of civic actors, an exclusive group then as ever afterwards. With reference to this history, Simon Shepherd writes that 'the theatre is, and always has been, a place which exhibits what a human body is, what it does, and what it is capable of'[31] and, for the Greek theatre that was, proper education was a primary concern in relation to the capability of bodies.

Socrates, philosopher of education and dramatist at large during this moment, introduced a method of enquiry – usually called the Socratic method – that still forms the basis of educational theory today. The command placed on the mind to proper reason, which troubled Raymond Carver's soul, results, through the deductive, dialectic method in knowledge, in the form of irreducible conclusions, and shapes the intellect through the application by it of shared and immutable principles of reasoning.

For Plato, after Socrates, education of this form could provide the basis for a state-sponsored instructional training that would help to shape not only individual intellects but also a responsible society. Plato's system of public education aims to produce a ruling class to have stewardship of the Republic; the body politic will rest on the proper preparation of selected bodies.

Aristotle would appear to have been as concerned by practical expertise as by intellectual mastery and he stressed the importance of habit alongside reason. He also showed a greater interest in the education of children than Socrates, whose approach could be retrofitted to the uncultivated adult intellect, and in play and physical exercise.

The classical thinkers, Socrates, Plato and Aristotle, described training as fundamental to humanity, to the shaping of human bodies and intellects to moral ends. So, from this point, body, training, theatre, politics and ethics are aligned in the project of human happiness and virtue (which are the same thing in Aristotle's philosophy). Aristotle asks in *The Nichomachean Ethics* 'whether happiness is to be acquired by learning or by habituation or by some other sort of training'[32] and concludes that intellectual and moral virtue – right thinking and right acting – will only arise because of teaching and habit. Doing *the right thing* will habitually lead to more *doing of the right thing* but cultivating the intellect, which will be necessary for happiness, will require instruction of one person by another, and the responsibility for this training falls on grownups because, 'it makes no small difference, then, whether we form habits of one kind or another from our very youth; it makes a very great difference, or rather *all* the difference'.[33] 'The man who is to be good must be well trained and habituated',[34] wrote Aristotle, proposing an ideology that still holds strong even during postmodernism's decline.

Shepherd identifies the persistence of this ideology amidst the various patternations of cultures when he writes, 'many ideas about what is good, right, natural and possible are grounded in assumptions about what the body is, what it needs and how it works'.[35] In a postmodern moment, performance theory has been more often at pains to point out this fact than to take a particular position on what *is* good, right, natural or possible or even what the body is, what it needs or how it works in any given context.

Although postmodernism largely neutralized categories such as 'good' and 'natural', I do seek to take a position on the no less problematic 'sense of authenticity', in relation to training in this book. Through my approach to the body I aim to show not what is possible but what is necessary for embodied performances and to conceptualize what the body needs and how it works in relation to its environment today. These efforts will be formed by the particular patternation of my own cultural position and my own ethical and political concerns about training but they will also show the concerns within training itself, as an historic phenomenon and newly emergent ideology reformulating and reasserting Aristotle's claim about the 'good man' in a new contemporary context where 'good' is harder to define.

If in what I have said thus far there is a confusing co-mingling of training and education, then this represents not only both strands of Aristotle's thinking – about private habits and public responsibilities – but also the messy politics of bodies in relation to conceptual learning and skill acquisition. Aristotle argued that 'men of experience know that a thing is, but they do not know why it is, whereas men of learning know the reason and the cause'[36] and this distinction exists today in the opposition between 'academic' and 'vocational' training. This manifests in the global education economy as a differential between degree programmes and apprenticeships and, as we can see, is not a new phenomenon. The implied distinction between *real* learning and operational expertise, between knowledge and skill has a particular social history and I will be discussing this in *MOUTH, FOOT, HAND, HEART* and *EAR*.

This distinction between thinking and doing – which Shepherd has described as a subplot within Frank's narrative of the body, telling the tale of 'resistance to the assumed (masculinist) separation of body and mind'[37] – has a particular history within the specific scholarly field of performer training.[38] This history is tied not only to feminism, as Shepherd writes, but also to the dynamics of the theatre event and the enthusiastic ethnography of late twentieth-century training practitioners. I wrote about this in detail in *Training for Performance* and will have cause to say more in *FOOT*.[39]

Aristotle wrote that 'it is precisely [nature's] deficiencies which art and education seek to make good'.[40] In this way, art and education are projects concerned with being humans and becoming properly or more perfectly human. The philosophy of training that I advanced in *Training for Performance* is, in the chapter *HEART* in this book, shown to work as rehabilitation through the body of the deficiency inherent in the human condition, which has a renewed urgency in all areas of our lives today.

HEART, *HAND*, *FOOT*, *MOUTH* and *EAR* each provide a differently attuned meditation on practical, symbolic and metaphorical aspects of training. This anatomy of the body maps onto the anatomy of training – consistent of vocation, obedience, formation and automatization – and my anatomical approach in this book enables me to delineate the problems of having, or being, a body-in-the-world today.

Anatomy is a science, or art, of the physical body, but as a methodology it relates to both the physical and propositional body. Anatomy dissects bodies to isolate the operations of individual parts in the existence of the whole and this method can be applied to the body concept and its different constructs in order to show the interrelation between each. Analysing in detail the symbolic role of body parts in a range of training practices will help to explain the development and operations of constructs of the body by and through training.

Anatomy of the kind I am proposing, Anna Furse reminds me, has a particular and quite recent history, 'Western culture has…privileged objectivity and distance since the Renaissance when both the vanishing point in art and anatomical dissection in medicine elevated a perspective on nature and the world, not a commingling with it'.[41] This perspective, like all perspectives, is deceptive and ideological, reaffirming the prestige of the anatomist over the anatomized just as in art 'the private owner's position of power over the artefact and his judgement on its composition' gave it value as commodity.[42]

There is then a cultural dimension to my approach, and to my examples, which are drawn largely from what Furse calls 'Western' culture, even if this amorphous thing called 'Western culture' is, as Robertson has suggested, colonizing, absorbing, hybridizing and living parasitically within all cultures.[43] The category of training arises because of the human condition and the development of this category into an emergent ideology within a globalized culture reproduces particular values about humanness, and these are not innately human but culturally specific.

Training's role as an emergent ideology globally can be seen in the context of the volume of research into globalized culture, and more specifically the international New Age movement and its relation to 'mainstream' media and workplace culture. Personal growth, self-development and the realization of one's individual potential are core principals of the New Age spiritual movement, which, as the preeminent Paul Heelas has shown, is ever-expanding across the globe, so much so that 'to change for the better, has become so widely adopted that it might be said that our culture amounts to the "age of training"'.[44]

Working in this same area, Steve Bruce has shown that the spread of these values is not only measured by the explicit growth of spiritual movements and groups but also by the extent to which all people are influenced by the New Age in their everyday life.[45] Andrew Ross and Wendy Parkins have also indicated that these values are not confined to 'new agers' but that they permeate mainstream culture globally through television programmes and business management and consultancy training cultures.[46]

International studies by Paul Heelas,[47] Richard Roberts,[48] Hildegard Van Hove[49] and Adam Possamai[50] all emphasize the global reach of these values by showing a strong correlation between the New Age and neoliberal capitalism and globalized consumer culture in post-, or late-modern societies. I am interested in showing in this book how training embeds these 'propositional' values within culture through very particular activities of and with the physical body, and yet how the ability for training to circulate and entrench sociological values derives from its relation to the ontological human condition.

This book moves between these two contexts – the human condition and sociocultural values and constructs of humanness – and I will endeavour to signpost these moves clearly as they happen. In oscillating criticism and theory between these two positions analysis shifts from the local to the global and from the specific disciplinary and cultural to the general categorical. Sometimes disciplinary examples are discussed with reference to their own values, and the relation of these to training per se and sometimes specific disciplines are illustrative of a wider phenomenon of training. Again, I will try to make clear which is happening when and I hope that I won't be seen to compromise the specificity of each example as I expand and contract my focus.

All of the training contexts about which I write are participating in the global culture through which the training ideology spreads. There are practices and cultures not participating, or participating less fully, in this globalized culture and critics of this work will be right to single these out. However, this globalized culture and the attendant ideology of training helping to promulgate its values can consume everything, and perhaps will, and I aim to identify some of the ways by which this is being done, in *FOOT* in particular.

There is a socioeconomic implication to anatomy in the sense that my approach subjects practices and bodies and bonds them within an inverse power relation. (As if power relations are ever anything but.) As Furse writes, 'since power is maintained by acuity' in this model, and from a 'vantage point' from which *everything* can be seen, it might be associated with the belief that 'we also find throughout human history that the upper classes work … at a remove, whilst the lower class work' close-up, 'touching stuff'.[51] Furse maintains that this might still be the case in a technological age where this 'stuff' might be a keyboard in a call centre, although the democratizing effects of technologies such as the personal computer complicate this presumed division.

Either way, my anatomical method clearly brings some problems. Firstly, it is associated with a decidedly 'Western' paradigm that might place limits on what it can accommodate. Secondly and relatedly, it derives from research modelled on economic relations that denigrate difference and that exclude the objective intellect from the objects of its imagination. Thirdly (and relatedly), it has a particular class dimension whereby the viewer maintains power over the viewed, and this equation has precedents in theatre scholarship usually bound up with theatre architecture and the stratified pricing of seating, and terms like 'the gaze'.[52]

Each of these methodological problems can be seen as symptomatic of the global cultural paradigm which training is helping to generate and sustain. These problems represent ideological principles, which have been grown and exported by the assurgency of training discourse in an expanding service sector economy and the inculcation of class, gender and intellectual values internationally by this globalizing movement.[53] Pursuing the anatomical method as an attempt to reveal the operation of training in an epistemological context represents a self-evident problem of epistemological theorizing in general – that, as Harold Veeser claims, every act of unmasking uses the tools that it critiques, and risks falling prey to these.[54]

There is perhaps another, related problem in the sense that anatomical parts imply a whole and that anatomy is a science of uniformity and totality and human bodies are not, as each of us knows and experiences, uniform or total. This problem could be linked with the problem of theory itself and to what Emmanuel Levinas has called 'Greek thinking', in relation to the classical civilization. Greek thinking, for Levinas, is an 'ontological mode that seeks to describe the whole',[55] which takes objects 'captive with a "totalising" method that acknowledges only what conforms to its categorical scheme'.[56] In contrast to Greek thinking, Hebrew thinking is 'dialogical' and 'never complete'.[57] Methodologically, anatomy oscillates between these two ontologies – while it might presuppose integration and unity within the whole it operates by dissection and comparison, studying *the relations between* in a never-ending opening out of the body.

The Greek terms 'theory' and 'logic' have been conflated such that it is often thought that the former cannot exist without the latter; that a *theos*, or way of seeing, cannot occur without a *logos*, or a ground on which to be based. Thus, theory is grounded in rationality and rationality is predicated upon immutable logic, derived from repeatable results.

This historical view of theory contains anachronism – 'repeatable results' being a modern criterion for logical reasoning, as opposed to the more ancient attunement to values derived by reason alone. Greek thinking is not, of course, *classically* Greek but rather is an historical invention of the modern scientific method and the pervasiveness of this myth is testament to the totalizing power of the very idea of objectivity. Thus, all of the problems with anatomy that I have outlined so far are now tied together as problems of 'Western' thinking and the science of objectivity.

Entering the territories of training by a particular methodology, of the viewer-viewed dynamic (which of course relates to what has been said about acuity and the politics of spectating), might help to mitigate some of these problems. The anthropologist Tamara Kohn wrote of the so-called 'participant-observation' method as being 'born out of necessity' and becoming a defining feature of the discipline of anthropology.[58] The forms of knowledge generated by this method risk the imposition of the observer's ideas on the participants' experience as well as the production of generalized and subjective accounts shaped by the perspective of the participant, posing as apparently objective, observational knowledge. These anxieties not withstanding a participatory approach borrowed from anthropology has become the defining methodology of theatre research into training, carefully utilized, sensitive to these dangers, by many scholars, including and for example, Philip Zarrilli, Paul Allain, Alison Hodge and Rebecca Loukes.[59]

Where I beg difference from this group is in the respect that although I participate in disciplines of training I am not primarily researching or writing about *this* discipline, or *that* discipline, or even all disciplines but rather I am writing about what is common within these disciplines.

In previous work I have used a technique of writing, common to this specific field, of describing my own participation in training exercises and using this description as a basis for analysis. Alan Read has called this 'presentee-ism'[60] precisely because the implicit suggestion is that being present and involved at the site of training is equivalent to expertise in that training. In my previous book I used a technique of description, inspired by John Laws,[61] called 'allegory', which entailed exhaustive or eclectic descriptive accounts of isolated moments in training conceived to contain more information than was necessary for analysis, and so to show the incompleteness of the analytical theorizing. In this book I have tried to follow a slightly different approach in writing about research, and one more directly informed by philosophical writing than anthropology, ethnography or social theory. This involves description of a premise, situation or event as representative of an abstract problem or proposition and the intent is to talk about the problem or proposition abstractly by writing about the event or premise.

This technique is common in philosophical writing where there is no requirement for the author to be *in* the description or even to describe real historical events. A good example of the approach can be found in the writing of the social justice philosopher Adam Hosein. In his essay 'Being Yourself'[62] Hosein describes set-piece moments from teen movies and stage plays to outline the different dimensions of the social expectations placed on teenagers. His intention was not to speak *about* these moments, as would a film or theatre theorist, but rather to speak *through* these moments about the values that they express or contain. Hosein suggests that this 'standard philosophical approach', which he calls the Method of Cases, might be developed by drawing examples from art because 'we sometimes find that art pushes our moral sensibilities in one direction or another rather than just reflecting our "common sense" reactions'.[63]

This particular approach can be seen to derive from a Foucauldian epistemological philosophy where the episteme is a formation within history whose structures of thought shape everyone and everything within a culture.[64] Describing events or facets of culture necessarily entails describing ideological aspects of the episteme, which is contained within and expressed by all cultural activities.[65]

Following this convention I have chosen to begin each chapter with a vignette from a training or performance context. *HAND* begins in the seventeenth century with Galileo Galilee and *FOOT* somewhere in West Wales in the 1990s. The millennial deep-diving of Audrey Mestre and Francisco 'Pipín' Ferreras provides the premise for *HEART*, while Tom Daley's Olympic high diving begins the chapter *EAR*. A fictional description of the actress Sarah Bernherdt in character for a role that she never played leads onto an historical account of John the Baptist in the chapter *MOUTH*.

These vignettes come from different historical contexts, and thus different epistemes, in the strict Foucauldian sense. Although not a historian by training, my contention is that training, because it relates to innate human conditions, is a part of every episteme but that in the current episteme it has a particularly explicit ideological role. With attention to the different role of training in practices of performance, and society more generally in each historical moment I hope to tease out the ways in which training occupies a unique position in social life across the globe today.

My interest is primarily in the recent and current contexts of training but I am historian enough to recognize that this context has antecedents and that these must be appreciated in their specificity in order to make sense of the contemporary. With regards to Galileo, Bernhardt, Mestre and Ferraras, Tom Daley and John the Baptist – I hope that I have described them well enough within the terms of their own historical moments to make the vignettes productive here and, more importantly, I hope that they would not mind me speaking *through* them about training.

The eclecticism of my approach to the real-world premise might lead some, such as Camille Paglia, to see me as one without the sufficient 'critical talent or broad learning in history or political science' to stay on subject but, while I might lack historical training, I hope that I am not, as she has accused certain New Historicists of being, without 'historical sense'.[66] While I feel I should pre-emptively apologize to *proper* historians, I also suspect that my anatomical approach may irritate some within the theatre training research field who have insistently argued for conceptualizations of the body as a whole, and so-called psychophysical unity. This thread of theory has, apparently, been labouring to undo the social damage unleashed on the body by a Cartesian thinking that carved the joint between body and mind and so, how frustrating to have somebody now set about severing every body part from every other.

Anatomy is a metaphor here, providing a methodology in relation to the embodiment concept that I suggested might supersede the mind–body paradigm. Besides which, anatomy, although dissectory is not really interested in parts but in how the whole works. It is telling that anatomists only set about dismembering once the whole has ceased to function as a whole. The training ideology is alive and strong internationally today although its promise, as I will suggest in *HEART*, may be unfulfillable, but this is not an autopsy. If certain sub-cultures have oversold the potential for training to make us better, or overcommitted to this possibility and are turning moribund others are renewing their commitment and pushing training ideology into fields where it has not predominated before. For now, this is not a necropsy but a vivisection.

Anatomy provides a structure for investigating and theorizing the role of the body in training by looking at the actions of each of its parts. Writing specifically about touch but making a point that holds true for any method one might bring to bear analytically upon the body, Constance Classen writes, the history of touch 'continually overflows the boundaries of any scheme of interpretation'.[67] This can be seen to be true quite literally in the case of anatomy where one part flows into the next, a simple fact most pleasingly illustrated by James Weldon Johnson's *Dem Bones* song – 'toe bone connected to the, foot bone/

foot bone connected to the, leg bone…' – as well as in the imagery of the Valley of Dry Bones, from the Old Testament book of Ezekiel, which inspired Johnson's lyric.

The overflowing of actions, such as touch, across parts of the body means that actions will elude the anatomist who looks for all causes and consequence in one place alone. Accordingly, the subjects of my chapters are not the body parts in isolation but some of the actions and uses made of that part, or exemplified and represented by it. My anatomy is as much about holding, walking, speaking, hearing and feeling as it is about hands, feet, mouths, ears and hearts.

Accepting the fact that bodies and body concepts will overflow the anatomical scheme, I should still account for my choice of these parts – hand, foot, mouth, ear and heart. In the afterword, *SECOND CUT*, I will consider how I might add to this list of chapters in the future and accumulate more parts to my *Anatomy of Performance Training*, refining the arguments I make in relation to the claims outlined at the start of this chapter but there are specific reasons for starting this project with this small selection of body bits.

Hands, feet, mouths, ears and hearts feature prominently in literature on acting, which is the central theoretical field of reference for this project. Furthermore, the actions of each of these parts have been formally codified in relation to meaning-making in theatre literature from the first century to the present.

Quintilian codified hand gestures in their relation to meaning in the first century, while the face provided Darwin with the basis for his catalogue of *The Expressions of Emotions in Man and Animals*, of 1872.[68] The mouth and the ear in relation to oratory and rhetoric have the oldest tradition in acting literature, first formalized in Ancient Greece and more recently reinstated and their primacy to acting reasserted by Sanford Meisner in his insistence on 'listening' to one another on stage.[69] Furthermore, mouth and ear are sense organs and interest in the senses has been rejuvenated following the phenomenological turn in performance studies. Martin Welton's excellent *Feeling Theatre* and his subsequent forthcoming sense books exemplify this fact.[70]

Discourse on feeling is, as Welton points out, not only about perception but also about emotion and the shingling of the two in something we might call sensation. The heart has a privileged position in these discourses and a long association, both symbolic and physiological, with emotion, and more recently the love emotion. Emotion remains a key discourse in acting practice and theatre theory and as an axis for this thought the heart is unsurpassed.

Furthermore, the heart is popularly conceived of as the centre and essence of the body; in common parlance, we speak of 'getting to the heart of the matter' when we really want to ascertain the crux of a situation.[71] Thus, the inclusion of the heart should remind that each part overflows into the other and that while they have distinctness they also have coordination and interrelation.

Each chapter overlaps with the preceding chapters as I refer back to ideas in previous chapters throughout the book. This overlapping of information is perhaps indicative of how the phenomenon being investigated overflows the analytical schema proposed. The overlapping of ideas within chapters and in relation to different practices and body parts also has a reverberating effect; as ideas accumulate, the image of training as integral to a particular ideology of the contemporary becomes more resonant.

So, the anatomical method can be used to investigate the physical bodies that we all have as well as the propositional bodies that we all share in. In between and in relation to these two – physical and propositional – is the philosophical concept of the human. This concept derives from the physical bodies that we possess and it feeds into the propositional concepts that generate on and around bodies. We all, by virtue of being human, share bodies in common and, although our individual bodies differ, we each share in philosophically-defined characteristics associated with our human bodies. It may no longer be viable to speak about human nature but I would suggest that training is an activity of the human condition, which is something that we all share in. As Hannah Arendt eloquently explained, humans are characterized by plurality, and this means that we are each the same in a sense that does not preclude our infinite differences and singularity.

In addition to plurality, we each possess a significatory capability. In fact, according to Judith Butler, we (or rather our social selves) are pre-existed by signification and the ephemeral, propositional bodies of post-structuralist theory are predicated upon this fact. Judith Butler's influential theory of the performativity, and thus relativity of gender is one good example of the importance of our significatory capability to human life, and human life today in particular. As Butler writes, 'if identity is asserted through a process of signification, if identity is always already signified and yet continues to signify as it circulates within various interlocking discourses, then the question of agency is not to be answered through recourse to an "I" that pre-exists signification'.[72]

Our significatory capability thus causes us some trouble – *Gender Trouble,* in the title of Butler's book – and also differentiates us from other creatures, which achieve meaning for us only when they fall within our schemas of meaning.[73] In relation to our positioning amongst other creatures, humans share a capacity to *do less* than that which we are capable of. Humans have to ask themselves, and to decide, how to act, and can choose to do or not to do what is sufficient technically, ethically, aesthetically and so on. This is what Raymond Carver was meditating on when he wrote about the soul. Mastery of this ability may be an ambition of those self-consciously undertaking training but participation in its problematics is not optional, as Butler has persuasively argued.[74]

In addition to plurality and a significatory capacity, I follow an old line of thinking in this book, that potentiality is also integral to the human condition. That we have potential to *get better at doing things,* to accumulate new expertise and to thereby shift enduringly our experiences of being in the world is an idea at least as old as Aristotle's philosophy of education and as contemporary as the immortal wisdom of the proverb, 'practice makes perfect'.[75] Our experience of being in the world is, as Arendt pointed out, a prerequisite of our existence and thus part of our, inherently plural, human condition. Being in the world doesn't only mean being amongst other people, it also means being amongst stuff – objects and things – and this is also an important aspect of our human condition. We might talk about this as the ecological reality of our existence, and our requirement to live in this ecological reality means keeping the physical body and its propositional constructs alive by utilizing, but also not being harmed by, all the things in the world other than us humans. I refer to this in the final body-part-chapter of this book, *EAR,* as the metabolic nature of our human life. Plurality, potentiality, signification and metabolism are the aspects of the human condition that I see as directly related to the ontological category of training. Through training, these inherently human conditions give rise to socially determined experiences of being human today as we live under the fading star of postmodernity.[76]

Finally, and in introduction to this book, I would like to say that I have ordered the chapters that follow in hope that their sequence will develop arguments in relation to training running within each of them. As the accumulation of ideas occurs, and as they connect and resonate with one another, I see a picture developing of the participation of training within a newly emergent ideology. After *HAND, FOOT, MOUTH, EAR* and *HEART*, I hope to have produced a *BODY OF WORK* that will be able to justify the challenging claims that I made at the beginning.

3
HAND

Towards the end of his life, when arthritis prevented him from writing for himself, Galileo Galilei appointed a Florentine teenager named Vincenzio Viviani as a live-in companion. Viviani, a gifted mathematician himself, wrote letters for Galileo and helped him to reconstruct his earliest scientific experiments. The dexterity of the young man's hands were more necessary to the aged Galileo than the nimbleness of his mind and perhaps equal, if Viviani's biography of his teacher is to be believed, to the pleasure of his company.[1]

Viviani records a mutual affection between the two men, with the younger man idolizing his acclaimed and notorious teacher and the older appreciative of his young protégé's many intellectual gifts.[2] Viviani had received teaching at a Jesuit school under a scholarship from Grand Duke Ferdinando II de'Medici before his appointment to Galileo, but it would appear that in the months he spent with him, Viviani learned a lot.

Following Galileo's death, Viviani developed into a respected mathematician and astronomer in his own right with a lunar crater and two mathematical theorems – known as the Viviani Theorem and the Viviani Curve – named after him. Seemingly besotted with his teacher until his own death in 1703, Viviani sought to rectify throughout his lifetime the insult of Galileo's burial, without state ceremony and contrary to the wishes expressed in his will, in a modest tomb in the novices' chapel of the Franciscan church of Santa Croce. Unsuccessful in his own lifetime in attempts to see Galileo's remains glorified, the childless Viviani left all his worldly goods and the responsibility of the cause to his nephew, who, three decades later, also died unsuccessful in this endeavour. Viviani's property passed finally to a Florentine Senator, Giovanni Battista Clemente de Nelli, who achieved satisfaction for

Viviani in 1737. Galileo's remains were exhumed and reburied in an ornate monument opposite Michelangelo's bust in the main basilica of the church.

Viviani viewed his teacher as the scientific counterpoint to Michelangelo's artistic genius and promoted the belief that Michelangelo's spirit had transmogrified from the dying artist into the infant astronomer in the few hours that separated the former's death from the latter's birth. Disinterred ceremonially, Galileo's many followers all carried Galileo's coffin the distance from the novices' chapel to the main basilica so as to permit all the honour of being his pallbearers. From Galileo's remains, the hand that Viviani had replaced was removed for posterity.[3]

Special importance would seem to have been given to the digits of the right hand in possessing some of the power of the great, dead teacher and their preservation would suggest a belief that his expertise resided there. Immanuel Kant, an intellectual descendent of Galileo the astronomer, who discovered the true shape of the Milky Way, would go on to claim 100 years after Galileo's death that 'the hand is the window on to the mind'.[4] If this is so, then in his palliative and remedial role as substitute for the great man's great hand, Viviani would seem to have obtained some insight into his teacher's wisdom.

That knowledge and expertise is transmitted through training is perhaps the least contentious belief associated with training. Precisely *how* it is transmitted, and precisely what is, or should be transmitted is moot. The broad and open field of the Western tradition of philosophy of education can be roughly divided into two factions: those seeing education as transmission of knowledge and those seeing education as the development of autonomy (of thought and action) through the acquisition of skills of inquiry.[5] At moments throughout this tradition, training, as a physical or technical education, has been association with the former position and learning, as a mental activity, with the latter, and the development of reason has served as an enduring, and in this case differentiating aim.[6]

In this generalized account I am following the guidance of Alfred North Whitehead, himself a philosopher of education and author of the still influential *Aims of Education* (1967), in seeing the 'safest general characterization of the European philosophical tradition' as 'a series of footnotes to Plato'.[7] In addition to the argument between conservative (knowledge transmission) and progressive models of education (acquisition of reason) running through this tradition, Plato introduced the question, 'how is learning possible?', and, in relation to human anatomy, I suggest that one answer to this question is, *by the hand.*

The hand possesses a symbolic association with expertise and this has given the hand a symbolic and practical function in knowledge transfer. There is an historic dimension to these functions in craft practice, where knowledge transfer was formalized as a commercial operation: in craft practice, the hand of the expert represents expertise itself. A good example of this might be the practice of assaying metals whereby the skilled craftsman determines quality through touch, rolling and pressing alloys and feeling for the imperfection that signals impurity. In the present, this skill has been somewhat distanced from the fingertips but can still be found in the laboratory practice of the experimental chemist. Another example can be found in orchestral music, where the hand dominates in stringed instrument sections and vies for pre-eminence over the lungs in woodwind, where the hands of the conductor impose ultimate expertise over all other hands in performances celebrated by the clapping together of yet more, probably less skilful, hands.

In some training practices wherein performance is not solely or even primarily associated with the competence of the fingers and palms, the hand still represents, metaphorically, expertise: while the trainee is all 'fingers and thumbs', the expert has a 'firm grasp', a 'good grip' on the practice. In training, expertise is, in part, constituted by the ability to 'get a feel' for the strengths and weaknesses of trainees, to know when to 'let go', and to guide or lead them, symbolically by the hand, through training and to expertise.[8]

The capacity of the hand to reach out and to touch, to affect and to move is symbolic of the transmission of competency from expert to novice. This is also represented in the fact that the expert will usually be recognized in such a context by his or her 'first-hand' experience of performance; he or she will have been moved and affected and so can now communicate that experience 'second hand' to others. This hand-in-hand chain is itself symbolic of the continuity of practice and the experience of knowledge transfer.

Thus, the hand is associated with right, expert judgement and this association is, historically speaking, before the association between right judgement and the eye. The contemporary preoccupation with an objective, scientific view of phenomena was produced and excited by visual technology that distanced the hand from objects. The eye monopolizes judgement during an age of the lens – telescopic, microscopic and photographic – where one can look deeper, further, closer and again at the world but prior to this moment expertise resides in the hand that can touch that which is nearby; close at hand.

Although the ancient world 'prefer[ed] sight, generally speaking, to all other senses' because, as Aristotle wrote, 'of all the senses, sight best helps us to know things, and reveals many distinctions',[9] even the ancients knew that this sense could deceive. Plato, after all, used a visual allegory of the shadows on the cave wall to represent the inadequacy of human perception. Indeed, for the early moderns veracity was held in the hand; as the theatre theorist Denis Diderot put it, 'if you want me to believe in God, I will have to touch him'.[10] While for contemporary performance theorist, Peggy Phelan, the ontology of performance is its evanescence, as performance theorists as far back as Aristotle have argued, ontology itself is a matter of touch because the flesh is the most corporeal of the sense-organs.[11]

Today the phrase 'the camera never lies' sounds quaint and ironic – perhaps it always did – and in the sphere of training, now as before, expertise in practice is as much about spotting problems and seeing opportunities as it is about getting a feel for the right and the wrong way to do things.

Feeling, which has been central to discourse on actor training since ancient times and which found expression as a paradox in the writing of Denis Diderot, is psycholinguistically linked to the hand. The Roman writings of Aulus Gellius provide probably the first recorded example of an actor transposing personally felt emotions to the stage and matrixing his own feeling within the fiction of a play: he tells us that the actor Polus, playing Electra mourning her brother, brought on stage an urn containing the ashes of his own dead son. As Electra spoke, Polus fixed his gaze on the urn, weeping real tears and forcing the audience to weep with him.[12]

In more recent times the casting of famous actors in roles that mirror their own life stories, or even casting an actor to play herself, has achieved a similar redoubling and complication of meaning, and feeling, in performance. The paradox that an actor might feel high emotion and yet present to an audience as impassive (or vice versa) was, for Diderot, a matter of sensibility: 'sensibility', Diderot tells his reader, is 'that disposition that accompanies a weakness of the organs' and cautions that if we 'multiply the number of sensitive souls ... in the same proportion you will multiply good and bad actions of all kinds, exaggerated praise and blame'.[13] In his article *Elements of Physiology* (1778), he strikes an even more alarmist tone stating that each passion is different but 'there is none of them that may not end in frenzy'.[14] Diderot's advice to actors might be boiled down to this: 'get a grip!'

Although the hand may not technically be a sense organ, our sense of touch being located in the skin that covers, the hand that feels its way, gropes about, establishes a hold or looses its grasp provides a semantic field through which we understand and experience our emotions. Following the thinking of the analytical philosopher Max Black, on so-called dead metaphor, this may be the most literal way of understanding certain emotions.[15] Is there, for example, another way to think about, or to feel, receiving helping hand?

Some well-known late twentieth-century actor training techniques entail the isolated use of the hand. Throwing and catching have been significant to a number of twentieth-century actor training approaches, notably Meyerhold's biomechanics that entails hand-held stick use as well as the miming of projectile actions, most famously shooting a bow and throwing a stone.[16] This, perhaps, has something to do with the interest shown in 'real' objects in theatre. This interest might be understood in relation to naturalistic staging conventions of the nineteenth and twentieth centuries but might also be put in the context of the Renaissance troupes that signalled the appearance of the professional actor, and with him, the emergence of actor training, in Europe.

Actors in these troupes usually supplied their own costumes but these troupes functioned as cooperatives and maintained stage 'property' collectively, the etymological origin of today's 'prop'.[17] Although it took until the twentieth century for actors to organize themselves into something called a guild – 1913 for stage actors (Equity) and 1933 for film and television (Screen Actors Guild) – the model of collective used by the troupes owed something to the guilds that had invented apprenticeship in the preceding medieval age.

Pressing back to this historical point from closer to the present day might start with the American and European traditions of improvization where mime is known as 'object work' and the handling of objects, both real and virtual, forms a part of a number of performer training approaches. One example of the use of real objects in training can be found in the so-called Meisner Technique, developed by a member of The Group Theatre, Sanford Meisner. Meisner's approach to acting is summarized by him in his description of acting as the 'reality of doing' and, according to David Krasner, the emphasis of one of his more famous exercises, 'independent activity', is on 'a task that is real (no mime)'.[18]

The exercise is usually constructed for two participants. One is absorbed in a 'real' task that he or she must complete and the other interrupts the completion of this task pursuing an objective of his or her own. The aim of the exercise is to impel the participants to listen and respond to each other even while pursuing their own individual interests and David Krasner's example of a 'real' activity suitable for such a task is stringing a guitar.

This will entail a participant bringing a guitar and strings to the studio. In my experience of working on this exercise with students, their enjoyment in the task comes in part from bringing into the studio 'real-world' things that are otherwise excluded from the sterile studio space. The things themselves appear as a sign of authenticity and demand to be handled 'for real', de-emphasizing the mimetic qualities of acting and placing a premium on 'doing'. Students scrub, chop, wash, whittle, organize, dress and undress, iron, blow-dry, knit, eat, draw and, on a memorable occasion, construct Airfix models, the apparent authenticity of their handiwork reinforced by the handling of real objects.

Viola Spolin, another twentieth-century American actor-trainer, also used objects real and virtual in her training exercises. Her book *Theatre Games for Rehearsal* details countless exercises involving objects, some real, as in the case of an improvization task involving a table laid out with balloons, feathers, sand bags, egg beaters, rubber bands and party toys, from which actors choose 'spontaneously, the moment the player needs it, to show a feeling or emotion'[19] and some imaginary, as in the case of the 'space objects' which must be handled (mimed) by players during scene improvization. To take a British example, Clive Barker's *Theatre Games* entails the use of real and imaginary objects and an entire section of his book of that name is devoted to exercises with 'external objects' and 'ball games'.[20]

The use of real-world things and objects by some mid-to-late twentieth-century practitioners might be seen as an effort to connect (or result of connecting) theatrical training with industrial work and artisan crafts, giving it a sense of tradition and purposefulness and realigning the class distinctions associated with art. This agenda might also be seen in an emerging taxonomy of the late twentieth century that renamed 'rehearsals' as 'workshops'; Joan Littlewood's 'Theatre Workshop', where Clive Barker played his theatre games, gives us one example of a theatrical institution with a social politics appealing for the 'working classes'. To return to an early twentieth-century example, Meyerhold's biomechanics connotes industry and biology simultaneously and in his pursuit to reproduce acting as a 'technical discipline',[21] as Jonathan Pitches has shown, he synthesized 'the theatrical, industrial and psychological'.[22]

In response to mid-twentieth-century politics, some British theatre strived to become more proletarian in its formation, locations and discourse so that it could sit alongside other forms of manual labour (from *manus*, meaning 'of the hand'). This produced some unexpected consequences and, in the present moment, the irony of a proscenium arch framing 'political dramas' about the lives of citizens without access to this theatre (or political process for that matter) has been reproached by the authenticity of 'site-specific theatre' and its spaces. Site-specific theatre's efforts to make the theatrical experience more immediate and relevant as practitioners and audiences descend from the upper circle to the factory floor, office block and supermarket may have, paradoxically, made theatre even less accessible: confirming theatre-going as elite by renewing the premium on exclusive knowledge in and about theatre, not only in the logistical sense of 'where should I go?' and 'what should I wear?' but also in the more insidious sense of 'where should I look?' and 'what does it mean?'

In one sense, this form of theatre is revisionist, referring to the traditions of the travelling Elizabethan troupes coming to a marketplace near you but, aesthetically speaking, it is codified by the nineteenth- and twentieth-century practices of theatre-going and audience behaviour. Theatre-going, as opposed to theatre-coming, has, throughout the twentieth century, and perhaps always, assumed a good deal of cultural capital and the emergence of the site-specific phenomenon in theatre has served only to underscore this socioeconomic relation. In Britain at least, theatre retains its recent historic association with polite society and the upper classes, even if today's jobbing actor lives hand to mouth, and the proximity of theatre spaces that are socio-geographically close at hand remain nonetheless beyond the reach of much of society.

The increasing proficiency of hands in performance training exercises is emblematic of increased efficiency per se and exercises that are begun with the isolated use of the hand can be transferred to other limbs, organs and regions of the body. For example, Yoshi Oida the actor, director and author, describes a training exercise in *The Invisible Actor* in which two performers hold a conversation each using only the actions of one hand to communicate with each other. Lorna Marshall and David Williams, in an article discussing Oida, argue that the exercise exists to provoke concentration in each actor and a particular kind of attentiveness to other actors, and to an audience – to draw attention to an 'invisible networks of relationships'.[23]

With reference to the transferring of this hand exercise to other body parts, Marshall and Williams assert that 'all such exercises can, and should, be remade for particular contexts' and thus the exercise could be 'exclusively vocal … or it could involve any parts of the body'.[24] Arguably, it is not the hand as such that is important in exercises such as this but rather that the exercise serves to estrange a participant from his or her own body and customary habits of using it.

This is representative of the interest, and tautological discourse of 'de-training' in late twentieth-century performer training practice.[25] The efforts to defamiliarize the trainee's own body is quite elegantly described in Oida's instruction to participants in this task: the actors should avoid referential actions, 'like sign language or a game of charades' but rather conceptualize their own hand as a 'strange animal trying to communicate with another equally strange animal'.[26] The metaphor is pertinent because the hand, according to Martin Heidegger, *is* a strange animal and that strange animal is a human.

Heidegger tells us that man does not *have* hands because man *is* hands, because, 'the hand is, together with the word, the essential distinction of man'.[27] No, man does not have hands but 'the hand holds the essence of man, because the word as the essential realm of the hand is the ground of the essence of man'.[28] In part, the association of the hand with expertise results from the association of the hand with language. If, as Heidegger argued, to have language is to be human then to have mastery of language is to be more fully and more perfectly human. In this sense, the hand is literate and the more proficient the hand the more literate is the owner.

The hand plays a practical as well as symbolic role in training. While the hand *is* language – *is* human – there is also a pre-human illiteracy to the hand in practice. My hands labour, as the philosopher Hannah Arendt has it, at those activities that sustain my survival.[29] Hands grow strong, calloused and rough through labour and those callouses signify proficiency, as any academic who shakes hands with a farmer will know, will feel. As Richard Sennett, a philosopher of craft practice, has suggested, 'we might imagine the callus doing the same thing for the hand as the zoom lens does for the camera'.[30] In principle, the callus should deaden touch sensation but in practice it appears to do the opposite for those skilled practitioners who use their hands. The callus might make using the hands in a particular way less hesitant and may facilitate a habitual way of using the hands. Practice shapes the hands in these cases and the particularly shaped hands of practitioners represent and impress upon others the skill that they embody.

In knowledge transfer the hand is corrective as well as evaluative. The skilled hand rescues the failing pot spinning on the novice's wheel and the expert performer takes in hand, figuratively, the neophyte actor.

One aspect of knowledge transfer is demonstration; the expert will show, in some cases specifically with his or her hands, how to perform a particular activity. Even in cases where the activity does not involve hands or handling, the hand still represents a practical corrective capacity to reshape objects and outcomes in a way that other body parts do not. The expert's hands complete the work of the novice's hand; the expert's hand intervenes. The hand is, arguably, the body part most capable of manipulating things – objects, in the world (as opposed to manipulating perceptions of those objects).[31] As phenomenology has shown, all of the body affects the world around us but this capacity to affect is, perhaps because of the forceful hypotheses of evolutionary biology, epitomized by the human hand, complete with opposable digits.

Contrary and prior to the Darwinistic view of the hand as an evolutionary outcome, the anatomist and theologian Sir Charles Bell saw in the hand what might now be called, intelligent design: seemingly self-justifying evidence of a more powerful creator. Despite difference with Bell, Darwin agreed with him that the hand was an executant. For Darwin, 'man could not have obtained his present dominant position in the world without his hands which are so admirably adapted to act in obedience to his will'.[32] Following logically from this assertion, Darwin would probably have appreciated the hierarchical organization of hands (and their owners) in the craft workshops of the Middle Ages where skilled hands that implement the will of the expert attain a dominant position over unskilled hands that execute but poorly the will of the novice.

Bell writes in the Fourth Bridgewater Treatise,[33] *The Hand: Its Mechanism and Vital Endowments as Evincing Design,* 'in the human hand we have the consummation of all perfection as an instrument'.[34] Bell argues, citing Galen, that the hand's excellence lies in its capability to execute 'whatever man's ingenuity suggests'.[35] Although Bell is careful to single out *ingenuity* and not its *instrument* as the reason for man's superiority over animals, he follows an earlier Bridgewater Treatise author, John Kidd, then professor of Medicine at Oxford University, both by quoting ancient authority and by emphasizing the originality and perfection of the hand as instrument: 'the hand is the organ of the organs, the active agent of the passive powers', Kidd quotes Aristotle as saying before arguing that hand is 'the instrument antecedent to, or productive of, all other instruments'.[36]

In knowledge transfer the hand is instrumental. Just as an expert may intervene to correct the mistakes of a novice, they may also put a novice in their own place, in training. As in the story of Galileo and Viviani, the novice may become the executant of the expert's will – may become the expert's hand. This might be a formal and ongoing arrangement whereby the novice serves as 'handmaiden' or 'right-hand man' – names deriving from the domestic and military spheres, respectively – to the expert. In these cases learning comes from 'acting up' to the role to which one aspires or is impelled, from executing tasks one is not fully capable of executing yet. Learning 'on the job' and 'sink or swim' pedagogies describe this phenomenon.

Equally, becoming the expert's hands may be a temporary experience in which the trainee's hands work alongside the expert's hands to complete a task together. Working on different parts of the same task together with a more proficient performer can help a trainee learn skills while contributing towards a particular outcome. This kind of learning might be described as 'supported' and an example of this might be the guitar teacher who fingers chords while a student strums the strings. Learning here entails a proximity to the expert and a mutual investment in a given task. In this example the student and the teacher work together, simultaneously, but the same phenomenon no doubt took place when apprentice artists completed undercoats and colour sections of frescoes, while masters worked on composition, detail, figures and faces.

In the context of the tradition of the philosophy of education briefly described earlier, we can see the emergence of weaknesses in the two principle models of education within supported learning. Conservatively, such practice may lead to over-reliance upon expert assistance – and the stunted development of trainees – and the perpetuation of unhelpful or outmoded orthodoxies of practice. Progressively, the supporting teacher models for the student the parameters of independent and autonomous practice within a safely circumscribed task or exercise and, assessing the extent of the support and the rate of its withdrawal becomes, in itself, an expert skill imbibed by the student alongside the skills germane to the given task. Over-reliant, or perhaps more likely under-supported, students or simply incapable teachers bearing weighty responsibility might be the perils seen to be stalking this approach. The metaphorical association between the hand and expertise suggests that the expert will have a feel for the right time and rate at which to provide or withdraw support. Where this is not so, training might be seen as little more than a process of enculturation, or of the blind leading the blind.

The need for training to perpetuate values and practices through time – what, as I explained in the previous chapter, Dewey called the 'social continuity' of human life – apparently calls for training to be both conservative and progressive; not only to pass-on expertise but also to pass-on the ability to pass-on expertise, and to modulate expertise in response to changing demands. The torsion between these two realities are emblematized by the hand's function for both holding tight and letting go.

We also find the corrective and exemplary touch of the teacher in the laying on of hands. This may be diagnostic, for example in the case of physicians, or it may help to complete what the novice could not complete on their own. A good example of this can be found in the 'corrections' offered by yoga teachers to their students whereby the teacher will manoeuvre the novice into postures and poses. The expertise of the teacher's touch is not only corrective but also pre-emptive; the ability to foresee error and to correct before this even comes into being.

This particular ability is intimately associated with the hand because a primary skill of the hand is prehension. This is seen in the ability to shape and control the hand in preparation for the object that it is about to receive; hands reach for water glasses cupped ready to hold them, hands grip nettles gingerly and reach out for other hands palm open and thumb lifted making way for another, opposing, thumb.

This proficiency is taken to extremes in racquet sports where the hands of professionals tilt and twist racquet handles in preparation for the swerve, power and direction of a ball not yet struck by an opponent. In this way the expert who appears to be able to see the future through his or her hands takes the human skill of prehension to extremes.

The potential to foresee or to anticipate that resides in hands generally is acute and pronounced in the hands, and bodies, of experts. This is a function of experience and repetition (and perhaps also of the more dimly understood talent, that I will come to discuss in *EAR*) and helps to explain the economy of the expert; that the expert and the novice may arrive at the same outcome but that the expert will arrive there sooner, less wastefully of effort and having made fewer mistakes.

Developing this proficiency leads to increased effectiveness within a closed system and to a decreased ability to innovate. The expert's hands are the hands for *this* job and not for *all* jobs.[37]

Prehension develops as a consequence of comprehension. Coming to understand the relationship between cause and effect in any given discipline or activity allows practitioners to make better use of available information and to better anticipate probable outcomes. This is what we talk about when talking about experience and this proficiency is championed in those with apparent preternatural abilities for given tasks.

The cultivation of prehension can be seen to be a consequence of experience and the expert can use his or her experience to develop prehension in the novice. In this respect, the story of Viviani is emblematic of training: Viviani served as amanuensis to his teacher, in effect copying his expert practice by recreating his experiments for him.

The word 'amanuensis' is Latin in origin and was coined by Roman noblemen to describe their personal servants – 'his secretary' from *ensis*, meaning 'belonging to', and *manu*, meaning 'hand'. For the Roman nobility the term came to describe a trusted servant, usually a freedman, capable and responsible enough to conduct the master's affairs. The word is often used now to describe a person taking dictation for another or reproducing the works of another with their permission. This meaning derives, in part, from the position of *secrétaire de la main du roi* in the French Royal court – an incongruously humble position responsible for reproducing the sovereign's signature on official documents.

The *secrétaire de la main du roi* role developed into the *secrétaires d'état,* the first permanent portfolio ministers – the prototype for the British Secretaries of State – who act as amanuensis for the Prime Minister in specific matters, not only enacting the Prime Minister's wishes but also developing policy and taking action according to their own expertise and intentions. Thus, the hand, by virtue of its association with expertise, also conveys, symbolically and practically, authority and the signature becomes prima facie of power.

A briefcase, that contains the pen and is held by the hand, symbolizes the role of the Secretary of State in Britain today but the triangulation of civic power, knowledge transfer and the hand dates back over 3,000 years. The Babylonian Code of Hammurabi, a law code from 1772 BC, provides that artisans should pass their skills on to younger generations, thereby enshrining apprenticeship in law as a civic responsibility. The symbolic association between the hand and the authority integral to law and to this particular paternalistic diktat is embodied in this code, the most complete original of which is carved into a diorite stele seven and a half feet tall in the shape of an index finger.

The evolution of this role says much that is paradoxical about the value of authenticity and originality in art and craft objects and practices. Signatures can be forged, indeed scholars still contest whether the famous Seven Moon Bifolium is by Galileo's own hand or whether the astronomical drawings and the signature that authenticates them is, in fact, forged.[38] While the hand might operate authentic power, it can also mislead and deceive, as in the example of the *secrétaire de la main du roi*.

Despite its association with right judgement, in the field of performance, the hand can dissemble. While it took until the nineteenth century for the neurologist Guillaume Duchenne to show how the electro-neurology of the facial muscles can produce deceiving effects, simulation has been the preserve of the hand since the first known literature on performance.

In his macabre experiments with patients of facial muscular dystrophy, whereby Duchenne attached electrodes so as to produce expressions on otherwise expressionless faces, Duchenne, inadvertently, revealed another dimension to Diderot's famous paradox of acting: that outward appearance and inward sentiment might discord was a self-evident fact but that this discord might result from electrical activity in the tissues of the body was unknown.

Duchenne, misreading the significance of his own discovery, believed that outward facial expressions could be codified into one universal taxonomy of inner emotions. Duchenne argued that God had created 'this language of facial expression' and had given 'all human beings the instinctive faculty of always expressing their sentiments by contracting the same muscles', thus this language was 'universal and immutable'.[39]

Amongst the earliest known writers on performance technique, Quintilian has primacy, and Duchenne was following in his footsteps when he began photographing and documenting the language of the face. The twelve books of Quintilian's first-century treatise *Institutions of Oratory* spell out 'correct' delivery and presentation of self in exacting detail and in book XI the author states, 'though the peoples and nations of the earth speak a multitude of tongues, they share in common the universal language of the hands'.[40]

Quintilian's principles of performance formed the basis of seventeenth-century Jesuit education and they were still widely discussed at the time when Macklin and Garrick are said to have introduced a modern style of acting in the eighteenth century.[41] Thus, the canonical history of the philosophy of acting passes back to Quintilian, and through him to Cicero and Aristotle.

Aristotle's interest in the hand as executant is codified by Quintilian (c. 35–c. 100) to show precisely *how* hands express sentiment. Book XI of *Institutions of Oratory* lists hand gestures to show assertiveness, condemnation, refutation, modesty, surprise, inquisitiveness, invocation, approval, remorse, anger, revulsion, objection, apology and gestures to emphasize, explain, clarify and accumulate one's thoughts, feelings, ideas and arguments.

The hand, for Quintilian as for Aristotle, is expert and can be trained to serve the human will not only in the execution of survival tasks but also through the accumulation of social power. The hand can protect by defeating one's enemies in combat and by the soft force of persuading others. By codifying the actorly skill of using one's hands to rhetorical affect, Quintilian gives predominance to the stage over the social and civic realm. When he writes that 'the trembling hand really belongs to the stage',[42] he makes a point about overacting and about the origins of the hand craft of rhetoric. Indeed, Hamlet appears to make the same point when cautioning the players to 'not saw the air too much with your hand'.[43]

By the eighteenth century and the writing of the first modern textbook on acting, *The Rules of Oratory Applied to Acting*, the author, Charles Gildon, felt confident in stating that the hands are 'the chief instrument of acting, varying themselves as many ways as they are capable of expressing things'.[44] In his instructions to actors, Gildon follows a long tradition of knowledge transfer and the hand: Quintilian wrote his *Institutions of Oratory* for children, specifically for his own dead son as a posthumous memorial to the fraternal advice that he would have provided if the boy had lived, and the Jesuit fathers used this book to educate the young in schools and universities.

In 1750, forty years after Gildon's largely successful book, Francois Riccoboni wrote a poorly received manual for amateur actors called *The Art of Theatre,* in which the 'commonplace rule[s]'[45] laid down in Quintilian were still being reiterated. Many of these 'rules' are still taught to politicians and public speakers who self-consciously modify hand gestures to show assertiveness and non-threatening intent. The online newspaper *The Huffington Post* produced a satirical article, 'Blair's best hand gestures', to lambast the former Prime Minister's insincere self-presentation at the 2012 Leveson Inquiry, arguing that 'whether it's saluting, straight shooting, clasping hands in prayer-like mode or repeatedly jutting his hand out to stress each syllable of a word, the former Prime Minister has a plethora of gestures'.[46] Captions to the countdown of images showing Blair gesturing included, 'pets an imaginary dog', 'puts a spell on you' and accompanying a pinching gesture of the thumb and fingers that Quintilian deemed suitable for displaying modesty Blair is captioned, 'my integrity is this big'.

The association between hand gesturing and dissemblance, which has a contemporary manifestation in political speaking and in the indignant gesticulations of professional footballers receiving thoroughly deserved red cards, goes back at least as far as Quintilian. That one can train the hands to perform a rhetorical function is one thing but that the hand itself has long been associated with the very idea that one can train at all is quite another.

The hand then has definitive symbolic and practical roles in the process of knowledge transfer. Symbolically, the hand has an historic association with expertise and authority and these attributes are personified in the expert and embodied in his or her hands. This is especially true in practices that utilize the hands in specific, skilled activities but is true more generally because the hands symbolize the capacity to affect – to affect outcomes and also to affect others.

The hand that affects has occupied, since ancient times and into the present day, a privileged place in theories and practices of acting. With regard to acting, the hand provides a semantic terrain in and by which emotion is experienced and understood. So central is the hand to our experience of feeling that, psycholinguistically, it is conceived *as* a sense organ. The metaphors of feeling directly or indirectly associated with hands are numerous – being touched, moved, gripped, handled, lifted up, put down, wrung out, pulled apart, squeezed, soothed, smoothed over, passed over, dragged under and manhandled – and belie the biological and phenomenological reality of sensation and sensibility.

The hand possesses, exemplifies, the ability to execute human will. This is because the hand, as Heidegger shows, is uniquely human and because it is, as Aristotle argued, the *first* thing that can do this. The ability of other body parts, objects, tools and machines to perform willed actions derives from the capacity of the hand.

The relationship between the hand and the will has a temporal dimension with unique qualities. This is because the hand can, in effect, see into the future and take action in response to events that have not yet occurred. The human ability for prehension, exemplified by the hand, is cultivated through training and accounts for one aspect of expertise, namely the economy of proficiency.

When knowledge is transferred in training, this economical ideal is communicated from one person to another, often by the supplanting of the expert's hands by the novice's or by the shared handling of tasks. The callusing of expert hands fits them to given tasks, promoting efficiency and inhibiting innovation. As expertise is handed on, practice ossifies, like thickened, hardened skin on a callus, and this helps to ensure the continuation of training institutions and values while simultaneously threatening them with obsolescence.

Biographers of Michelangelo, Galileo's posthumous companion, have commented that the sculptor's father failed to hand on to his son the family business of banking. His father, Ludovico, nonetheless provided the first influence upon Michelangelo's artistic training by sending him to live with a stonecutter working in one of his quarries during the prolonged illness of the six-year-old's mother. One biographer, Charles de Tolnay, quotes Michelangelo as saying, 'If there is some good in me, it is because I was born in the subtle atmosphere of your country of Arezzo. Along with the milk of my mother I received the knack of handling chisel and hammer, with which I make my figures'.[47] Although Michelangelo served several formal apprenticeships to painters and sculptors in Florence, as a young man he attributed his talents in no small part to the hands-on experiences in his father's marble quarry.

Perhaps two of the most famous creations of the artist entail hands: his statue of David depicts a disproportioned youth with over-sized head and enlarged hands, especially the right. In his fresco for the ceiling of the Sistine Chapel, God's right hand reaches out to touch Adam's left. Both masterpieces are an exercise in scale and time. Adam is depicted in the 'moment just after'; the moment just after God brings him into creation and imparts a soul into his considerable body. David, on the other hand, is shown the 'moment just before'; in contrast to the triumphalism of earlier depictions of David, which show the young warrior standing over the slain giant, Michelangelo's statue depicts a slightly anxious figure in a pose of false confidence.

In the context of this discussion of knowledge transfer, the Sistine fresco shows the 'prototypical executant' emblematic of the instrumentalism of the hand in training, which, for Bell, was handed down from God and which for Darwin has caused an aspect of our humanity by placing us atop the food chain and apart from the animals. The latter image, of the apprehensive David before the battle, represents the hand's capacity for prehension, which is central to expert practice. The ability of skilled hands, such as David's on the sling, to foresee and manipulate outcomes is representative of the agenda of training to develop capacity.

That this capacity is transferred from one hand to another through shared and vicarious execution is testified to by Michelangelo's homage to the stonecutter. Viviani's zeal, until his dying day in working ceaselessly to see his teacher laid to rest opposite Michelangelo in the church of Santa Croce, suggests that he knew that the expertise he possessed was acquired at the right hand of his teacher.

4
FOOT

At night, along a sandy forest track in Poland, and on a cliff top path in Wales, they are running. They are running as a group.

A car passes, its headlamps throwing shadows of branches heaving in the wind and leaves across the track and everybody running, stops. They sit quietly till the car passes. The shadows of the branches and the leaves slant and extend along the track as the car corners past the group, headlamps illuminating the unspeaking figures. A passenger in the car sees feet, rows of feet and then some legs and then some waists with hands dangling beside as the momentary light of the headlamps spreads up to and over the group. Five people certainly, and maybe as many as twelve or fifteen.

The red, round rear lights equidistant beneath the glow from dashboard instruments contained within the image of the rear windscreen diminish and shrink away from the group around the corner. When the triangle of lights blurs into a faint glow and dissipates the group get to their feet and, in the quiet of the night, the syncopated footfalls are the only noise to be heard.

Two runners break away to run downhill at a faster pace before returning to the shuffling crowd. Someone else cartwheels. No one speaks. Occasionally someone sings.

As the group shuffles onwards down the track a glow appears in the distance, further down the track. The group advances towards the glow: it is not the rear lamps and the dashboard lights. The glow, it will become clear, is a building and the building is alongside the track.

When the group reaches the building, which will take another half an hour at this pace, they will go inside. They will sense the 'energy and effort committed' and feel the 'heightened consciousness brought on by the activity and deep breathing in the dark night air'.[1] Before they start work for the night, they will massage each other's tired limbs and when they start work they will continue till morning. It is 1999.

At the end of the twentieth century many theatre companies and makers were eschewing signs of professionalism in their work. By the beginning of the twenty-first, the appearance of confidence, competence, deliberateness, assurance and control were being replaced by performances of uncertainty, ineptitude, accident and disorder as key aesthetical signifiers of the actor in the work of Josse de Pauw, Richard Foreman and Richard Maxwell to name three. According to Adrian Kear, Foreman 'has consistently articulated the desire for the stage to adopt the "authenticity" of amateur performers over and above the studied perfectionism of professional actor',[2] and in an early twenty-first-century moment, as amateurs flooded the stage it appeared that he finally got his wish. In de Pauw's production *Ubung* (2002) the amateur arrived to stage in the form of six child actors just beginning to enter their teens. They were all dressed in miniaturized adult clothes – suits, floor length dresses, slacks, cravats, shoestring gem stone necklaces and other jewellery. A film playing on a screen upstage behind the children, showing their adult doppelgangers 'the morning after the night before' of outbursts 'of drunken violence and infidelity',[3] undermines the sense of kids playing 'dress up'. As the children imitate the adults' on-screen behaviour and speak their lines for them, the grotesque adult world is mirrored and dispassionately parodied by the children. The 'adult' content – the clothes, the violence – is incongruous in the children's world, their imitation of the adults is without guile and this sense of a naive authenticity doubly condemns the petty and immature adult behaviour. In Richard Maxwell's *Joe* (2002) the amateur again appears in the form of a young teenager, while amateur and professional adult actors also have a go at playing the eponymous hero of the production. In total, five actors each in a red hoodie take to the stage to depict Joe, who seems to be a metonymic 'average American Joe'. In the show's unexpected finale a rather low-tech robot – closely resembling Johnny 5, the robot that comes to life in the 1980s *Short Circuit* films – rubbles and squeaks its way onto stage wearing Joe's signature red hoodie to speak a monologue and sing tunelessly from an electrical voice box. Even in the twenty-first-century theatre of professional actors, the aesthetic of the amateur, or rather of the *bad amateur* – bumbling, forgetful and inadequate – became key. Forced Entertainment's iconic performances of a-little-bit-rubbish-acting and Goat Island's currency as the-dance-company-who-can't-dance developed within a post-dramatic moment when, Nicholas Ridout claims, theatricality became 'a key and negative term' and 'articulating anxiety' about theatrical form became the central subject matter of theatre.[4]

The consciousness of the audience that paralyses the amateur actor, or incites her to 'ham it up' was reabsorbed within the professional sphere and recalibrated as a signifier of a studied irony. This enabled a parodying of professional theatre's more-or-less ineffective attempts at producing authenticity, which abounded in a different form on the amateur stage. In Forced Entertainment's two-hander *Spectacular* (2008), a histrionic actress, played by Sarah Marshall, made attempt after attempt to perform her 'big death scene' in an overt sending-up of (and perhaps homage to) dramatic and cinematic performances of dying: one single example of a theatre company from theatre scholar Hans-Thies Lehmann's 'namedropping'[5] list of over thirty companies and forty individuals situated within what he calls the post-dramatic panorama.[6]

Kear has suggested that the appearance of amateurs on stage might do something to disrupt the oppressive (and for some, depressive) sense of theatre as commodity and refer back to an, albeit illusory time of pre-commodified play: 'if the professional functions as the sign of art's irredeemable translation into the value of commodity, perhaps the space of its trans-valuation could be found within what might remain as the space of the amateur?'[7]

The effects of the *professional-playing-amateur* in relation to this equation are somewhat harder to pin down. At one end of the spectrum there is a sense of cruel mockery of the amateur and at the other a championing of her amateurism. At one end a challenge to the capital relations of commercial art and at the other a reassertion of these relations by the absorption of the periphery by the mainstream; where even the few remaining means of resistance to commodification became commodified and recapitulated as signifiers of commercial relations.

Following Foreman's thinking, Kear suggests that in the amateur, and perhaps even in the professional-playing-amateur, there abides a sense of fragile humanity exposed to view. This is perhaps why, he argues, in a late twentieth-century moment, 'the amateur performer seems increasingly to be professional theatre's newest form of "hot property" '.[8]

Coupled to the rejection, or reconfiguration, of professionalism and its aesthetic in contemporary theatre was, and is, a diminution of the significance of training to this art form. When the fragile humanity of the amateur becomes preferable to the studied perfectionism of the professional, the utility of training is no longer self-evident or even clear.

One exception to this amateurish trend in theatre that has received much critical attention was Gardzienice, a Polish-based theatre company-cum-collective that engaged in regular and rigorous training from their base in the village that gave them their name, and whose 'night-running' training exercise opens this chapter. So influential has this company been that it is, according to one of their leading scholars, Alison Hodge, regarded as 'something of a cultural paradigm'[9] in and of itself. Gardzienice now exerts an artistic influence on numerous theatre companies and practitioners, including in what Hodge calls 'mainstream and alternative theatre'.[10] The latter, rather undefined category - alternative - probably best encompassing *Ubung, Joe* and *Spectacular* as expressions of the turn-of-the-century post-dramatic, 'anti-theatrical' genre of theatre described by Hans-Thies Lehmann and Nic Ridout. Gardzienice's influence amongst this loosely assembled group is probably most keenly evident, as Kear's analysis might suggest, as an opposite – their aesthetic of 'technical virtuosity'[11] being the foil and counterpoint to the amateurish styles of children, robots, seemingly incapable actors and chronically uncoordinated dancers.

Hodge's 2007 article 'Gardzienice's Influence in the West' describes in detail the various means by which the company has been able to influence twenty-first-century European and American theatre practice, by workshops and collaborations with other companies, such as The Royal Shakespeare Company and through contacts with university departments. In a seven-year period leading up to 2003, Gardzienice visited no less than fourteen different US theatre departments and as recently as 2010 were still paying regular visits to Royal Holloway Drama department and Rose Bruford College of Theatre and Performance, as well as Manchester University, where they have jointly established an MA acting programme.[12]

Hodge also traces Gardzienice's influence on the British and Americans through the teaching and export of their 'training methodology', which includes 'the integration of voice and body' and exercises to emphasize 'mutuality within partnership work'.[13] This export has been accomplished through teaching of training techniques not only in Poland, at Gardzienice's 'Academy', but also in the United Kingdom and America. One example can be found in the relationship with the English theatre director Katie Mitchell, an Associate of the National Theatre and a director with companies including RSC and Paines Plough. Mitchell visited Gardzienice in 1989 and again in 1990 before inviting the company to deliver a five-day training programme to RSC actors the following year. A two-week training programme with RSC happened the following year with actors there commenting on the 'emphasis on the physical' in their work, which, they claimed, didn't exist in the 'British acting tradition and in current training in the UK'.[14]

Gardzienice's emphasis in training on the generation of virtuoso technical skills, especially in choral singing, is partly responsible for the influence that they exert today. Woldziermiz Staniewski, the director of Gardzienice, or Centre for Theatre Practices Gardzienice, is in essence continuing a tradition of actor training acquired through his own studies at National Theatre School in Krakow, but more specifically from his contact with Jerzy Grotowski. Staniewski collaborated with Grotowski throughout the 1970s until Gardzienice was founded towards the end of the decade.[15] Grotowski's influence on Staniewski and on the formation of Gardzienice is evident not only in the shared commitment to daily rigours of physical training but also in the model of the collective Staniewski formed.

In 1972, Grotowski's Laboratory Theatre acquired a farm about 40 km from Wroclaw, which got its name – Brzezinka – from the small village nearby. In rural isolation and away from the city context, Grotowski's 'paratheatrical' experiments got underway with a group of fourteen members, seven of the old guard from the Laboratory Theatre and seven new members, including Staniewski.[16] In 1977, when Staniewski established a company of his own, he did so with a core membership, living collectively in an isolated rural location in Poland and he named the group after the nearby village, Gardzienice.

Grotowski was not the only influence on Staniewski; he was much affected by Antonin Artaud's odyssey and followed his path to the Sierra Madre Occidental of Mexico, where he too witnessed the spectacle of extreme physical prowess of the Tarahumara, an ethnic group capable of extraordinary feats of distance running.

Running continuously through day and night Tarahumara people are reportedly capable of covering 200 miles without stopping. Like Artaud, Staniewski was 'struck by the magical beauty of the deep canyons' and the 'energy and physical prowess of the Indians'.[17] Artaud was looking for what he had called an 'organic culture' continuous with the environment and for him, as for Staniewski, 'nowhere was this more exemplified than in their [the Tarahumara's] running'.[18]

For Artaud and Staniewski this journey had 'immense spiritual significance'[19] but for the latter it also provided something practical. According to Paul Allain (whose detailed descriptions of 'night-running' with Gardzienice informed my opening vignette), 'one can see the obvious attraction in this for Staniewski: in the corporeal and mental ability, in the sympathy between them [the Tarahumara] and their natural surroundings personified in activity, and the combined practical and spiritual functions of their running imbued as a tradition'.[20] According to Allain, 'all of these elements were adopted and adapted for Gardzienice's night-running'.[21]

Thanks to Allain's descriptions, night-running is perhaps the most widely known of Gardzenice's training methods but it is not the only technique that Staniewski has lifted from ethnographic research.[22] In his more recent book with Alison Hodge, Staniewski relates this practice of (what he sees as) benign pillaging to his belief in a 'time [when] human being[s] referred to nature, its structure and its laws'.[23] Constructing his belief in this idealized humanity around Milton's idea and ideal of a lost paradise, he writes, 'this memory [the myth of paradise lost], which is somewhere in our genes, tells us that once upon a time there was a perfect world in which everything was based on simple, clear, pure, indispensible rules and ethics'.[24]

Recognizing the problems with justifying cultural copying on the grounds of a myth of 'truth' – even if he creates a new problem by embedding this memory in 'our' genetic make-up – Staniewski notes, 'on the one hand, it is a metaphor and on the other, in Milton's time, there were practical efforts to recreate, reinvent such idealism in society'.[25] 'Of course, I believe there is nothing like one fundamental truth' he states, 'but truth exists somewhere in small pieces... that's why I make expeditions to indigenous communities, to look for small pieces of something, the gesture, the word, the saying, the tone, the expressiveness of breathing, the devotion to that and only that place'.[26]

Staniewski's expeditions to 'indigenous communities' are motivated by a belief that in those communities that have been overlooked by globalization there remain fragments, 'pieces' to use his term, germs of a pre-cultural ideal. In the current practices of these groups, his argument goes, there is continuity with pre-cultural humanity – which, in this context means pre-modern-cultural – and 'you recognize one particular gesture as true because it has a geneology that has existed for millennia'.[27]

This ethnographic approach may appear to the anthropologist as somewhat risky. Indeed, the anthropologist Lucy Mair criticized her counterpart Stephen Corry for taking such an approach in a public spat conducted in the pages of *Anthropology Today* in the mid-1970s.[28] Mair described an ethnocentric fascination with indigenous culture as a form of 'pristine-ism', which essentialized so-called primitive cultures to construct Neo-Rousseauian fantasies of humankind's fundamental nature. Mair argued that such a pristine-ist approach was fascinated by the annihilation of historic cultures by modern ones and that exponents of this thinking sought to condemn the destruction without having 'made up their minds what it is they are condemning'.[29] A generalized bemoaning of progress ensues, claims Mair, from the position of those within cultures whose thought processes about culture has been shaped by progress. Furthermore, this assertion, of the continuing existence of 'untouched' cultures is self-contradictory given that it arises because of contact between these cultures and more developed ones. Maintaining the differential between so-called primitive and developed cultures is, argues Mair, ethnocidal in the sense that it inhibits access to new ideas and to the means to survive and adapt within a changing world.

To an extent, the anthropology of the later decades of the twentieth century gave the lie to the ethnocidal argument: in 2001, Cory 'updated' the exchange for the edited book, *Best of Anthropology Today* to say that while he still disagreed with Mair on key points, the situation on the ground, for indigenous communities, 'today is not so different from that in 1975'.[30]

Gardzienice was founded in the immediate aftermath of these anthropological debates and since then Staniewski's perspective (even if not his practice) has been more nuanced than the ethnocide that Mair critiqued. In the radical cultural upheaval of Poland and Russia in the twentieth century, Staniewski saw an attempt to 'kill the past in order to build a "brave new world"'.[31] Staniewski sees, in the postmodernism that emerged from the ashes of this dream, another attempt to kill the past. Postmodernism is prefect, he argues, to 'forget a sense and quality of the past'.[32] For Staniewski, 'purposely to kill the past is a very dangerous game'[33] because all 'reference points', be they moral, ethical or aesthetic are threatened or lost. His belief in residual fragments of a better past is, he acknowledges, 'nostalgic' but he pleads, 'even if truth is something nostalgic and sentimental which doesn't exist anymore, do not kill this sentiment in your psyche, in your being'.[34]

Staniewski is careful to not make clear whether he believes that fragments of authentic practice are recuperated from the ashes of the past or whether he believes in *inventing the idea* of such fragments of the authentic past, as preferable to a world without any stable sense of truth. Either way there is a strong sense of idealism in his writing, and of an appeal to something authentic in human nature. This appeal has found a practical outlet in Gardzienice's training practice where elements – pieces – of 'indigenous' cultural activities are rehearsed as training tasks, such as night-running.

There is something revivalist in this approach, like the battle re-enactment groups and enthusiasts who construct weaponry using historical methods. There is, perhaps something revisionist too, asking for reconsideration of the value of practices left behind by progress. There is also in Staniewski's essentialism around culture and humanity something essentialist in relation to training, and this is significantly located by him in the practice of moving on foot.

There is in the very idea of training an appeal to human nature. This appeal takes the form of a truism and predicated on this is the logic and values of training, and of education and of change per se for humans. This truism is that it is possible to improve – by whatever standards this improvement might be understood or measured, simply by virtue of being human. This truism can be traced right back to amongst the earliest extant writings on the concept of training, Aristotle's *Nichomachean Ethics* and *Politics*.

Like his teacher, Plato, Aristotle questioned the prevailing view that children were and should be treated as miniature adults and schooled as if their minds were adult, and held accountable for their conduct accordingly. Instead, Aristotle argued, children are fundamentally different from adults and should be treated accordingly. This belief persists to the present day and informs not only educational theory but also social and legal policy in general.

Aristotle, following Plato, kick-starts the modern notion of anthropomorphy by differentiating humans from animals on grounds of agency: 'we do not say that either a cow, or a horse, or any other animal is at all happy for none of them are able to share in such an activity [choosing to do noble things]'.[35] Perhaps surprising to the contemporary reader is that Aristotle uses the same justification to disbar children from full human status: 'it is because of this too that a child is not happy either: he is not yet apt to do such things on account of his age'.[36]

For Aristotle, human is a state to be attained and the conditions for its attainment are given to all humans, and this is constitutive of being human. Thus, the idea of becoming *properly human* – for Aristotle, a properly political animal or what we might call a social animal – entails working on and with our very nature. From this assertion derives the logic that one can improve oneself.

For Aristotle, improvement is first and foremost a matter of moral betterment. However, the logic established in relation to moral betterment supports, and is supported by, its manifestation in relation to technical practices, such as musicianship and athleticism: 'the serious person, insofar as he is serious, delights in actions that accord with virtue and is disgusted by those that stem from vice, just as the musical person is pleased by beautiful melodies and pained by bad ones'.[37] 'Suffering injustice is to have less and doing injustice is to have more' writes Aristotle, 'just as is also the case with health in medicine and good condition in gymnastic training.'[38]

Aristotle also uses running and wrestling as analogous illustrations of the logic of training in virtue and throughout the *Nichomanchean Ethics* the self-evidence of skill acquisition is used *as evidence* for the logic of self-improvement per se.[39] At the same time skill acquisition is understood as a less important manifestation of that logic in relation to moral conduct in Aristotle's writings.

Improving oneself, which Aristotle relates to the experience of getting-better-at-doing-things, results from the coordination of character with conduct: 'for some people become moderate and gentle, others licentious and irascible, the former as the result of conducting themselves in the one way, the latter as a result of doing so in the other'.[40]

Thus, moral conduct results from habituation, which works, according to Aristotle, through 'repeated action and the proper application of pleasure and pain'.[41] To be more specific, moral conduct results from training, from a structured and motivated engagement with human nature; from the coordination of living with the principles of virtue innate in humans.

In a description that might now read as quaint, Aristotle describes training (specifically moral training but also training more generally) as prudence: 'virtue makes the target correct, prudence the things conducive to that target'.[42] The real work is done by virtue – by human nature – which has the power to change humans but human work facilitates this principle by bringing the subject into right and proper contact with it; with itself. Thus, training is a human process both in the sense that it is controlled by humans and in the sense that it works on humans.

Particularly significant in relation to human nature and training is that Staniewski's attempts to reassemble fragmented human truth is conducted *on foot*, in relation to the particular training practice of running. Staniewski's efforts to revive, revise and revalue a particular kind of moving-on-foot can be seen as part of a more widespread revival, revision and revaluing of moving-on-foot per se taking place over the last century.

'Walking[,] in the last hundred years, has not only retained but perhaps even has gained – as superseded necessities so commonly do – an enhanced cultural significance in a riding society.'[43] Joseph Amato points out in his insightful book *On Foot: A History of Walking* that the human primary mode of locomotion – walking – has been superseded by successive technologies of travel, from horse riding to train travel and then the automobile. Paradoxically, the increasing obsolescence of walking as a mode of locomotion has resulted in an increasing significance being attached to this mode of transportation.

As Amato shows, the 'upper class' pass-time of promenading and strolling and the 'romantic' practice of rambling, both of which treat walking as a leisure pursuit (or indicator), re-value walking as an activity. The value of walking in these instances comes not from its practical function, as it once did at the origins of bipedal humanity, but from its symbolic significance in an age of global transportation.

The globalizing culture that Staniewski sees as destroying a shared past has grown by the expansion of communications systems, which requires the technology of transportation. The movement of people more quickly and further across the surface of the earth by improved road, rail and aeroplane travel has been complimented by the instantaneous and sometimes holographic sense of their movement accomplished by mobile telephony and Web-based video messaging. This technology has even done away with the need for movement whatsoever and forms of locomotion have received new significance, drawing much of this meaning from a sense of history and humanity. The value placed on walking by the ascetic pursuit of pilgrimage, for example, is rejuvenated as walking comes to signify leisure, or even resistance, as in the case of the 1932 Mass Trespass on Kinder Scout, to give an historical example.

On Sunday, 24 April 1932, 400 members of the Lancashire Branch of the Workers Sport Federation trespassed en masse on land controlled by the Duke of Devonshire and ascended to the highest peak in the Peak District. After scuffles with gamekeepers, arrests and short prison terms followed for some of the ramblers, unleashing public sympathy in favour of the ramblers' cause and leading to the establishing of National Parks in 1949 and, ultimately, to the Countryside and Rights of Way Act of 2000.

The conflict between trespassers and landowners, ramblers and gamekeepers had a class-politics dimension – the British Workers Sports Federation had been established ten years earlier by Clarion Cyclists, Trade Union officials and Labour party members and sympathizers. Throughout its early years it was dominated by Communist Party members and, after internal conflict, the organization regrouped under Trade Union and Labour party leadership. The new federation was formed in 1930 at the headquarters of the Labour party and it retained its goal to achieve international unity and peace through sport.[44]

The political aim of the Mass Trespass was to achieve access for all to land owned or controlled by individuals but, in effect, this meant increasing the freedom of the working classes and restricting the power of landowners. The harsh treatment of the ramblers by the criminal courts became emblematic of the association of landowners with the police and judicial system.

Retrospectively, the story of the Mass Trespass has been overwritten by the cause of conservationism. The trespass represented two related sets of political interests – left wing property politics and a broader 'humanist' commitment to access to nature – the former more divisive issue subsumed within the more inclusive latter, and it is the latter that has overtaken in the political afterlife of the event. The National Parks established post-war and in the wake of the Mass Trespass legal action, exist as government funded but politically independent bodies. They do not operate internationally and so the choice of name – National Park – emphasizes the rights of all to access nature. It also refers to the sense of history evoked by the Association of National Park Authorities that dates itself to the moment when Romantic poets, Byron, Coleridge and Wordsworth, captured the public imagination with depictions of British countryside. Wordsworth's claim that the Lake District was 'a sort of national property, in which every man has a right and interest who has an eye to perceive and a heart to enjoy' represents the politico-psychology that ultimately disarmed the more militant class politics entailed within the Mass Trespass.[45]

In the commemoration of the Mass Trespass by the Association of National Park Authorities is an appeal to our common and shared right to freedom of movement – to a pre-cultural ideal. The social politics of a movement that viewed property as theft has been sanitized by this interpretation to produce a cause that argues for preservation of natural habitats for the benefit of all.

This particular interpretation may have arisen because of the simple fact that the trespass was on foot, and feet, and walking, is something that humans, in general, rich and poor alike, share. Had the Mass Trespass taken place on motorcycles, the benign interpretation of the event might have found less traction today.

Indeed, walking and running for that matter, although implicated in numerous political acts from walkouts and protest marches to parading and civic pageantry, retains the sense of an apolitical act. In fact, it draws its political power from the sense that it is an apolitical act, thereby naturalizing the cause to which it is aligned and neutralizing the oppositional cause.

The primary nature of this mode of locomotion situates it, imaginatively or symbolically, prior to any given political framework or agenda and because of this walking retains an association with an, albeit specious, notion of pre-civilized human unity. Walking bonds contemporary humans to our early bipedal past by foregrounding in our imagination and our day-to-day experiences our human-animal-ness, just as the train, the car and the supersonic jet disentangle and remove us from this condition. Walking represents continuity of human experience.

Viewing Staniewski's conception of the Tarahumara running alongside the benign interpretation of the Mass Trespass, we can see in both an idealistic narrative of human nature. Both of these interpretations defy movements towards globalization where, as Staniewski puts it, 'there is no measure or scale of significance'.[46] Human nature becomes the ground on which the political resistance to forces of 'progress' can find a purchase, and by aligning a particular politics with the idea, or ideal, of human nature a conflict between past (when our human nature was still in tact) and present (where it is fragmented), between so-called primitive cultures and developed cultures and thus between ethnic groups and even generations arises.

In the story of the Mass Trespass the 'human nature' interpretation has had the effect of occluding the particular social politics innate in the event by over-coding them with a different, humanist politics entailing a unified view of humanity. In Staniewski's anthropology of the Tarahumara, a political attack on globalization, on the cultural context that he calls 'postmodern'[47] is conducted through the valorization of primitive culture. One culture is prized over others and one set of practices afforded a special, human status.

In the context of globalization, the pace of development of digital technology has been seen to estrange humans from nature and humankind from itself. This theme, the 'then popular problem of the "modernization" of third world societies'[48] emerged in publications by Roland Robertson during 1965–72, coinciding with the ethnocide debate and culminating the year Staniewski first joined Grotowski's paratheatrical experiments. During this period of theorization, globalization was seen by many as a symptom and cause of this estrangement and, through the expansion of media internationally, it is implicated in the spread of the story of this story also.[49] The story of globalization, as something different albeit related to colonization, is comparatively new and to what extent its various subplots – of cultures at war and of the strains of interculturalism – existed before this story was told is difficult to ascertain. As Robertson suggests, during this historical period 'the sense of what was supposedly common to all in an increasingly tight-knit world'[50] was sharpened and entrenched and the idea of 'globalization as a problem' emerged.[51]

Against these troubling narratives the concept of an innate human nature emerged as that which could allay strife and unify, avert conflict and promote mutual understanding and ethically good behaviour. It is not insignificant that nature features in this much-used phrase, 'human nature', emphasizing a natural, animal and pre-cultural understanding of our selves. Human culture, it would seem, is something different.

The appeal to common ground through aspects of human nature, even if this ground does not exist, attaches great cultural significance to those practices, which although superseded, are, or can be, meaningful to different generations. The sense of continuity offered by walking is related to this appeal.

Although this might suggest a particular 1970s politics to Staniewski's thinking about training, training's appeal to human nature is not entirely specious. In relation to training, Aristotle is able to refine this understanding of human nature in *De Anima* through the concept of potential. Analysing Aristotle's writing on the subject, Giorgio Agamben explains that there are two clear concepts of potentiality in Aristotle, 'generic' and 'existing'. What I have dealt with thus far through Aristotle can be understood as humans' generic potential; a person's potential, more specifically a child's potential, for self-improvement. This is generic because it is possessed by all, and it is this fact that makes training a distinct human category. Existing potential however, which Agamben calls 'impotentiality', is possessed only by the person who has acquired a given capability and now possesses the ability to choose to act, and crucially to *not act* in a certain way.[52]

We might think about it like this: I cannot run 200 miles through the night without stopping and so this is not a choice that is open to me. Neither can I choose to *not* run 200 miles continuously because there is no agency entailed in the differential between these two choices. A Tarahumara runner, by contrast, can choose both to run and to not run. Because of existing potential the Tarahumara can choose, they can assert their agency both by running and by not running. I posses generic potential to run like that, but not existing potential to do so; the Tarahumara possess both.

In practical terms, quite how the Tarahumara acquire the existing potential to run such great distances is not fully understood. Accounts of the Tarahumara, such as Chris McDougall's *New York Times* bestselling book *Born to Run*, tend to suggest that a combination of an energy-rich diet, running barefoot, or in thin-soled sandals and a long-standing tradition of running both for fun and for hunter-gathering necessity comprise the training methodology.[53] Increased joint strength and resilience acquired by absorbing shock through the limbs, rather than the padded insole of a running shoe, is a recurrent theme in McDougall's account of living with the Tarahumara, and the quasi-scientific hypothesis is, rather crudely, that running great distances is primarily a matter of remaining injury-free. The tendency in such descriptions to see the Tarahumara as the 'hidden tribe' or 'ultra-runners',[54] or 'a near-mythical tribe of Stone Age superathletes'[55] is strong. McDougall's retelling of apocryphal tales of Tarahumara catching deer on foot after 'chasing the bounding animal until it finally dropped dead of exhaustion'[56] seem in step with Staniewski's descriptions of an 'experience of a magical reality' on the 'earth of the Tarahumara Indians'.[57]

Returning from the practical matter of training methodology to the philosophical grounds for training's appeal to human nature, we can see how these two concepts – generic and existing potential – relate to moral conduct: I can only really be said to be acting good if I also possess the ability to act bad. Similarly, I could only be held accountable for bad actions if it was within my power to not commit bad actions. This, according to Aristotle, and to our own contemporary penal code is why animals and children cannot be held fully accountable for their actions. Neither a child not a cow can commit murder because they cannot posses *mens rea,* or 'guilty mind' even if they can commit *actus reus,* 'guilty acts'.

Generic potential is a human endowment and the very concept of training is predicated upon it. Existing potential arises because of and in relation to training methodologies, and existing potential, as we can see in Aristotle's technical analogies has been a rarefied commodity for at least 2,000 years.

As Aristotle shows, existing potential can be both morally good and bad, 'the former as the result of conducting [oneself] in the one way, the latter as a result of doing so in the other'.[58] Generic potential is value-free and in relation to humanity as such; existing potential is value-full, always in relation to ethical values and technical ideals. Staniewski has perhaps confused these two concepts in the process of a political redress of the 'postmodern' world, and by so doing has misconstrued certain value-full practices as value-free. In other words, to see certain social and culturally inscribed practices as more authentically human than others.

Staniewski did not invent this confusion, and in his case it is probably the result of the influence of Jerzy Grotowski on him. Grotowski's thinking can be situated within a 1960s cultural movement that, according to Simon Shepherd, 'embarked on a project to re-educate [the] body in order to recover its potential'.[59] If the state of the body is a measure of the state of society, then mid-twentieth-century body training practice in theatre and in self-presentation more generally argued that physical incapacity resulted from social discontinuity, and sought to rectify the two problems side by side.

The suggestion that society corrupts the body through learnt behaviours, which form as adaptations to social needs and pressures, appears in the thinking and writing of figures from F.M Alexander and Moshe Feldenkrais to Arthur Janov and R.D. Laing. Grotowski's concept of the 'via negativa' – a technique for recovering a more original movement lexis by eradicating the obstructions to this imposed on the body by culture – is one particularly theatrical version of a larger discourse on potential and the primal. The idea that a more authentic embodiment of our humanity lies beneath layers of socialization is central to Grotowski discourse on theatre training as a process of stripping back, 'not a collection of skills but an eradication of blocks'[60] an 'inductive technique...of elimination'.[61] This discourse has been strongly influential on twentieth-century actor training in the United Kingdom, and can be seen, for example, in the writings of theatre director Declan Donellan, who claims that actors can and should be 'taught how *not* to block our natural instinct to act'.[62] This influence has perhaps arisen because of Grotowkski's influence over Staniewski in the 1970s, and Gardzienice's subsequent influence on late twentieth and twenty-first-century theatre in the West.[63]

Training per se, which is to say the ontological category of processes that I defined in *ANATOMY* and all disciplines of training by the fact of relating to this category, appeal to human nature via Aristotle's concept of generic potential. This appeal results from and underscores the truism that improvement is possible. In some cases, notably the tradition of twentieth-century performer training well documented by Hodge,[64] this appeal has become corrupted to relate not to humans per se but to some humans more than to others. This is a potentially dangerous development because far from neutralizing differences on the common ground of humanity, it essentializes those differences and implicitly values some practices, and some humans over others. Rather than sharpening 'the sense of what was supposedly common to all [humans] in an increasingly tight-knit'[65] globalized world, it might drive a wedge between cultures and further entrench the estrangement felt in globalization rather than ameliorate its effects.

The self-evident logic of Aristotle's understanding of generic potential, which is fully inscribed within our own global collective consciousness today – which as Robertson suggests, from the 1960s onwards has included 'an intensification of consciousness of the world as a whole'[66] – is applied to the existing potential of some ethnic practice and groups. This gives the impression that certain forms of existing potential are, in reality, generic and thus suggests to some that borrowing cultural practices that cultivate such potential may sharpen a genuine sense of what is common to all humans in a shrinking world (or compressing world, to use Robertson's term[67]), where the increasingly forced meetings between cultural differences can lead to conflict.

The suspect anthropology of Artaud, Grotowski, Staniewski and of researchers of training methodologies outside of theatre, such as McDougall, can be understood as part of a broad cultural movement from the 1960s to the present. If we address the attitudes towards training and human nature in theatre in the last century to attitudes and beliefs in society more generally we find that they are, in significant ways, in accord.

Paul Heelas has shown that 'to change for the better, has become so widely adopted that it might be said that our culture amounts to the "age of training" '[68]. This dictum – to change for the better – has a very particular meaning in the late-modern and postmodern age of training to which Heelas refers because the concept of humanity to which it relates has been redefined. Whereas Aristotle reasoned that moral action was *sine qua non* human and essential to society, this reasoning lost some appeal to late-moderns and postmoderns for whom *good* was no longer a unified, objective and transcendental principle and society no longer a stable, or in some cases even a desirable, proposition.

Aristotle's understanding of human betterment was transposed into Judeo-Christian culture in conformity with a theistic worldview. In the twentieth century, as the certitude of that worldview was eroded, human betterment through training was superseded by a phenomenon called 'human development'. Human development is no longer attached to an objective truth and yet the commitment to change entailed by betterment is retained.[69]

The emergence of the concept of human development in society globally has been studied by several influential thinkers, perhaps chief among them Adam Possamai. Agreeing with Heelas, Possamai has seen the assertion of a 'change for the better' culture in relation to a syncretic belief structure – Perennism – which triangulates Monism (a paradigm which recognizes a single, ultimate principle, or force, underlying all reality), Spiritual Knowledge (a quest for knowledge of the universe, or the self, or both in relation) and human development in the form of what he calls the ' "Human Potential Ethic" … the teleology of a better or superhuman being, also referred to as self-development'.[70]

The spread of the Human Potential Ethic has been via the procreation of 'alternative spiritualties' and 'Westernized Eastern practices', what Bauman[71] has called the spread of 'postmodern religions' or 'consumer religions'.[72] These religions 'consume products for gathering and enhancing spiritual sensations' and one of their central characteristics is a belief in the Human Potential Ethic.

In relation to consumer religion the concept of the Human Potential Ethic is subtly different to most theistic notions of divinity in the sense that full 'potential' *can* be attained in this life, and this may or may not relate to an afterlife or another plane of existence.

Although this notion of potential is associated with the concept of divinity, it is not associated with the concept of salvation; it relates to enlightenment but is also grounded in 'worldliness' as a sense of 'greater self-insight, more bodily awareness' and definitively in 'personal growth and the development of latent abilities'.[73]

Paul Heelas has noted that the permeation of the concept of Human Potential Ethic throughout society globally is, in part, a result of the commercialization of New Age religious practices 'aided and abetted by training programmes in the business world'.[74] Following Ross,[75] who has identified the popularization of the New Age ideal of human potential through global talk shows such as *Oprah Winfrey* that emphasize personal growth and development, Heelas observes that 'business spends between $3 and $4 billion' a year on buying training in which personal development and the 'achievement of the human potential ethic' are core, implicit messages.[76]

In the workplace a shift in nomenclature from Personnel to Human Resources, and increased reference to and practices of staff and professional development, is concurrent with the spread of this concept through the global economy.

Furthermore, Possamai argues that the carriers of these new forms of spirituality are the baby boomers of the 1960s and 1970s and that one way by which they have cultivated and exported the ideal of the Human Potential Ethic has been by the global export of media culture, and its popularization of self-development narratives. Alongside business culture and talk-show morality, superhero stories in comic books, cartoons and later movies-of-comic-books 'may be thought of as agents for popularizing the human potential ethic'.[77] Or, rather for re-popularizing, or 're-enchanting' to use Possamai's term, the idea of improvement for postmoderns because, as Grixti has shown, since 'time immemorial' tales of Gilgamesh, Ulysses, Hercules, prophets and religious leaders and political and military figures from Alexander the Great to Napolean Bonapart have 'invited readers and listeners to admire, emulate and/or measure themselves'[78] against the deeds of the great, the perfected.

What is different about the late twentieth-century versions of these stories is that the heroes cease to be political or religious characters allied to objective values – of good, or simply power – and become, as in the case of the comic book superhero, *just like you or me*: not great warriors or demigods on just crusades but newspapers reporters, photographers and businessmen with very normal names like Kent, Parker and Wayne trying to apply increasingly ambivalent principles in a deteriorating world.

Significantly, Superman – whom Possamai cites as the prototypical superhero, emerging in America in 1938 – like most other superheroes does not have to walk; his superpower of flying releases him from the mortal realm, just as web-swinging and bat mobiles will for his comic book descendants. Tellingly, in Superman 'Grounded', a 2010–11 story arc of the comic book series written by J. Michael Straczynski, Superman *walks* across America through Philadelphia, Detroit, Ohio, Chicago, De Moines, Nebraska, Colorado, Utah, Las Vages, Oregon and Seattle, not flying in an effort to 'reconnect' with the everyday (human) people that he is committed to protecting.[79]

In the fruition of perennism in the current moment these superhero narratives are characterized by feet of clay subplots in relation to the character's alter ego and this dichotomy between development and decline motivates the polarized characterization of *real people* in the talk-show phenomenon, and lifestyle or gossip magazine culture. Here we see a faint echo of objective moral values reflected in the character judgements of a studio audience or a magazine readership – he is good, she is bad; she is right, he is wrong; once they were beautiful but now they are ugly.

We might see Staniewski's indigenous fascinations in the context of this broader cultural fixation: the compressing together, and exchange of cultural practices in a globalizing world and the demystification of human betterment into the concept of human development. Perhaps the appeal to a better version of humanity in Staniewski's training practice relates not to generic potential or existing potential as such, but to a corruption or hybridization of the two concepts by the postmodern world.

In the New Age there emerges an image of frustrated training, committed to human development in a context where no clear human ideals have survived. Training in a globalized world emerges as a simulacrum of pre-modern training restlessly reanimating its machinery long after the power has been switched off. The amateurish aesthetic of contemporary theatre is a meditation on this fact, while Staniewski's nostalgia and dissatisfaction with postmodernism is one, ironic, manifestation of this image.

In relation to this image, the attitudes of Foreman, Maxwell and de Pauw may be countercultural, or alternative, to borrow Hodge's term. Their rejection of the appearance of training augurs the futility of the teleology of human development and is incredulous towards the human concept, and thus any terms on which generic potential might be secured.

While this work might appear sceptical about the project of Human Potential Ethic, reminding its postmodern audience through an ironic pose that the very idea of humanity is not without its problems, it may in fact pursue this project through a more complicated and anxious search for a fragile humanity, which may or may not be there to be found.

Maybe their attitude is not countercultural but one more expression of New Age Perennism. As Kear has shown, in their work amateurs and amateurism appear only within a 'tightly orchestrated mise en scene constructed'[80] by a professional. The fragile humanity depicted in their work is, they sometimes remind us, not authentic and unmediated but rather mimetic, devised, constructed and represented. In this aesthetic complexity, there lives a hidden training, a hidden commitment to improvement and the continuation of the project of Human Potential by new means. When the sun comes up in Poland, and in Wales, and when those runners arrive at their destination to begin their work they may find that they are not in the ancient world they struck out for but in the postmodern one that they were running away from.

5
MOUTH

Dancing wildly with the freshly severed head of John the Baptist, Salome cries, 'ah! Thou wouldst not suffer me to kiss thy mouth' in life, 'well!, I will kiss it now' in death![1] In abandoned glee Salome taunts the decapitated head asking why the eyes that were so accusing moments ago do not now look at her; asking why the tongue that criticized her faults now falls limply out from between the lips. Rising in a fit of resentment, 'Thou wouldst have none of me...thou rejectedest me. Thou didst speak evil words against me...well, I still live, but thou art dead, and thy head belongs to me!'

Incensed, a woman rejected, she screams, 'thou didst put upon thine eyes the covering of him who would see God, well, thou hast seen God...but me, me, thou didst never see me'.

Me, me, she repeats demanding John's attention now, now. Her unrequited gaze enrages her more and more as she extolls John again and again to 'look at me!' and finally, distraught and incensed she violently kisses John's detached mouth: 'there was a bitter taste on thy lips'. Unsure of the taste – is it the savour of love or just the tang of blood? – Salome self-deceivingly insists, 'what matter? What matter? I have kissed thy mouth'.

'Divine Sarah, that was wonderful but, we have sad and regrettable news', interjects Oscar Wilde from the auditorium seating. Bernhardt's countenance turns quizzical and her shoulders drop from around her ears as she lets the prop-head fall to her side, banging hollowly against her thigh and betraying the fact it is cast from plaster. Tilting her head forward and scooping back the hair that has fallen madly over her face with her free hand as she straightens herself, 'pourquoi?' she replies.

Or perhaps it was Aubrey Beardsley who interjected with something a little less florid. Maybe he had been sketching Bernhardt in rehearsal and, rising from under reams of ink covered papers – drafts for the illustrations of the forthcoming *Salome,* the book, which *The Times* would describe as 'unintelligible' and 'repulsive'[2] – he might have said simply 'halt, please'.

Perhaps it was Bosie who took the news, whispered from a stage-hand who overheard the theatre manager; maybe he was there – this is, after all, three years before Wilde would begin an ill-judged prosecution against his father and Wilde and Bosie were still secure as lovers in 1892. How might he have paused the 'most famous actress the world has ever known'[3] mid-flow; might he have simply started applauding and, consummate actress, when she ceased speaking and stooped to bow he may have taken to his feet and offered enigmatically, 'such a tragedy that London will never see *this*'.

My favourite way to imagine the scene is with the Lord Chamberlain himself bringing the news, dressed officially and corpulently fat. Red-faced and carrying, no *waving* a wax-sealed parchment – 'Stop! Stop! Stop the rehearsal! Your play is banned!'

As a quirk of the now defunct system of censorship of the British stage, Wilde's *Salome* was not banned because of the gruesomeness of beheading and not even because of Salome's thanatological attraction to John but because it was, at the time, illegal to depict religious characters on stage.

In the Biblical account of John's beheading, Saint Mark depicts events somewhat differently to Wilde. In the gospel it is Salome's mother who desires John's death and Salome is little more than a pawn, ensuring that her stepfather acquiesces to this requirement. Feasting in celebration of his birthday in the remote fortress of Macherus, Herod Antipas, Salome's stepfather, is drunk. Salome's mother, Herodias, pushes her daughter to dance seductively for the drunk Herod. She does so, dancing what in later mythology will become known as the 'dance of the seven veils', the removal of each unveiling more and more of her flesh. Seemingly inflamed with incestuous desire for Salome, Herod swears an oath to give her anything she desires in payment for her entertainment up to half his property.

The plan working, Salome refers to her mother, the ex-wife of Herod's brother, what precisely to request. Incensed by John's public criticism of her remarriage to her dead husband's brother, Herodias takes the carefully constructed opportunity for revenge and tells her daughter to ask for the head of John the Baptist on a silver platter.

This appears to sober up Antipas, who knows what effect this will have on John's numerous loyal followers. Outmanoeuvred, he is forced to consent. John is murdered, decapitated and his head presented to Salome on a platter presumably already to hand from the feasting. Mark does not record Salome's reaction, except to say that when they 'brought his head on a platter, and gave it to the girl; the girl gave it to her mother'.[4]

In Mark's version of the story, largely corroborated by the Jewish historian Flavius Josephus, John is put to death for political reasons even if there might be personal enmity involved. John's public criticism of Antipas's remarriage to his brother's widow is secondary in Flavius Josephus' account to John's ability to command a devoted crowd to rebellion and the historian has it simply that, Herod 'thought it best'[5] to put him to death.

In Wilde's dramatization of events the erotic theme raised by Mark takes hold and Salome becomes the licentious and jealous architect of John's harrowing punishment, which is violently concluded with a necrophiliac kiss.

Both versions of this story develop themes from the image of John's mouth. Wilde's *Salome* cultivates an erotic theme and the carnality of the mouth comes to the fore. The dramaturgy of the story points towards a carnal reading in both versions; John is decapitated where others are eating, and possibly even while they are feeding, presumably intemperately, at a celebratory feast. John's head is placed on a plate, perhaps recently cleared of food by a now sated diner but, for Mark, the carnal symbolism of mouths feeding is secondary to the allegory of mouths talking, and John's mouth represents his prophecy and public speaking. In his narrative, John's statements about Herodias' remarriage to Antipas leads to his imprisonment and motivates Herodias to revenge. John's prophecies have also angered the Pharisees, who will later hand over Jesus to Herod for making even more inflammatory public statements.

The power of Jesus and John's public speaking appears to shake Antipas, who, seemingly chastened, will later refuse to judge Jesus, returning him to his subordinate, Pontius Pilate, afeared that 'this [Jesus] must be John the Baptist. He has risen from the dead. That is why these powerful works are done by him'.[6]

The power of speech to entrap is visited on the iniquitous as well as on the righteous in Mark's telling of the tale: John speaks the truth and is punished for it, while Herod speaks in haste and regrets at leisure.

The mouth is not, of course, solely responsible for speech; speaking results from an entire vocal apparatus, but the mouth stands symbolically for the voice. This symbolism is rife in the Bible and in common parlance relating to speech – shut your mouth, plum in the mouth, shoot your mouth off, big mouth, smart mouth, and for the foul mouthed, *wash your mouth out with soap*! – and John and Jesus provide heroic illustrations of the sagacity of Proverb 21, which cautions, 'whoso keepeth his mouth and his tongue/keepeth his soul from trouble'.

Wilde himself delivered a rather more vainglorious embodiment of this wisdom: the mini-drama I have imagined for Bernhardt and Wilde – because much as I would have wanted the banning of *Salome* to have occurred histrionically amidst a cast of stereotypes I don't suppose that it did – takes its melodramatic lead from the theatre of Wilde's later trial and incarceration; Delighting the gallery and indicting himself with every witty rebuttal he offered, becoming the subject of his own barb about the man who goes through life with his mouth open and his mind closed.

These two themes – speaking and feeding – emerge in the story of the beheading of John the Baptist through retelling in secular and religious texts and both feeding and speaking have a particular relationship to training via the philosophy of human work.

Hannah Arendt, whose philosophy of the human condition was outlined in *ANATOMY*, categorized humans as homo faber – 'man the maker' – and animal laborans – the 'labouring animal'. These categorizations derive from her sense of the different forms of work open to humans by virtue of their embodiment per se, and their embodiment of social roles.[7] *Animal laborans* is associated with 'labour', with the task of keeping the body alive and represents the necessity of feeding and the labour of all activities required for biological survival. For Arendt, *animal laborans* becomes dangerous because of a capacity to make things also; she calls this 'work'. In work human beings produce things, insert objects into the world and the irreversibility of this process threatens social and biological survival as the world fills up with increasingly useless, outmoded, ill-conceived and broken stuff.[8]

Most dangerous of all, the things produced potentially supplant humans, and thus ethics, as their technical (and therefore morally neutral) imperatives drive human endeavour. Making *better* stuff becomes more important than making *good* stuff and creations such as the guillotine, the gas chamber and the atomic bomb result.[9]

Homo faber counterbalances this danger. *Homo faber* represents our capacity to reason together and, importantly, to promise and to forgive – two techniques Arendt finds in human exchange for overcoming the dangers of production. *Homo faber* conducts a form of work called 'action', which is germane to the experience of training.[10]

Action is a collective, Arendt would probably say, social, form of work. Action does not make things and does not maintain existence, rather action provides a social existence for humans that outlasts the individual biological condition, and gives rise to new possibilities – Arendt says, 'beginnings' – that could not be achieved by one person acting alone.[11]

Life is the activity that corresponds to labour, worldliness the condition that corresponds to work, while plurality – the fact that we are all human and each different – is the basis of action. Action concerns communication and interaction and social movements, uprisings and perhaps even community itself can be understood as a consequence of action.[12] In the case of training, action connects practitioners to one another and sustains practical expertise through time.

The idea of training itself maintains a particular sense of community, which can be seen as encompassing the more specific institutions and groups within which training often takes place. Training in a given practice, for example acting, or more specifically the body-based fitness and flexibility regimes that have formed part of twentieth-century acting discourse, such as yoga, will not only bring trainees into contact with trainers within a given setting but also relate trainees to a broad body of knowledge, practice and people. Overarching bodies, such as The British Wheel of Yoga,[13] will connect underlying groups to each other and the interrelation of institutions and individuals will maintain and develop *the practice*.

Even within practice that has overarching organizing, accrediting or regulatory bodies, a sense of connection between individuals and groups pertains to simply sharing in the same activity. In the case of yoga, this can be understood in relation to the phenomenon described by Mark Singelton as modern, transnational Anglophone Yoga. 'Asana' – literally 'throne' or seated posture, but referring to a canonical schema of yoga postures – is the 'foundation stone of transnational yoga'[14] connecting together yoga practitioners in a 'great number in virtually every city in the Western world, as well as, increasingly in

the Middle East, Asia, South and Central America, and Australasia'.[15]
The practice – asana – provides the basis for a sense of transnational
community and provides, in effect a shared language through which
social exchange and interaction can occur between practitioners.

Arendt argues that action has a 'linguistic structure'[16] and that
language is the primary condition of action. Arendt elucidates her
concept of work with reference to the images of work in the book of
Genesis and thus places work *first* by developing her ideas relative to
the originary myth of the Old Testament.[17] Man *labours* as punishment
but God *works* to create the earth. The creative potential of communal
action has most in common with this latter image, because this is an
image of a beginning; of something new that is not augured or bound
by what came before.

Chronologically, John's birth is the first event in the narrative of
the New Testament, recorded by both St Luke and St John and the
biblical character of John the Baptist is associated with speaking from
the moment of his conception.[18] In Luke, John's birth is foretold to his
aged father Zachariah by the angel Gabriel. Incredulous, Zechariah asks
the angel how he can be sure that his wife will bear a child, because
she too is aged and has been unable to give birth. In punishment for
his disbelief, Gabriel tells Zachariah, 'because you did not believe my
words', 'you will be silent and not able to speak until this day [John's
birthday] happens'.[19]

As a small child John has mastery of language and a preternatural
ability to read and interpret scriptures. In later life, John preaches and
attracts a significant following through his speaking. Shortly before his
imprisonment by Herod, John is challenged by the Levites to account for
his baptist practices; they ask him, who are you to be doing this? And he
replies, quoting the Old Testament prophet Isaiah, 'I am the voice of one
crying in the wilderness, "make straight the way of the Lord"'.[20]

Social speech, such as John's prophecy, is quintessential to
community, as Arendt understands it, but can also give impetus to
movements by and within community, producing irreversible effects
and new 'beginnings'.

Community is, in one sense, conventional and reactionary and
social speech can have the capacity for maintaining values and also
reproducing behaviours. This is common to training practice – this
is the essence of the 'conservative' model of education outlined in

HAND – however, in the context of training, John's speaking can also be understood as a vocation – a voice crying in the wilderness as a calling to his followers to live out life in a very specific way, a way that is, in the Arendt-tradition of action, disruptive to community and its prevailing orthodoxy.

In the biblical story, John has a very specific vocation to 'make straight the way of the Lord', and to inspire and convince others to perform this same task. John's vocation – from the same etymological Latin root as voice; *vocare* and *vocalis*, meaning 'of the voice' – sets a precedent for the religious life of monastic communities that will develop in the deserts of the Middle East following the crucifixion of Jesus and, as Max Weber puts it, provides a model that will come 'to dominate worldly morality [and] the tremendous cosmos of the modern economic order'.[21]

Vocation, in the specific Christian sense, entails a personal experience of a calling to live a certain way. This calling has propositional and performative dimensions; not only to testify or believe in certain moral or spiritual values but also to embody these values through socio-behavioural techniques of living.

The Catechism of the Catholic Church states that '*love* is the fundamental and innate vocation of every human being'[22] but in the Roman Catholic Church vocation is still used narrowly to refer to the specific calling to the priesthood.

In common usage, vocation refers to an occupation to which a person is especially suited or an occupation that he or she finds particularly gratifying. The transit of the idea of vocation from religious to lay communities has been accomplished through training institutions. Larry Cochran, who has written a humanist psychology book called *The Sense of Vocation* analyzing the life experience of twenty individuals who felt strongly that they had a vocation to particular work, describes the common sense of vocation as 'an elevated story [that] the person lives'.[23] John Stuart Mill gave a similar definition when he defined his vocation as, having 'an object in life'.[24]

Max Weber showed how our common sense of vocation as a performative commitment to activities giving significance to life, personally felt, derives from the life of John the Baptist and more specifically the Protestant Reformation of the idea of his vocation in the sixteenth century.

Martin Luther's theology protested that most secular occupations could posses a sense of diving calling.[25] Weber's seminal *Protestant Ethic and the Spirit of Capitalism* shows how Luther's reinterpretation of the concept of vocation contributed towards the evolution of capitalism in Northern Europe as people began to undertake work *for its own sake,* and not merely to perpetuate their current living conditions, thereby driving capital.[26]

Weber showed how the circulation of capital described by Marx was facilitated by social conditions arising out of religious doctrine, and how theological concepts came to influence secular life, especially in the area of economics. Leland Ryken, a scholar of Christian literature, has suggested in *Work and Leisure* that the 'arbitrariness of one's choice of work',[27] emphasized in Marxist philosophy of work, is offset by Luther's understanding of vocation and that many people in Northern European economies still hold to the idea that particular kinds of work can be of special value to them personally, and that any work might be of such value to an individual, at least hypothetically.

As with action, religious vocation has the structure of language; is dialogic by its nature positing God and Man in relation to one another. God calls, Man answers. This language structure is well illustrated by John because the call of John's voice is a command – *make straight the way of the Lord*.

Weber unpicked the complexities of this structure with reference to the different theologies of the church but in his own interest in the vocations to science and politics he chose to describe the agency entailed in linguistic call-response equations with the word 'hingeben', which entails a sacrifice and a 'giving over'.[28] In their introduction to Weber's 'science as vocation' and 'politics as vocation' lectures, David Owen and Tracey Strong describe how Weber understood vocation as both passive and active – passive in the sense that the calling comes from beyond oneself and active in the sense that it requires a response: 'one must freely give oneself to that which calls one, which by the acknowledgment of that call appears as and becomes one's own'.[29] Thus, vocation is not only a 'free act', 'defining of the person' but also a 'necessary act', 'expressive of the person'.[30] At a personal level, vocation has nothing of the instrumental but is an end in itself; it is the 'freely chosen commitment of individuals to their own particular fates'.[31]

At the level of social structure this free and necessary act becomes instrumental as the commitment of individuals to their own fate becomes modelled within social institutional structures. This is the basis of the novice–master relation which comes to dominate institutional training contexts and which is personified by John.

The position of the novice, and the dynamic between novice and expert – between the one who knows or *does* and the one who knows not, or does not – is central to the contemporary ideology of training. John is a novice in this loose sense of not knowing – Matthew records Jesus as saying, 'among those born of women no one has arisen greater than John the Baptist; yet the least in the kingdom of heaven is greater than he'[32] – but John is a prototypical novice in a more specific sense relevant to training ideology and practice.

By the mid-fourteenth century, 'novice' had come to refer specifically to a member of religious orders but its derivation lies in the Latin word *novous,* meaning 'new'. In old French (C12th) *novice* broadly meant 'beginner' and the common meaning of 'inexperienced person' is attested from the fifteenth century. The first period of time spent in a monastery today, before solemn vows are taken is called the Noviciate and the rigours of living in the Novitiate refer would-be monks back to John's vocation in the desert.

John had a special calling, a vocation to ascetic living; this is made clear in the story of the angel Gabriel's prophesy to John's father, Zechariah. In the gospel of Luke, the angel foretells that John 'shall be great in the sight of the Lord, and shall drink neither wine nor strong drink; and he shall be filled with the Holy Ghost, even in his mother's womb'.[33] In other words, John will be an ascetic from birth.

John's ascetical image is probably most strongly felt in popular culture through depictions, such as Wilde's of his execution; John's martyrdom represents an ultimate expression of his self-denial, which is often regarded as a key signifier of asceticism. Al Pacino adapted Wilde's play into a 2011 film under the title *Wilde Salome* and, to the extent that John's image, and not just his death, resonates in popular culture, he is commonly depicted as an austere figure. This image probably derives from Mark's description of him wearing camel hair clothing and a leather girdle, and eating only locusts and wild honey.[34]

John's dress is significant in the synoptic[35] gospels because it depicts John as both a revolutionary and an anachronism – as something radically new but also with the authority of tradition. In his appearance he resembles the Old Testament prophets and not the religious figures of his day – the Pharisees. He extends their nazirite asceticism to a lifelong ministry under conditions of deprivation and homelessness, destined to end in martyrdom. John's lifelong vocation is expressed in living a certain way; living as a perpetual novice, an eternal beginner and student and so doing in a way that constructs a sense of shared history with earlier prophets. In this way, John's way of living represents the continuity of values and John's way of living will be used to produce an institutional model for the monastery that will ensure the social survival of ideas.

Today we see the dynamic of expert and novice thoroughly encoded within training institutions so much so that it appears as an a priori condition of training. The story of John reminds us that this dynamic is not a natural condition but a method of training, which in many of the lay communities of what Max Weber called the 'tremendous cosmos of the modern economic order'[36] results from the secularization of the concept of vocation and its associated performative techniques.

Calling, in this religious sense, entails a subjection to higher powers: the called subject to the caller and this subjection is formalized through conventions – in John's case of dress and diet – which might in today's parlance be called 'lifestyle choices'. These lifestyle choices develop into daily rituals and through this ascetical way of living John provided a proto-typical model for living a religious vocation to the monks, the so-called Desert Fathers, who would follow him into the wilderness in the third century.

Superficially, John's attire and diet influenced the ascetical dress and fare of the monks descending from him but more importantly John is the first New Testament eremitic – from the Greek *eremia*, meaning a wilderness or desert. His retreat to the desert to live under avowed conditions of deprivation is prototypical for Anthony, Pachomius and the other so-called Desert Fathers who will follow him into the wilderness to establish monastic communities and, importantly, Rules.[37]

These communities, first formalized under Pachomius' Rule and later reasserted and popularized through the Rule of St Benedict, will produce those conditions that Weber says come to dominate the modern economic order: 'for when asceticism was carried out of the monastic cells and into everyday life, and began to dominate worldly morality, it did its part in building the tremendous cosmos of the modern economic order'.[38]

The concept of vocation is disseminated to the lay community from the monastery, as Foucault points out, by the export of techniques that form part of these Rules. Techniques, such as timetabling, become central to the institutional experiences of learning (in schools) and correction (in prisons).[39] In Weber's history of work, John's vocation gives rise to techniques of living and learning that govern what Alphonso Lingis has called the 'disciplinary archipelago'[40] of the late-modern world, which encompasses so many places where training takes place, from factories to offices and workplaces, hospitals to barracks and leisure centres.

Along with the training techniques of the monastery the ethos of vocation was exported globally to lay communities. Weber shows that through the several histories of vocation it has for centuries retained a connection to Christian doctrine. In the second and third centuries, as scholars such as Tertullian began to translate the biblical texts into Latin, concepts key to Christian theology, for example the Trinity, emerged.

Tertullian, 'the founder of Western theology',[41] would appear to have been responsible for translating the Greek, *Klesis* – meaning 'an invitation' – into *vocatio* in his renderings of the gospels, and thereby aligning the concept of a spiritual inclination, duty or aptitude with the concept of speech. The sixteenth-century Protestant Reformation in Europe finally displaced the notion that vocation, or calling referred only to God's work (or rather, monk's work) with an ideal of the sanctifying power of worldly labour.[42] Martin Luther concluded that one could experience a *spiritual calling* to eternal salvation in heaven and an *external vocation* to serve one another in the world. The first remained associated with the soul, while the second entangled the soul with the body, grounding spirituality in human corporeality and more specifically, labour.[43]

As the two-way dynamic of vocation implied by spiritual notions of calling is transposed within a worldly disciplinary context, other relations complicate it. Although the novice has a particular relation to the Abbot in a monastery, he (it is a he in this historical case) also has a relation to other novices, to other monks and to the lay community.

The language structure of vocation, introduced by Tertullian into Christian theology and discourse and today central to techniques of asceticism propping up Weber's tremendous economic cosmos, is not simply duologue but also dialogue, and entails attendant communal relations. Regarding Luther's concept of vocation, this structural function of language exists in the sense that one is called to work in the world, amid each other and amongst things. The monastery provides a tangible framework for this language structure where individuals are positioned institutionally relative to one another and where each individual and the group relates to other individuals, concepts and events, and this tangible framework is reproduced within the various institutions of the disciplinary archipelago.

The monastic institution provides the model for subsequent social institutions, especially of education and correction, both of which relate to the mission of perfecting the self. The communal relations within institutions take form within and with relation to overarching schema of practice and doctrine, be this religious or secular, as in the case of asana and transnational yoga.

The prototypical training institution, the monastery, cultivates a particular form of commitment to its values, doctrines and techniques through the convention of promising. In his prophesy to Zechariah about John's abstinence, Gabriel is referring to an extant convention of promising associated with a class of individual called a nazirite.[44] In the Hebrew bible nazirites took vows, especially to avoid alcohol but more specifically any drinks deriving from grapes, to refrain from cutting their hair and to avoid graves and any structures containing corpses. Nazirite vows were made by spoken declaration and would normally last a prescribed length of time, culminating with burnt offerings in the temple.

Monks still profess vows today but it is less common for secular trainees to profess commitment to practice in this way. However, training is generally thought to entail a certain level of ongoing commitment to practice, as Cochran, Mill and Weber all make clear. This performative commitment reasserts the Aristotelian belief in the perfecting effects of prudence, which I discussed in *FOOT* and which holds strong in the contemporary ideology of training where 'practice makes perfect'.

We can see that, in relation to Arendt's philosophy of the continuity of social life and values, that the promising required for sustaining action may take a less than explicit form. In Arendt's macro example of community as national political life in democracy, exercising political rights and performing political duties constitutes a form of fidelity towards sociopolitical values. Each time I choose to obey the law rather than to break it, or to register my vote in an election, or to pay my taxes or use a state service I, in essence, assent towards the values of the system in which I live and make a form of promise towards their upkeep. In the micro example of training community, ongoing participation in practice, and the maintenance of communal relations and values through this, also entails fidelity, and a form of positive consenting towards given conditions. Practice makes perfect, according to the saying, but continued commitment to perfecting practice also ensures the permanence of practice.

Particular practical techniques and values attain a social life because of individual efforts but these techniques and values also achieve continuity through time because of a sense of their essentialness. This is well illustrated in the prototypical example of John – the implication of Gabriel's comments are that John's naziritism will not be time-limited but will be lifelong and, importantly, that it is preordained from the moment of his birth. Thus, John radicalizes the nazirite promise of abstinence and gives impetus to the Reformation ideal that vocational talents are predetermined at birth, which still holds sway in the popular imagination today – he or she has a 'natural talent' an 'innate ability' and was 'born to do it', whatever 'it' might be in any given context.

The centrality of this belief to the contemporary ideology of training is well illustrated in the phenomenon of the rejuvenation of the talent show format in the global media. Emblematic and definitive of this media phenomenon is the *X Factor* franchise, licensed by SYCOtv to TV networks in forty-nine countries across every continent on the globe, whose stated aim is to uncover and then to cultivate a mysterious, rarefied talent that exists to a finite amount and resides disproportionately within a small group of the populace. It is perhaps not as significant as I might like it to be for the elegance of my argument that, in this example, the voice predominates in this discourse on talent.

We can see how through this ideological belief in the predetermination of talent and the necessity for the cultivation of novices by experts that the secularization of the theological concept of vocation gives rise to some pretty serious social dangers in the case of training institutions. In the religious example novice and expert positions are maintained in relation to the concept of God: God provides talents and, owing to his benevolence, this is done fairly and equally, and the relationship between God and individual is primary, supervening on subsequent institutional versions of this dynamic. Luther's transposition of spiritual vocation into the body and the world left the residue of this belief, which, untethered from the supernatural, lingers in the form of the ineffable 'talent' and, in relation to training, talent becomes a central plank of the heroic narrative of the expert practitioner. This narrative trope retains the arc of John's story in the sense that the call–response structure of language is still part of the experience of vocation whereby individuals must subject their (novice) talent to convention, and this will probably be done within an institutional context whereby the will of one person becomes subject to the will of another, institutionally senior person.

The socioeconomic world order described by Weber, resulting from the secular ideology of vocation has been seen to lead to alienation within society.[45] This results from the interpellation of individuals by various institutions, which maintain asymmetric social conditions through the regulation of the division of capital and labour. Here the secular concept stands at a philosophical crossroads: in one direction self-fulfilling work enriching the life of the individual that feels especially called to this work, in the other alienating labour damaging the psyche of the individual 'best suited' to dreary or hard labour.

The concept of God residing in Luther's theology could recuperate all work to a divine cause and a life ever-after but with the secularization of his ideas and the rejection or diminution of the concept of God even an ideological belief in this possibility evaporates. The secular understanding of talent now only serves to underscore the disparity between individuals in society. In this thinking inequality becomes a natural condition of human existence, although, as outlined in *FOOT*, many 'new age' systems of spiritual thought seek to overcome this difficulty by mobilization of a generalized and amorphous monistic principle – a force, not God, benevolent and pre-existent and governing life on earth and not life ever-after.[46]

Navigating the intersection between self-fulfilment and alienation is made more problematic by the fact that inherent within the concept of vocation from its earliest origins are the notions of predestination and supervening agency. As Weber neatly illustrated, to be called to specific work is not the same as to want to do a particular kind of work, or even the same as enjoying that work or being unusually good at it. The Calvinist assumption that we are each endowed with particular talents to suit each of us to worldly occupations, for reasons of our own self-fulfilment, remains common in secular ideologies of work[47] but in a secular society that cherishes personal choice and individual liberty, the idea that abilities and occupations are predetermined is distasteful.

In training institutions there is no reliable safeguard against the threat of unethical subjection through work-based relations.[48] This does not mean that those in positions of power institutionally knowingly oppress those in positions of subjection, but rather that the context itself does not protect either party from alienating or being alienated.

Trainers may not knowingly oppress or manipulate trainees but by virtue of a residual sense of the predetermination of talent, and the fact that vocation does not seem to arise from agency in the same way that other actions do (because of the historic theistic context of calling), trainees must look outside of themselves for confirmation of their own abilities. The judging panels of SYCOtv productions, and imitators of this format have exploited this need and the requirement for external confirmation puts both parties – trainers and trainees and the practice they share in (singing pop music in this case) – in a precarious situation.

The problems entailed by the contemporary secular ideology of training erupt across all training institutions, and not just within global media phenomena. In analysis of the training of psychoanalysts, James Davies has suggested that 'trainees quickly learn that they are judged on something more intangible, less easily quantifiable' than examination performance.[49] Rather they are judged on 'a vaguer kind of "suitability" as defined by those socially positioned as responsible for adjudication'.[50] Trainers determine talent, or 'aptness', as Davies calls it in this context. Even though this aptness may be determined with regard to objective criteria, these criteria might 'remain mysterious'[51] to trainees and criteria maintain a 'certain degree of interpretation',[52] subject to the agenda of given 'schools' each asserting ascendency over the others.[53] Thus, 'talent' becomes embroiled in institutional-cultural competition and professional rivalries and no one agreed definition of aptness in such a context could emerge.

Often, as Davies points out, the mysteriousness of talent leaves trainees feeling uncertain about their own capabilities and reliant upon trainers for confirmation that they posses the relevant qualities. Approval, if it comes, can bring relief from anxiety but may reinforce the power dynamic between trainers and trainees. The delaying of judgement implied by professional training (only when one gets one's professional qualification is one finally judged 'apt') reinforces dependency on trainers and renders trainees susceptible to manipulation and suggestion through training.[54]

Davies' analysis of training suggests that the asymmetric dispersal of aptness between trainers and trainees – trainers *have* aptness and trainees *may or may not have* aptness – can give rise to negative 'fantasies' for trainees. The fantasies develop from the anxiety that they *may or may not* be judged suitable to a given occupation and this renders trainees susceptible to conform to institutional values embodied by trainers. This relates to what Davies calls the 'ownership of concepts'; that the 'debate about trainees' suitability transpires in a discourse of concepts only the evaluators [trainers] are qualified to employ but whose authority both parties accept'.[55] Davies states that in this situation 'the game favours the leaders', leaving trainees 'vulnerable to a discourse which can impute destructive unconscious motivations to their ostensibly innocuous acts'.[56] Referring back to the dynamic of vocation, naturalized by secular institutions as an a priori condition of training, Davies observes that this 'vulnerability is heightened by the fact that trainees are socially positioned within this discourse as "novices" and so "unqualified" to wield these concepts in their own defence'.[57]

Following the research into the effects of stress in the experience of learning conducted by the pioneering Anthony Wallace,[58] Frank and Frank illustrated how trainees' dependency on supervisors' guidance inclines them to 'imitate' the values and behaviours of trainers.[59] This 'modelling' has been shown to be instrumental in learning, especially of children[60] and Davies has gone on to claim that within this context trainers 'stand as the "embodied answer" to the question, "what do trainers want?"'. In this way imitation can be a palliative for the fantasies evoked by the novice–master dynamic and beneath the ostensibly benevolent communication of skills between trainer and trainee runs a psychodrama of dependency within which neither party is able to correctly divine the others' motivations or understanding of practice.

One way by which trainees become modelled on and by their teachers is through the instruction they receive and the way in which they respond to this. Language may in itself provide the structure for relations between trainers and trainees and thus calling might typify training per se but, although Luther grounded the language of calling in the body and the world investigations beginning with the body-in-the-world appear to show that, in training, the body is the basis for language.

Frank Wilson, a neurologist working with patients of apashia (loss of language comprehension skills) and apraxia (loss of skilled physical movement), has shown that in clinical cases of patients suffering with both disorders treating apraxia first may lead to improved language comprehension, especially in relation to physical instructions.[61] The philosopher of craft Richard Sennett suggests that Wilson's clinical discovery has suggested 'more broadly that bodily movement is the foundation of language'.[62] For Sennett, this discovery motivates an inquiry into the forms of language used in training.

In analysis of written instructions for performing practical tasks, such as following a recipe, Sennett shows that there may be at least four different ways of expressing instructions: 'dead denotation', 'sympathetic illustration', 'scene narratives' and 'instruction through metaphors'. Sennett sees the three latter modes as different solutions to problems caused by the first.[63]

Dead denotation is problematic because it 'tells rather than shows'[64] how to perform a task. Dead denotation is characterized by verbs issuing commands the full context of which will only be evident to he or she who has already performed the task and understands the challenges it poses. 'Knot your shoelaces', to use a generic example, is a perfectly comprehensible instruction to someone who wears lace-ups every day, but to a child in Velcro, it conveys nothing of the loosening, pulling, weaving and tugging entailed in the act of tying knots. Dead denotation issues commands; it does not explain how to perform tasks and thus it may not be suitable to the teaching of new skills.[65]

Sennett argues that attempts to break practical tasks down into smaller, more detailed commands may well result is similarly deadening results. Sticking with the illustrative shoelace example, commanding a class of children to 'cross the two laces over one another', 'pull the laces in opposing directions' or 'loop one lace and cross the other lace around this loop' will result in very mixed results, even in a group with strong language comprehension skills. Conversely, a child reading these instructions to a room full of adults in lace-up shoes will probably find that every adult in the room follows these instructions to knot their laces correctly, in essence because they are not really following the instruction at all. Prior experience of the task enables the practitioner to interpret what is *really meant* by the instruction, and to understand instructions as shorthand for particular prior experience. Commands such as these are reliant on other commands and experiences for their meaning and in this sense dead denotation is both perfect and redundant.

Analysing the phenomenon in the specific case of what Mark Singleton calls modern transnational yoga – a fitness regime and part of a twentieth-century generic 'well-being' or leisure paradigm – shows how injurious, in many senses of the word, dead denotation can be.

In physical training dead denotation often emerges as a kind of acronym for more detailed expansive instruction or as a touchtone to familiar tasks. Taking the example of yoga, the instruction 'touch your toes' may be a perfectly sufficient command to a room full of students used to postures such Pada Hastasana (hands to feet, forward bend) or Paschimothanasana (hands to feet, seated forward bend) but the familiarity of such language, and associated practice, can also become deadening in sustained training. Biomechanically, the task of stretching hamstrings is more complex than the simple instruction 'touch your toes' conveys. The tendency to arch one's back when straining to follow the instruction to 'touch your toes' can redirect the stretch away from the hamstrings and may lead to postural problems. In order for the instruction to be executed as intended the student will need to be aware of these potential problems and equipped with expertise to address them as and when they arise.

In this small example, in effect the instruction says, 'touch your toes; *you know how to do this*'. This can lead to misunderstanding and misguided practice if the student does not in fact *know how to do this*. Instructional language such as this opens a lacuna between embodied doing and description. How much more complicated does this problem become for trainees when language is describing 'higher-level' skills or communicating subjective and specific values and not providing for mere 'technical' tasks? Where yoga is practised as part of a spiritual system rather than as a leisure activity, how does a trainer communicate the profundity of experience accessible through postures and poses? In another context, is there a better way for John to say 'make straight the way of the Lord'?

Then again, perhaps as David Torevell has argued in relation to religious worship, it is precisely the attentiveness to technique that gives on to spirituality: 'ontological changes' arise through and because of 'involvement in liturgical performances'.[66] Terry Eagleton has criticized atheistic and agnostic criticism of religion by pointing out that faith 'is not in the first place a matter of subscribing to the proposition that a Supreme Being exists ... it is for the most part performative rather than propositional'.[67]

Perhaps this language will not lead to problems where the same sense of what 'embodied doing' means in a given context is shared by trainer and trainee. In the shared context of a vocation perhaps the propositional is already accounted for and all that is left to maintain is the performative. Perhaps, in this example, dead denotation merely represents the ineffable nature of our physical experiences and perhaps such instruction respects this nature, and in its perfect redundancy reinforces the private and individual reality of physical experiences. If so, all well and good but the problem remains for trainers and trainees, how to communicate about practice?

Instructional language such as this opens, or at least points towards a gap between embodied doing and description during training and this may lead to, or perhaps more importantly mask, misunderstanding between trainer and trainee. Every time students respond to dead denotation with actions resembling those intended by the instruction, the impression that trainer and trainee understand one another is reinforced, for the trainer and potentially for the trainee. In a sustained training process this might lead to ongoing misunderstanding and malpractice and might reinforce for trainer and trainee the erroneous conclusion that all is well. Malpractice can become entrenched and go unchecked, with stultifying results for students and institutions.

Sympathetic illustration is a mode of instruction that aims to suggest that 'a new gesture or act is roughly like something you have done before',[68] and thereby engender confidence. This mode of instruction is intended to dispel anxiety in the trainee by rendering new and unfamiliar tasks familiar but this mode also establishes a sympathetic bond between trainee and 'instructor' because it requires the expert to recall, or imagine, his or her own novice state of vulnerability, prior to expertise. Here authority is undermined and expertise is presented as the consequence of experience, and not the sole consequence of 'talent'. Here the subjection to other powers entailed by vocation arises in conformity to training protocols. Talent must be supplemented by hard work and so the discourse of the inexorable logic of training gathers momentum.

Sympathy may be expressed by foreboding: the instruction, 'stretch down to your toes but remember, forward bends live in the back!' does not state the consequences of stretching 'from the front' but it implies, subtextually, that there will be negative consequences. This instruction is a 'lesson' rather than a command; it has been 'learned the hard way' by the teacher and it offers the student the benefit of this experience, sharing knowledge with the student as opposed to simply imposing rules on him or her. Sympathetic illustration might also take the form of loose analogy, equating new experiences with old ones: 'Tying your shoelaces is difficult but it's a bit like tying the drawstring on your pajamas, and you can do that!' a father might say to a child or, 'reaching for your toes can feel painful but it's a bit like stretching out in the morning, and think how good that feels once you've done it'!

The success of such instructional language depends largely on a trainer's capacity to recall a state of vulnerability and ignorance prior to expertise. This can be motivational, as in the example earlier, but relies primarily on a sense of shared experience. Success also depends on the trainer finding an effective way to communicate about this shared experience through comprehensible and profound illustrations. The impact of such illustrations will also be determined by the particular responses of students to given analogies. Obscure analogies will not necessarily be less effective and multiple analogies may confuse as much as they may edify. As with dead denotation, sympathetic illustration may lead to misunderstanding but given that part of the purpose of such language is to consider the conditions of ignorance, this is not entirely inappropriate.

Possessing of similar weaknesses to dead denotation, sympathetic illustration may counter its own shortcoming simply by undermining the certitude of the instruction, and the trainer. Imagining a shared space of inability and unknowing, as opposed to imposing certainty, may give a trainee confidence in his or her own ability to 'figure it out for myself'. This contrasts the culture of 'clinical certainty' in which expert knowledge is infallible and which numerous research projects have shown to have detrimental effects in the case of therapeutic treatment.[69] Projects, such as Davies', are aimed towards the 'de-ideologization' of vocational training by dismantling cultures of clinical certainty by reconsidering how candidates are selected and trained, and language usage is one area in which this might be accomplished.[70] The aim of the scene narrative is to tell you, the student, a story: to 'grab your attention, get you outside of yourself, rivet you in an arresting scene'.[71] The scene narrative does not attempt to give detailed technical information or familiarize students with new tasks.

A scene narrative that places the storyteller, ethnographically speaking, *there* while the student remains *here*, for now, might reinforce authority. The aim of this mode of instruction is to 'jolt' the student and radically defamiliarize the task they are about to perform; it is the opposite effect to the sympathetic illustration. The more 'indelible the message, the less direct will be the connection between the scene…and the moral'[72]; the scene narrative is to training what the parable is to religious contemplation.

A yoga teacher introducing students to Ashtanga, for example, might begin with a description of the unique cultural significance of this form. This description might emphasize the uniqueness and difference of these traditions and the historical and sociocultural context in which they emerged, whether or not the description has an Orientalist tone. Or a trainer might describe the people and contexts in which she or he first encountered the techniques they are about to teach. Or a yoga teacher might begin a class by chanting in Sanskrit, or teach poses using their Sanskrit names. The lack of technical information conveyed by such description and instruction may lead to anxiety as well as confused or erroneous practice. Perhaps such 'instruction' is not sufficient by itself to teach new skills and techniques. Such language might be seen as invitational – as inviting the trainee to enter a new or different context and to accept the possibility of new practice and expertise.

Clearly, the opposite of clinical certainty is clinical uncertainty, and this is no less detrimental to practitioners than the 'retrogressive dependency upon the theoretical faiths of the past'.[73] In de-ideologizing institutional training by challenging the knowledge of experts all knowledge, and knowledge itself can be eroded.

The ethnographic interest of scene narrative instruction might draw students into the practice they are being offered or may alienate them from that practice. Scene narratives that reiterate structurally the anthropological myth of 'first contact' – the descriptions of unfamiliar and 'strange' people and contexts – may risk 'othering' newly encountered practices. This othering may well be thrilling for students but may also pose cultural complexities and cause unhelpful veneration or denigration of practices on the basis of perceived cultural significance. Mark Singleton has made this point compellingly in *Yoga Body*, in which he argues that the claim to centuries-old Indian heritage made by 'transnational Anglophone yoga' is fallacious because, 'in spite of the immense popularity of yoga worldwide there is little or no evidence that asana [postures] ... have ever been the primary aspect of any Indian yoga practice tradition ... in spite of the self-authenticating claims of many modern yoga schools'.[74]

Instruction through metaphor might aim to 'magnify the mundane' tasks of a given exercise or regime and arouse strong emotions or associations.[75] Instructions issued as metaphors drive intense contemplation, add symbolic value to tasks and can help to clarify the essential objective, as opposed to the technical stages, of a task. The imagery of metaphor can deliver brevity in instruction and direct concentration to precisely where the instructor wishes to direct attention.

In the simple task of touching one's toes directing the stretch to the hamstrings requires maintaining a straight back and one metaphorical way to encourage a straight back in a person performing this stretch is for an instructor to say, 'you are a hardback book. You fold in the middle, at your pelvis. Close the book by bringing the two covers together – don't turn into a paperback!' The image is simple and familiar (in literate cultures) and the metaphor here can prove particularly powerful because both things – human beings and books – have spines. It is, of course, equally possible that such an instruction will confuse or cause associations that blur the intended instruction but there is scientific evidence for the effectiveness of metaphorical imagery in training.

Ineke Vergeer and Jenny Roberts, of University of Durham and University of Sunderland respectively, conducted a study into the effects of imagery in flexibility training and published their results in the *Journal of Sports Sciences*.[76] Vergeer and Roberts studied thirty volunteers in a four-week flexibility training programme, dividing the volunteers in three groups that would each receive a different mode of instruction. Group 1 participants were asked to imagine moving the limb that they were stretching, group 2 participants were asked to imagine the physiological processes going on during stretching of a limb, at a molecular level and group 3 participants were not given any cues to mental imagery while stretching.

In practice this means that participants in group 1 were instructed by the trainer leading the flexibility exercises to imagine continually moving the limb that they were stretching and 'suggestions were given about how to imagine the movement in different stretching positions'.[77] It was 'emphasized that the participants needed to try both [using imagery and not using imagery] to see and feel the movements'.[78]

Participants in group 2 were instructed to imagine the muscles lengthening at a cellular level. The 'cellular level imagery involved picturing the sliding movements of the actin and myosin filaments to create a lengthening of the muscle fibres'.[79] This imagery was first explained verbally, then the sliding action was demonstrated by the movement of the trainer's hands and finally the participants were shown diagrams of this action in a medical textbook.

Group 3 provided a control group wherein the participants were offered no imagery but only technical instructions concerning stretches. At the beginning and end of the flexibility training programme all participants were assessed on both active and passive range of motion and participants provided ratings of 'vividness' (of the imagery) and comfort (in the stretch) throughout the programme.

Although Roberts and Vergeer do not offer extensive documentation about the issuing of the instructions, perhaps it is possible to classify the three groups according to Sennett's type of speech: group 1 perhaps represents a form of sympathetic illustration whereby the trainees' imaginations are engaged and empathy is promoted as the trainer draws on her own experience of exercising to produce illustrative description, for example, 'imagine continually moving the leg … by repeatedly flexing the knee, bringing the heel to the buttocks'.[80] Going beyond technical information and into imagistic territory the instruction to imagine the continual movement of the leg in the stretch position directs trainees' attention to a particular aspect of the task and avoids merely denoting the task – 'bring your heel to your buttocks'.

The form of instruction experienced by group 2 represents instruction through metaphor, or perhaps, a version of scene narrative with the intention of riveting the trainee in a compelling tale. In this instance, the tale comes from the biology lesson rather than ethnographic experiences 'in the field' but it nonetheless attempts to defamiliarize the experience of stretching for the trainee and to jolt their attention. Group 3 experienced something like dead denotation – a technical instruction on how to perform a given stretch.

Pertinently, Vergeer and Roberts found significant increases in flexibility over time in all of the groups with no notable differences between the groups. However, a significant relationship between improved flexibility and vividness ratings was found in group 2, and groups 1 and 2 scored significantly higher than the control group on levels of comfort, with group 1 scoring higher in comfort levels than group 2. In other words, there was no significant difference in the levels of flexibility attained as a consequence of a particular kind of instruction but there was significant difference in terms of how flexibility was experienced.

According to Vergeer and Roberts, results appear to show that there is potential for 'enhancing physiological effects by maximizing imagery vividness'.[81] This argument, that 'mentally imaging specific changes in a selected physiological process can produce concomitant changes in the process',[82] supports the findings of earlier research into imagery in physical training.[83]

Imagery may have a direct physiological effect on processes, or it may have an indirect physiological effect by influencing other factors, such as motivation and enjoyment, or it may have no physiological effect but be beneficial in a psychological way by making training more pleasant and fulfilling or at least less painful or dull. The higher levels of comfort achieved by the groups working through imagery-based instruction (most notably the sympathetic illustration) may have considerable impact on long-term training even if, as Vergeer and Roberts suggest, imagery may have a stronger psychological effect than physiological effect.

Whether the effects are physiological or psychological is important to scientific research and relevant to philosophical inquiry. However, while this study of flexibility and other studies in the context of sports training and injury recovery dispute the relationship between language and physiological process, there would appear to be compelling evidence for the existence of a relationship, even if this relationship is mediated pyschologically.[84]

In Vergeer and Robert's case study 'comfort' might be viewed as insignificant by those trainers and trainees interested only in increased flexibility. Interest in comfort in this context might be revived for this group if further studies showed that increased comfort leads to longer-term participation in flexibility training, which in turn leads to increased flexibility. In contrast, some trainers and trainees might view comfort as more significant than increased flexibility if, for example, these exercises were used as part of a therapeutic process, or 'well-being' lifestyle, as opposed to an elite results programme. So, irrespective of subjective judgements about the value of outcomes of training it would appear that language usage in training is pertinent to outcomes, and may with a degree of control, be used to effect certain outcomes.

In all four modes of instruction, dead denotation, sympathetic illustration, scene narrative and instruction through metaphor, trainers can have little notion of the extent to which trainees actually understand the language used, or the exercise in question. Following Davies' train of thought, one susceptible novice may understand instruction as it is intended while another may fail to understand and yet seek to conform in order to salve anxieties or imitate the trainer and her values. A trainer has no means of differentiating between these two students given that either one may or may not produce practice that 'looks like it should'. In fact, the second trainee may well produce practice that 'looks like it should' without understanding why or how they have done this, reinforcing the erroneous conclusion for the trainer that she has communicated effectively and further sinking the trainee in a relation of dependency.

One means to overcome this problem with practical teaching might be to facilitate a freer discourse between trainers and trainees and to promote questioning and discussion. To borrow and make use of Sennett's classificatory approach to language in training contexts, perhaps there are types of speech associated with *responses to* verbal instructions. Some types familiar to trainers and trainees might include 'insights', 'observations', 'complaints', 'conversations' and 'silence' and ultimately each of these types implies a question about the experience underway, even if this question has not yet found interrogative form.

Questions might be technical, theoretical or philosophical, or might even probe at the intention or ethics of an instruction or exercise. 'How do I get my heel to touch my buttocks?' is an example of this type of speech and so is 'why are we doing this anyway?'

In the context of the twenty-first-century leisure paradigm, which will usually posit students as 'users' of a given service, teachers may seek to elicit questions from trainees in an attempt to ensure user satisfaction. However, within the health and fitness lifestyle craze, as with the global media talent show phenomenon, certainty and expert knowledge are central to profit generation and autocratic cultures of novice–expert relation can satisfy both student desires (for a *good workout* or *sound advice*) and financial imperatives for health clubs, fitness studios and production companies. The recent phenomenon of the Personal Trainer, an expert capable of pushing gym users to achieve what they could not achieve on their own, is culturally modelled on the Drill Sergeant. Here expert knowledge and authority coalesce as individuals surrender their bodies to the will of holders of institutional power, often in ways that secular society at large claims to find abhorrent.

Inviting and prohibiting questioning in studio represents two distinct strategies in relation to feedback. The former emphasizing the collective endeavour of training associated with democratic ideals purported cherished in transnational context Singelton writes about and the latter reasserting the hierarchical structures of training institutions and a sense of obedience usually regarded with distaste in these cultures.

Also, there is, perhaps, always a policing of questions in studio training where trainees learn techniques as opposed to learn *about* techniques. Sustained training in a particular practice leading to expert status may require a minimum level of commitment to that practice by trainees. Questions that undermine, or might potentially undermine that commitment may be seen as unhelpful. This commitment might be seen in relation to the personal sense of calling entailed in training.

The students in the yoga class may find their questions bracketed or answers postponed. 'Why does it matter if I arch my back when I touch my toes?' has both a long and a short answer and, in the context of modern transnational yoga, it is probable that the short answer will have to suffice if the instructor is to serve all students equally and finish the class on time (both techniques – communality and timetabling – arising from monastic living). Furthermore, questions that interrogate the foundational values of a given practice may be discouraged or dismissed, may lead to 'vituperative arguments'[85] if they question the 'authenticating claims', concepts or histories of a given practice, as Singleton shows.[86]

We could choose to see this as the consequence of the rigorousness with which time-keeping has been embodied by secular institutions in the wake of the monastery and conclude that open and wide-ranging discussion on the theoretical arguments around foundational concepts might be apposite to informal discussion, but detrimental to what the trainer is trying to do *right now*, in the studio. Thus, when questions contravene the agenda of a studio class, trainers may practise a form of hygiene that keeps certain questions out of the studio and protects those practices held within it. This hygiene may or may not spread beyond the studio.

We might equally choose to see the policing of such questions as the self-maintenance of Weber's global economic order: as Mark Singleton has shown, yoga is a multibillion dollar business and has been used to sell everything from yoghurt to mobile phones, its ability to do so resulting from core hagiographies of training which may or may not have a basis in history, and challenges to these hagiographies represent challenges to the economic relations propped up upon them.[87] Thus, decorum, in the general sense of 'good manners' (social mores), in the more specific sense of studio etiquette (training specific behaviours) and in the insidious sense of mendaciousness (economic relations) may influence the kind of questions proposed by trainees.

In the context of studio hygiene, trainers may respond very differently to questions according to the ways in which a question threatens the practice that is underway – socially, context-specifically or economically.

Practice, the maintenance of its values of talent through institutional structure, shows training to be a conservative phenomenon. Added to this is a significant social threat lurking within the experience of vocation, surfacing within language usage in training. In institutional practices and discourses of training, this generalized hazard to all novices properly emerged in the wake of John the Baptist's vocation.

John's life, in the context of Christian spiritual training, is prototypical of the experience of novitiate. The secularizing of John's story, and more importantly of the techniques for living that he developed, has produced our contemporary understanding of talent as a predetermined condition prior to but also subject to the will of others. The idea that certain individuals possess innate predisposition towards certain tasks derives from the doctrine of religious vocation and the Christian ideal that we are each personally called to a spiritual life. Max Weber has shown that Martin Luther built the bridge for this idea to transit from theology to philosophy and that monasteries accomplished this task practically by institutionalizing and then exporting the nazirite model for living embodied by John.

Perhaps the auteurs that retell the story of 'the voice of one crying in the wilderness' are drawn to this tale because they, as artists, are cast by society within a particular subplot of 'talent', innate and self-sabotaging. I am not talking here about the association of genius and madness, which, as Steve Connor has shown, 'is an ancient one, from Plato and Shakespeare onwards'.[88] Neither am I talking about what Connor calls the 'distinctively modern feature' of this idea – the expectation that 'performing genius ... will be accompanied by physical or mental deficiency' – which has been well used in the critique of talent show contestants' personalities and capabilities. I am talking about a much, much broader cultural phenomenon by which we each embody the notion of talent; a deterministic principle that impels us to conform within social institutions and which predisposes each novice to listen to the expert. The principle, innovated in the wilderness 2,000 years ago, is now thoroughly embedded in the creative consciousness of training in a contemporary transnational context. Today we all, each of us, live in the wilderness.

However, as John's story shows, communal relations have power that individuals do not. As Arendt has explained in relation to the remedial techniques of promising and forgiveness, communal action contains the potential to disrupt values ossifying around any given practice and, 'without the faculty to undo what we have done and to control at least partially the process we have let loose, we would be the victims of an automatic necessity bearing all the hallmarks of inexorable laws'.[89] Indeed, the very possibility of action depends upon each of us continually considering and releasing one another from what we have done, perhaps unknowingly.[90] In essence, the reactionary effects of talent, novice–master relations, language usage within institutions and the very idea of practice in a broad sense are vulnerable to the revolutionary potential inherent in doing things together.

Thus, for the training ideology spreading by the expansion of techniques across the disciplinary archipelago, given values will predominate and then decay and be replaced. Individual lives, such as John's will end but, through institutions, the values embodied through techniques of living will attain a social existence outlasting the private one, even if not an eternal one. History suggests that ideas and ideals of talent, what it means in a given context and what should be done about it will come and go but that the philosophy of vocation, because of the economic imperatives now bound to and within it, will ensure that training itself has life after death.

6
HEART

The average heart beats between 50 and 100 times per minute but in 'highly trained apneists the heart rate can drop to values well below the average – as low as 30-40 beats per minute – with great advantage to apnea'.[1] In apnea, or freediving, the practice of diving to extreme depths underwater on a single breath, a low heart rate can enable individual divers to swim under water for five minutes or more and to plunge to depths of over 500 feet.

Diaphragmatic control (giving higher oxygen intake to the lungs) and breathing techniques to supress the urge to inhale, slowing the heart rate and enabling the body to metabolize its oxygen stores more conservatively, provide the fundamental basis of apnea, or freediving training. The rudiments of these techniques appear to feature in humans as far back as 10,000 years, where palaeontologists have found evidence that settlers on the coast of the Baltic Sea were able to feed themselves on shellfish from the bottom of the ocean. Apnea remains a professional necessity for divers and fisherman across the developing world but in the developed world today 'single breath diving' has become a leisure activity and extreme sport with superstar practitioners.

Amongst these, the husband and wife duo Audrey Mestre and Francisco 'Pipín' Ferreras were foremost – a glamorous French marine biologist and her maverick Cuban husband between them sharing world records and sponsorship deals with global brands, such as Seiko watches. Three years into their marriage, Pipín and his younger, and third, wife, Audrey, set out to break a newly established world record freedive of 525 feet (160 m) set by British Caymanian Tanya Streeter, another celebrity of the sport with global sponsorship deals and mainstream media exposure.

On 12 October 2002, off the coast of the Dominican Republic, Audrey Mestre would dive to an unprecedented depth of 558 feet (170 m), thereby eclipsing Streeter's dive and claiming the men's and women's world records for deepest 'no limits' dive on a single breath.[2] Mestre had achieved the depth several times in training prior to the official dive and so the team had every reason to be confident, except for the fact that a worrying tension was bubbling up between the husband and wife and was becoming increasingly evident to Carlos Serra and others in the team.

'Obviously something was just, not right', commented Serra, Pipín's then business partner who would go on to write a damning account of Pipín's involvement in the dive called *The Last Attempt*. 'Something was not right. Pipín was very nervous. He was like, all over the place' said Angelo Cordero, a photographer charged with documenting the dive. Prophetically, Pipín later wrote that on that morning he 'awoke from uneasy dreams'.[3]

Pipín described Mestre's waking on that morning in contrast to his own disquiet: waking to find her husband nervously surveying the moody weather a cheery Audrey stretches her 'long limbs', 'don't worry', she says, 'it'll clear up'.[4] ' "Relax", she said "don't worry. It's going to be great." '

In Pipín's description, Mestre is her 'usual self' – 'completely unflappable'[5] but this is not the figure fellow freediver Paul Kotik, present at the record attempt, saw that morning: '[Audrey's] mood was bizarre … it was troubling … there was a lot going on, it didn't feel quite right but it just, like a Greek tragedy, ground on toward this end that everyone could see coming'.[6]

After descending calmly to the record depth along the dive wire guiding her to the bottom and past her two safety divers positioned underwater and breathing from compression tanks, Mestre reached the record depth. As is customary in freediving, she reached for the pony tank – a small tank of compressed air contained within an inflatable 'lift bag' about the size of a small rucksack that she would ride to the surface – suspended above her on the dive wire and opened the valve. As the air rushes from the valve of the tank, it powers its way towards the surface filling the bag and trailing the diver, hanging onto the tank by a steel handgrip, upwards. A pony tank can bring a diver to the surface of the ocean from a depth of over 500 feet in less than one minute but only when it is full of air. At 558 feet Mestre opened the valve on the pony tank to find that it was empty.

After frantic and disorganized efforts, when her safety team finally got Mestre to the surface seven minutes later pink foam was spewing from her mouth and nose and she was unconscious, but her heart was still beating.

On deck of the dive boat the onboard doctor turned out to be a dentist. It took another twenty minutes to get Mestre to the onshore infirmary, carried across the beach on a makeshift stretcher fashioned from a sun lounger. When she arrived there the medics had no knowledge of the record attempt and the small hospital was in disarray because it was being painted and redecorated that morning. When Mestre finally arrived to a doctor in the hospital, it was more than thirty minutes since she had been pulled to the surface by her husband, who had risked potentially fatal decompression sickness diving 90 m down to Mestre as she slowly ascended on an improvised lift bag made from a safety diver's air regulator.

In the controversy surrounding Mestre's death, failures in safety procedures quickly came to light. Under-resourced and seemingly poorly planned the dangers inherent in the dive were legion – only two safety divers spread over a 200 m distance, no spare pony tank or lift bag, no qualified onboard hyperbaric medic, no shoreline medical team, no recompression chamber and no organized or rehearsed emergency protocol but the crucial safety failure, and the one that brought to light all these other inadequacies was the fact that the pony tank in the lift bag had not been filled with air.

Trauma in the freediving community turned to scandal as suspicion that Mestre's death might not be accidental arose. Pipín, as leader of the team, husband to Mestre and as the individual responsible for filling the tank with air, became the subject of furious speculation in online apnea forums; had Pipín neglected this crucial duty deliberately?

Carlos Serra pursued this question in *The Last Attempt*, following two hypotheses: '1.) Pipín forgot to fill the tank … or, 2.) He consciously failed to do so'.[7] Serra concluded that Pipín did not intend to murder Mestre but rather that he had sent her down with an empty pony tank so that he would be able to rescue her heroically from drowning.

Pascal Bernabe, one of Mestre's safety divers and the one who brought her to 90 metres and within range of Pipín, doubts Serra's conclusion and Pipín has never been investigated for the crimes of murder of manslaughter.[8]

In the ten years that have passed since Mestre's death, Pipín has become an increasingly divisive figure. Several of Pipín's former dive team left his organization, the International Association of Freedivers, which foreclosed due to lack of funds two years after Mestre's fatal dive. Serra is a public critic of Pipín and his actions on the day of the record attempt and numerous media articles have speculated over Pipín's actions and motives.

In 2003, the Hollywood director James Cameron announced that he was to make a movie on Pipín and Mestre, with Salma Hayek positioned for the role of Mestre. As part of Cameron's research for the proposed film, as yet unmade, Pipín agreed to perform an homage dive to his wife on the first anniversary of her death. He descended to the record-breaking depth of 558 feet off the coast of Cabos San Lucas in Mexico, the place where Pipín and Mestre had first met. The dive was successful and following the dive, Pipín retired from the sport.

Pipín goes some way towards addressing the controversy surrounding Mestre's death in the book he wrote in retirement, *The Dive: A Story of Love and Obsession*. The cover image for *The Dive* shows Pipín and Mestre in an underwater embrace and the first thank you in his acknowledgements is to 'Audrey, who taught me the true meaning of love, and who showed me that the end of life as we know it is simply the beginning of another journey'.[9] He concludes by offering, 'a heartfelt hug to all members of all crew we ever assembled. Neither Audrey nor I would have made it without you'.[10]

Pipín confronts the accident in chapter 1 of his book and the promotional copy that was used to market the book emphasized this element of Pipín's story – other parts of the book were autobiographical and about Pipín before he met Mestre – over all others. 'A world-champion competitor in the deadly sport of freediving tells the heart-wrenching story of his life with and without his beloved wife', is a typical example. The 'human angle' of Pipín and Mestre's love for one another elevated this sporting disaster story to the level of allegory and its 'heart-wrenching' qualities attracted journalists and film producers alike. In the parlance of film promotion, this story 'has heart'.

The semantic and iconographic capacity of the heart to represent human emotion, and more specifically love, is evident everywhere from greetings cards to graffiti, and evenly latently in the blinking heart symbol of the pulse monitors ubiquitous in freediving. Even when deployed to represent the heart as an organ, the heart symbol packs an emotional punch and the earliest known depiction of the familiar heart shape in coincidence with a metaphorical meaning of love appears in a thirteenth-century illuminated manuscript version of the French text, *The Romance of the Pear*. Contained within the letter S, a young male figure offers something heart shaped (and perhaps a bit pear shaped) to his female lover initiating an iconographic convention, which six centuries later will give rise to the infamous and much parodied 'I ♥ New York' tourism ad campaign.[11]

Although the heart stands, iconographically, for love, this symbol also represents emotion more generally, of which love is one example. The heart is symbolically representative of the emotional life of humans, and this capacity for emotion, often in place of expediency and even survival, has been seen to be definitive of humanity and a key differentiation between the human animal and other animals.

'In life-changing and mundane ways, emotion is a fundamentally *human* quality',[12] wrote Stephanie Shields in her book *Speaking from the Heart: Gender and the Social Meaning of Emotion*. Although the human animal exhibits a capacity for untrammelled emotion, which can jeopardise both social standing and biological survival, this animal also possess the capacity to manipulate representations of emotion and by so doing to augment emotions in others. Emotion occurs in humans as both a sign of authenticity and duplicity, a dichotomy that Shields covers in historical detail.

Taking the case study of the 2000 American presidential race between George W. Bush and Al Gore, Shields suggests that despite the diametric opposition of the two politicians' policies, in the final stage the competition boiled down to which candidate could 'better persuade the public that he was a genuine, feeling human'.[13] This is of course not the same thing as *being* a genuine, feeling human, although it might be.

'The question of emotional authenticity became critical to winning the election' and ultimately the American public elected the candidate that they thought 'projected the more authentic and heartfelt persona'.[14]

In addition to duplicitous representations of emotion, Shields notes how the image of emotion can carry negative consequences when, for example one is described as being 'an emotional person' but in this election there was also a 'positive side to the image of emotionality, too: a person who "speaks from the heart" is far more credible than someone who merely speaks'.[15]

Following Bush's election, and Gore's heartfelt concession speech, Shields contrasts the strategic use of representations of 'gendered emotion' in the election campaign and its aftermath. Sheilds sees Bush's tears on the *Oprah Winfrey Show* on national TV as pivotal in delivering his 'compassionate conservatism' message and documents the spontaneous 'public expression of intense emotion' in response to the terrorist attacks on the Twin Towers one year into Bush's presidency.

Shields point out that although the familiar gender stereotyping around emotion – she is 'emotional', he is not; she is upset, he is angry – might seem like a modern invention, it can be dated back to the *Phaedo* and Plato's account of Socrates admonishing his weeping friends for behaving like women at his state-mandated suicide: 'really, my friends, what a way to behave! Why, that was the main reason for sending away the women, to prevent this sort of disturbance'.[16]

The association of the heart with emotion has an even longer history in physiology than it does in iconography. In the fields of medicine and physiology, the association goes back to 200 AD and Galen of Pergamon, who formalized a theory (now often referred to as Galenic theory), popular right into the eighteenth century, that the heart was a kind of furnace exciting and diffusing the humours, originating in the liver, that percolated through the body giving rise to emotional states or rather, *passions*.

The proportion of the humours in each individual was thought to be partly inborn and partly the result of individual behaviour and lifestyles. The humours were produced by the co-combustion of *pneuma*, inhaled from the atmosphere with blood in the heart in a process sometimes partially and sometimes fully beyond individual control.

When medieval iconography depicted the heart in its now familiar scalloped, pointy shape it was the Galenic heart that was being depicted – consistent of separate chambers but connected by a porous septum. This pear shaped heart blended together humours and was rumbling, leaky, gaseous and animal. By the late sixteenth century this vitalistic heart was becoming increasingly mechanized as mixing, heating and cooling turned into dilation, suction and compression.

It is a profound anachronism that human beings discovered pumps before they discovered that they were themselves pumps; suction pumps would appear to have been invented in Egypt in the third century BC but it was not until the seventeenth century that the English physician William Harvey described in detail the circulation of the blood around the body resulting from the pumping of the heart's valves.[17]

The shift from vital to mechanical caused a concurrent movement in the understanding of emotion as a bodily experience, located both physiologically and later symbolically at the heart of the body.

Great scholars from ancient Europe, Persia and Syria all contributed to the pneumatic model of the heart that predominated until the mid-seventeenth century. Until the Renaissance revival of anatomy, Aristotle's observations of chick embryos formed the basis of the model, in which the heart was described as the most important organ and the seat of intelligence, motion and sensation.

Two centuries after Aristotle, in his book *On the Usefulness of Body Parts,* Galen reaffirmed commonly held beliefs about the heart, describing it as 'the hearthstone and source of the innate heat by which the animal is governed'.[18] A careful anatomist, Galen contradicted Aristotle's assertion that the heart was the centre of the nervous system but concurred with him in seeing the heart as the body's furnace, combusting humours in air and blood and driving human emotion and sensation.

Medieval Islamic scholars, Avicenna and Ibn al-Nafis, sought to bring the pneumatic system into line with current anatomical findings about pulmonary transit and thereby reconcile differences between these two ancients. Although Avicenna (980–1037) and Ibn al-Nafis (1213–88) pointed the ways towards a circulatory theory in which the heart is the pump, others, including Leonardo (1452–1519), a committed anatomist, agreed with Galen that the toughness of the dissected heart explained why being 'of such density' the fires that burn within 'can scarcely damage it'.[19] Right up until the end of the seventeenth century, when Harvey's conceptualization of the heart as a pump finally achieved critical mass, the heart was understood to be a creaking, leaky engine room producing human emotional states through combustion and diffusion.

How much more compelling must the art of acting have seemed when audiences were able to witness physiological pyrotechnics on stage; in place of the psychological gesture of today's actor, yesterday's board-treader almost literally walked hot coals to entertain his audience.

Although theatre mythology is filled with tales of actors succumbing to the neuroses of the characters they play, the threat inherent in feigning emotion within a pneumatic physiology is so much more serious because, as Joseph Roach has shown in great historical detail in his studies of seventeenth-century acting, 'a surfeit of a humour' could be 'frightening in physiological consequences and violent in its psychological effects'.[20]

Excessive passion, such as might be demanded of a Renaissance actor portraying Ophelia in her final crazed scene before her suicide by drowning, could cause the 'coagulation of humours around the heart, leading to disease, madness and worse'.[21] Robert Burton, in his beautifully titled nineteenth-century book The Anatomy of Melancholy, explains how sorrow, resulting from excessive 'black bile' sloshing about in the body, congeals the blood and hinders all of its operations causing 'melancholy, desperation and sometimes death itself'.[22]

For the pneumatic body, feigning emotion and feeling emotion is one and the same thing and the former is apt to lead to the latter. Where received medical wisdom extolled frequent drainage, through blood letting of various kinds, to help avoid build up of unhelpful humours, the pneumatic actor dices with internal drowning each time he sets out to portray an emotional state. How thrilling for an audience to know that the actor playing Ophelia, who 'beats her heart'[23] as she loses her mind, might at any moment expire in front of them as the 'stinking carcasse'[24] of flesh with its 'juice-filled sponges of various shapes and sizes'[25] stagnates or overflows with passion.

By the late eighteenth century, Harvey's pumping circulatory system had displaced the heart somewhat from the emotional life of humans. No longer the permeable furnace of passion, the heart was becoming the floodgate of a closed circulatory system. The 'new' science of electricity was taking over in the explanation of human emotion and action. By the late eighteenth century, Luigi Galvani's theories of animal electricity (1780), developed from the observation that a dissected frog's heart could be made to beat posthumously and outside of the frog's body by the application of static electricity in the atmosphere, were signalling a new physiological paradigm. The instantaneity of electrical transfer was being used to explain the dynamism of emotional transformations performed by actors such as David Garrick and the pleasure in spectating on acting was transmuting from a pleasure in one's proximity to physical jeopardy to awe at the control and 'technique' of practitioners such as Garrick.[26]

I would err to suggest that passions and emotions are one and the same thing, or that a history of emotion in relation to the heart could be easily drawn. In line with changing physiological paradigms the shift from passions to emotions does not merely represent changing semantic moods. Thomas Dixon has shown how this shift is representative of broader transformations in philosophy and theology moving the status of emotion towards human artefact.[27]

In contemporary parlance, a passion is perhaps better thought of as a kind of seizure. Although we retain the idea that emotions go beyond individual control and have physiological effects, we seem generally confident that the effects proceed from mental states, although these states may be incited by bodily experience more generally. In both passion and emotion psychological and physical experience arise together but, in the former the content of experiences is thought to derive from a physiological process without cognitive basis, whereas in the latter the cognitive is thought to precede or predominate over all other processes. The psychologist Elizabeth Duffy commented how emotion is most typically associated with a 'felt' quality – with experience. She wrote that emotion is generally understood as that 'vivid, unforgettable condition which is different from the ordinary condition'.[28]

Shields, in summary of definitions in emotion research comments that 'classic definitions' of emotion generally entail response to a precipitating event and or readiness to respond to events.[29] Many definitions also note the special cognitive qualities commonly associated with emotion, such as absorption in the subject of the emotional response. Behaviourist approaches to defining emotion tend to see emotion as short-term and tactical rather than long-term, static and goal-oriented. Reaching for a concise workable definition of emotion Shields concludes that emotion is 'taking it personally' and that 'something about the *self* is at stake in emotion' (italics in original).[30]

Today the emotional life of humans is associated with the intellect, the imagination and with corporeality through the nervous system, whereas for the ancients passions result from the relative quantities of substances moving within the body and between body and environment.

Perhaps the fact that for 1,800 years the heart was thought to generate passions explains why, until the present day the heart is associated with the origins of emotion. We are as familiar as the ancients with the fact that our outward self-presentation might mask our inner most feelings but the idea that the heart contains or expresses our 'true' emotions is evident in symbolic representations of the heart as well as in proverbial language about the heart. We extoll one another to 'listen to your heart', 'follow your heart' or to do only what's 'in your heart'.

Our current mechanistic physiology recapitulates the heart as a truth organ because it has now become the barometer, and not the engine of our emotions. The pneumatic physiology had the heart producing passions, while in the mechanistic paradigm the agitation of the heart muscle is in response to emotional shifts occurring elsewhere in the nervous system, largely in the brain.[31]

The mechanized heart has led to the invention of other attendant machines such as electrocardiograms and polygraphs (or, lie detectors), which can monitor emotional states such as stress and anxiety as well as devices such as the pace maker, which can induce or alleviate these states by stimulating the heart.

In apnea, controlling the heart rate through breathing and visualization techniques can help to calm anxiety and suppress the fear of drowning enabling humans to dive deeper for longer. Pipín's long-time competitor, Umberto Pelizzari, has co-written a definitive training manual for apneists, *Manual of Freediving: Underwater on a Single Breath*, which contains detailed information on training techniques to lower the heart rate. The heart is 'of the greatest importance to the apneist, it gives the rhythm for preparation before apnea, for the dive itself, and for the recovery between one performance and the next'.[32] Pelizzari is able to descend to depths lower than the Holter (the instrument used to record the electrocardiogram) is able to go and still function and he maintains that, at these depths, his heart rate slows to only nine beats per minute.[33]

Bradycardia (reduction in heart rate) can be induced by techniques of relaxation training[34] and 'autogenic training and Meditation, Yoga and Pranayama [breathing], Mental Training and Visualisation are all the bread and butter of top level apneists',[35] according to Pelizzari. However, there is research to suggest that simple immersion of the face in a bowl of water is sufficient to stimulate the so-called 'dive reflex' and to cause reduction in heart rate in most humans.[36] This reflex is found strongly in human new-borns deteriorating through infancy as we each become more accustomed to life in the air rather than aquatic life in the womb.

The 'forced apnea' of some dive specialists, in which hyperventilation is practised to 'pack' maximum oxygen into the lungs before a descent is opposed by the 'relaxed apnea' of Pelizzari who, following the French apneist Jacques Mayol, uses relaxation techniques from yoga and its 'westernized versions (autogenic training and mental training)'[37] in dive preparation. The emphasis here is less on total oxygen content prior to diving and more on oxygen vascularization during a dive.

Vascoconstriction, or the lack of tissue oxygenization is a recognized side effect of increased heart rate and a positive disadvantage to apnea and so the focus of training in Pelizzari's Apnea Academy is on relaxation and anxiety reduction, promoting bradycardia and maximum efficiency vascularization.

Increased heart rate can result from fear or anxiety underwater and much of the focus of Pelizzari's Apnea Academy training programme is on developing and practicing techniques to combat these stresses. Thus, the heart can be seen to both respond to nervous activity and also lead it, and this perhaps explains why it is now commonly thought of as a measure of emotional excitation.[38]

In this relation to our emotional life, the heart has been seen to represent our 'true' emotional state, and we are familiar with the idea that the truth of such states may exist only in the sense that they are truly manufactured. As the apneist manufactures calm, she becomes calm and from a physiological perspective there is no difference between manufactured calmness and calmness arising 'naturally'.

This question of causation has a long history. In *FOOT* and *MOUTH*, I described how Aristotle's understanding of prudence – that acting virtuously would make one virtuous – is entailed within training ideology, ensuring the social life of practice. This philosophy is echoed in the contemporary advice to, 'fake it till you make it', as well as in the continuing confusion between how I *really feel* and how my body responds to, represents, masks or directs those feelings. The 'inner' and 'outer' dynamics of this question, which vexed thinkers such as Denis Diderot, are now even more vexatious since the 'outer' representations of my 'inner' emotional self are now dispersed across terrain beyond my body – Internet photo media – and have a global, commercial dimension.

The eighteenth-century philosopher Denis Diderot juxtaposed the actor who 'feels' the part with the actor who 'shows' the part, opposing feeling with representation in the formulation of artistic technique.[39] Diderot's polemical *Paradoxe sur le comédien* (or, usually, The Paradox of Acting) remains probably the most well-known and influential philosophical account of the practice of acting. On the one hand, a technical vivisection of the art of playacting, the text also expanded from its theatrical findings to make arguments about the authenticity, or lack thereof of self-presentation in everyday life. Experiencing emotion could make representing emotion difficult and, as Diderot suggested, the question of whether or not my 'heart is true' has always had technical as well as ethical facets but increasingly it has economical ones, too.

In the days of the humours, training in the management of passions was the preserve of the actor and rhetorician but today professional training in the management of the heart is socially all pervasive, as Arlie Hochschild showed in her seminal book *The Managed Heart: Commercialization of Human Feeling*.

Hochschild documented how the expansion of the service sector in twentieth-century America had led to a new form of work, which she called 'emotional labour'. For months Hochschild observed the Recurrent Training Programme delivered by Delta airways pilots to stewardesses and was struck by the emphasis placed by the pilots on projecting a certain emotional state to passengers. The professional necessity to 'smile like you really mean it'[40] was central to the training programme as it was, and has become central to training programmes in the service sector more generally.

Hochschild attempted to use Stanislavski's acting theory as a paradigm to explain the difference between 'surface acting', wherein an individual knowingly presents an emotional state publicly that they do not feel privately, and 'deep acting' in which the presentation of an emotional state publically gives rise to feelings privately, each maintaining the other. Limited in its reading of these theories,[41] *The Managed Heart* achieved its influential status by showing the complexity of how institutions manage the way that individual workers feel, for commercial purpose.

Synthesizing ideas from Erving Goffman with her reading of Stanislavski, and her own research data from Delta airways, Hochschild introduced a new layer of complication to earlier writing on emotional self-presentation by asking not only 'how do institutions manage personality?' but also 'how do institutions control how we "personally" control feeling?'.[42] Hochschild added to Foucauldian descriptions of how institutions surveil and control behaviour by describing ways by which institutions surveil and control emotions, and how this might determine how emotions are privately experienced.

Hochschild found discord and confusion amongst employees, such as air stewardesses who had been trained to present emotions contrary to those they expected to feel, or to those felt to originate 'authentically' from within. The fact that when faced with aggression from a passenger the air stewardess who smiles discovers that she can induce in herself and others a calm emotional state was not an original finding but the recognition that this skill had now become the basis of a global service sector commercial economy was.

The reality that the practice of this skill had potentially detrimental effects on the psyche of individuals seems like a reassertion of ancient fears that acting an emotion might lead to the emotion itself, which I described in the first chapter of this book. Adrian Kear has suggested that this fear is less concerned with the emotional deterioration of individuals than it is with the Pandora effect of mimesis itself – its capacity for pure potentiality and thus for rendering all options relative and thus destabilizing 'certain' values, of ethics primarily.[43]

Hochschild was suggesting that the 'management of the heart' was no longer the preserve of the actor alone but that in the twentieth century it had become the sine qua non of the global economy. Skills that once dominated the arts economy now dominated the economy per se and more than that, these skills now increasingly dominated private life also.

Professional institutions, such as Delta airways, had developed training techniques to teach staff to manage emotions, while changing social demographics had caused families to find new ways to interact emotionally in response to increasing geographic dispersal and newly defined terms of intergenerational dependency. Hochschild foresaw that emotional labour was increasingly occurring *between* the traditionally understood categories of 'home' and 'work', 'private' and 'social' as new jobs in the 'care economy' proliferated. 'Affluent time-bound working parents'[44] increasingly outsourced the care of their young and elderly relatives and even the management of the day to day running of the household, or the organization of family events such as birthdays and weddings. Even shopping for intimate and personal items, such as underwear, could now be outsourced to what Carmen Siriani and Cameron Macdonald dubbed the 'emotional proletariat', in their 1999 essay 'Emotional Labour since *The Managed Heart*'.

Now, as Hochschild puts it, we live in an age of the 'marketization of private life', or within 'marketized domesticity' where someone – sometimes ourselves and sometimes others – must manage emotions professionally that were once germane to the private and non-commercial realm.

Having conceived of the heart as a truth organ capable of revealing our 'real' emotional life, mechanized physiology now finds that truth claim tested as we each labour to control the heart, often in confusion about how I should *really feel*.

As Hochschild writes, in reference to new research with people paid to help families in difficult situations, such as bereavement, 'they all face the bewildering task of figuring our how, exactly, to feel? – like a professional expert, a surrogate sister or a visiting aunt?'[45] In the globalized world the confusion redoubles: 'if a sister, in the spirit of which national or religious culture?'[46]

In a global culture uncertain about the very idea of authenticity, the truth claim made on behalf of the heart has an abiding appeal. Or, as Hochschild puts it, 'the more the heart is managed the more we value the unmanaged heart'.[47] The notion that the heart is prior or resistant to socialization and can thus tell the world, and probably more importantly, us, how we *really feel* beguiles. In the rapid oscillation between public and private, work and home necessitated by the global economy the ideal of the unmanaged heart seems fallacious, or this at least seems to be the conclusion that all of Hochschild's research is driving, inevitably towards.

Not only is this ideal of the true heart become increasingly fragile we can also increasingly see how the residue of this ideal in conventional wisdom can be used as a new means of social control. That this social control strikes on behalf of the usual perpetrators, and at the usual victims of historical oppression as unfailingly as it always has, as Adam Hosein has shown, probably will not surprise.

In his essay *Being Yourself*, Hosein uses Ophelia as an example of one of the facets of what Shields calls gendered emotion. One aspect of the stereotype that women are 'emotional' is that women are more apt and adept than men at the kind of emotional duplicity that apparently won George W. Bush the American presidency. Shortly before Ophelia apparently succumbs to madness and drowns herself, Hamlet is shown berating her for her various failings, which he sees as 'a symptom of a widespread disease, turning his criticisms on women in general'.[48] His central complaint, according to Hosein, being that 'women refuse to be themselves or to act authentically'.[49]

In subsequent analysis of the female heroines of 'teen movies' Hosein shows how the advice or complaint that 'you should be yourself' is most often levelled at women and especially so at teenage girls.[50] This seems relevant to Hochschild's documentation of how women work disproportionately in the new service economy, with about half of all working women sampled by her employed in jobs that call for emotional labour.[51]

In *Being Yourself*[52] Hosein shows how individuals, and in this case, women and girls are advised to conform to a certain set of norms as opposed to others – in the teen movie genre the preferred set of norms usually involve familial obedience, filial loyalty and diligence in work or study. These norms, associated with her 'true' or authentic self are favoured over other norms – in this genre these other norms probably include seeking popularity or/by sexual promiscuity.

As Hosein explains, there is no basis for seeing the former norms as 'natural' and the latter as 'social' and so the only philosophical basis for this complaint can be that the woman in question is acting inauthentically because she is acting in accordance with norms that she herself claims to abhor. This is what Hosein calls 'authenticity as self control'.

This too has a 'dark side' because, as Hosein points out, conforming to accepted norms can be 'destructive when we ignore the costs people must endure to follow the values that they endorse'.[53] Ophelia's suicide serves as an example of the irreconcilability of the loyalty demanded from her by both her father and Hamlet. This case illustrates Hosein's conclusion that 'not all failures to follow those values [we each claim to endorse] are mere failures of will; many are responses to serious personal costs and pressures',[54] a fact obscured by the 'happy ending' narrative trope of teen movies.

A darker side still to Hosein's studies in authenticity is that women, in this example, might not only be expected to conform to certain moral norms but might also be expected to *genuinely feel* that these norms are morally right. Disapprobation awaits she who fails to acknowledge this fact, as is well illustrated by Hochschild's case study of the child reduced to tears by the realization that her busy working mother had outsourced the 'emotional labour' of planning her birthday party.[55] Yet, this disapprobation is at odds with the social-cultural reality of how we live, and must live our lives now. We judge ourselves and each other by moral standards appropriate to a social context with clear duties and behaviours rather than uncertain obligations and ambivalent response.

Hochschild's observations of the expanded service sector and the rise of emotional labour puts training, as I am describing it, into a global context – increasingly, in public and in private at work and at rest we are each being *trained* to perform this labour. What is more, it is not only the emotional life of ourselves, and others, that we are training to manage but also the concept of authenticity itself, which is allied to emotional life.

Hochschild suggested that emotional labour developed to exploit an emerging condition of the twentieth-century globalizing economy. I suggest that the multiplication of trainings to manage authenticity (our own sense of authenticity as well as others' perceptions of our authenticity) arises because it is increasingly called for in cultures in which the concept of authenticity has lost all purchase.

In the world after postmodernism, where post-structuralist thinking and the proliferation of simulacra as mediums for our encounters with everything from architecture to clothing, history to family have undermined the stability of the authentic, training can be used to suture the wounds between our social and private selves and stabilize a sense of self through the maintenance of identity, personally felt.

In her essay on the 'aesthetics of asceticism', Patricia Cox-Miller provides a meta-definition of asceticism as 'attempts to control the play of the body as signifier; it attempts to reimagine how the body can be read and what it can say'.[56] Cox-Miller is not alone in reading asceticism as a paradoxical process whereby the embodiment of social roles *as social roles* is challenged propositionally while in the process of reconfiguring these roles practically; Averil Cameron compares the act of 'self-creation' entailed by asceticism as an 'act of literary or artistic creation'.[57] With regard to historic Christian discourses, Cox-Miller suggests that the body is problematic not because it is a body as such but because it is a body of plenitude, and this condition of plenitude, ancient as it may be, has been made even more plentiful by the global economies and cultures that we live in today.

As techniques of training have moved outwards from the monastery to secular society so too have these tenets of asceticism. 'Self-creation' has produced a narrative marketed through everything from food products and gym equipment to fashion and hairstyling, and the most stable and enduring self-creations are thought to arise from ongoing maintenance of diet, exercise and self-presentation, a fact paradoxically reinforced by the 'miracle effect' trope inherent within much of this marketing. A significant and growing subgenre in the magazine industry for 'lifestyle publications' that effectively monitor and comment on body transformations of celebrities – crash weight gains, extreme weight loss, 'beach', 'summer' and 'post-baby' bodies all photographed, often covertly and judged according to a binary formula of 'hot' or 'not' – testifies to the reach of these tenets.

The reconfigurations of my 'private' and 'social' selves that I must undertake to live in this culture serve only to remind me of the instability of both positions and the absence of any 'authentic' ground on which I might be able to ground these categories.

In *Training for Performance* I suggested that one way by which training offers a way out of this perilous state of affairs (and this is surely partly responsible for its monstrous expansion across so many areas of social life) is by ensuring that the reconfigurations I perform at least enable my self, my body, to act as a signifier of a unity and not of a discrepancy, to myself and to others. It is the voluntary and committed attempts we make to ensure that ourselves and our bodies can stand as signifiers for completeness – for doing the job right, striking the right emotional balance, and most importantly for being *right for the job*, whatever that job might be in any given context – that typify our contemporary commitment to training for performance and set this activity, training, apart from the discipline that characterized an earlier episteme.

A mutual need to correct a discrepancy in identity had drawn Pipín and Mestre together six years before Mestre's final, fatal dive. Gary Smith, who wrote a *Sports Illustrated* article titled 'The Rapture of the Deep' about Mestre and Pipín and 'the last attempt', suggests that 'both of them felt trapped inside their bodies' and that freediving training would become the means by which they were both emancipated.[58]

At fourteen Mestre contracted typhoid fever, which gave her a scoliosis of the spine and she had to wear a hard plastic corset for many years to help to correct this. The only time the teenage Mestre was allowed out of the corset was when she was in the water with her spear-diving fishing champion Grandfather. 'For Pipín, a lot of this [his interest in freediving] goes back to when he was a child; the body he was born into' claimed Smith. 'He's got deformed legs and feet, he's got orthopaedic shoes, he's got asthma, he's got really bad eyesight, thick glasses and kids make fun of him'. Pipín discovers, thanks to an uncle, that 'he can swim before he can walk'.[59] As Pipín grew, the water became his place of work, first as a spear-fisherman and later as a professional freediver. In the water, through dedication to apnea, Pipín healed his body and also the wounds in his identity caused by feeling that he did not belong in his body, transforming from an awkward youth on land to a confident and capable man underwater.

According to Smith, Mestre and Pipín recognized in each other the role that diving had played in liberating the private identity each felt strongly, suppressed beneath the biological and social reality of their bodies. Through dedicated practice Pipín and Mestre had brought their social identities into line with their private sense of self so that the body of each acted as an exemplary signifier of unity. New signifiers of a completed and competent identity – global sponsorship, world records and media exposure – had displaced the lack signified by the corsets and glasses of their youths. This narrative of training, as with so many, entails the individual becoming through training more perfectly *what they already feel themselves to be*.

In his freediving manual, Pipín's long-time professional adversary, Umberto Pelizzari, stresses the hazards of psychopathologies such as inferiority and superiority complexes in causing 'absent-mindedness and traumatic incidents'.[60] One of the key dangers he alerts trainee apneists to is the psychological effect of 'humiliating experiences' in the past on freediving in the present, and the likelihood of these jeopardizing safety on a dive. Before addressing breathing technique, relaxation visualizations and underwater body formation, Pelizzari claims it is necessary to ascertain 'psychological fitness'.[61] He writes, 'by [psychological] fitness we mean the capacity to recognise and control emotions connected with the specifics of apnea (for example fear of water, of depth or loss of control) as well as emotive factors ingrained in man'.[62] He writes that apnea does not 'lend itself well to competiveness', which now reads like a cautionary note on Mestre's hasty dive response to Streeter's new record. 'We must be able to recognise weakening in our emotional defences', says Pelizzari, 'so that we can intervene to control the emotion.'[63]

Smith suggests that the need to maintain the cult-like status Pipín had achieved through freediving may have driven him to take unnecessary risks with Mestre's final dive. 'I was the king of freediving [prior to the attempt]' wrote Pipín, 'I was in the business of endorsing diving products, filming underwater documentaries, and setting world records.'[64] On the morning of the dive Pipín could not relax despite Mestre's best attempts to calm his anxiety prior to the dive; 'how could she expect me to relax? Our reputations would be riding on the sled with her'.[65]

Pipín suggests that following Mestre's dive he was expecting his 'protégé [to] become [his] successor'[66] but Carlos Serra concludes that Pipín, who cherished and aggressively promoted his 'king of freediving' image, was in the process of producing one final grand semiotic gesture by saving Mestre, that would signify the perfection of his identity and its predominance over all other identities, even hers.

Speaking after Mestre's death for a television documentary called *No Limits*, freediver Paul Kotik said, 'Pipín is a product of his own imagination. The Pipín we see is the character "Pipín" in the movie, "Pipín" written, directed and produced by Pipín.'[67] As a personal necessity and later to professional advantage Carlos Ferraras had created "Pipín" and for the imaginative creation of the cult character "Pipín" the romance between Pipín and Mestre served as an emotive and powerful signifier of the unification of the self with itself.

Pipín, who described himself as 'her polar opposite',[68] depicted the attraction between the two as magnetic and Mestre and Pipín's marriage appeared to serve only to emphasize the uniqueness of each and the romance and wonder of the fact that two so unique individuals could find in each other someone so different, and so alike. As Pipín put it, 'I was a bald, outspoken, macho Cuban with a gift for pissing people off; she was a beautiful, auburn-haired goddess',[69] who seemed to Pipín 'like a different species' altogether, a superwoman 'ahead of the rest of us on the evolutionary scale'.[70]

The larger-than-life characters Pipín described bear all the hallmarks of comic book heroine and anti-hero, with Mestre exemplifying female beauty and poise and Pipín typifying male power, its virtues and foibles. Pipín wrote that, for Mestre, freediving was about self-discovery, whereas for him it was about competition and the empowering feeling of beating all challengers.

Journalists, and even Pipín's close friend Serra, often made 'beauty and beast' comparisons, which Pipín seemingly drew dark pleasure in recounting. James Cameron picked up Pipín's superhero theme, writing promotionally for Pipín's book, 'Pipín has gone so far beyond what scientists said was possible [and]…his quest – to go beyond, to become a true creature of the sea in body and mind – is nothing less than inspirational'.[71]

In the years following Mestre's death, 'Pipín' had come to represent a deficiency once more. For the character 'Pipín' this wound could be closed as the ghostwritten *The Dive: A Story of Love and Obsession* recast him as a lovelorn and guilt-racked widower whose complete identity consists in being one remaining half of a whole. The 'opposites attract' love story was being redirected into another no less familiar narrative trope: the pathotic tale of the 'one left behind'.

Linda Robertson, Pipín's ghostwriter seems exasperated in footage of her for the documentary *No Limits*. 'The main problem I had with him [Pipín] as a writer was that he was kind of a [sic] unreliable narrator.'[72] Pipín had lived a rich and exciting life but also felt the need to tell tall tales about his exploits and edit from his image those aspects of his personality and life experience that did not conform to the image he was creating. Paul Kotik said that the bits 'left on the cutting room floor' were probably not as interesting as the bits Pipín chose to show you.[73] In her punning blurb for the book, Robertson describes 'a unique and complicated tale of love and obsession taken to extreme depths'. In person she bemoans the unknowable character of Pipín; the self-constructed hero of her 'heart pounding adventure'.

7
EAR

The bodies of Olympic athletes are national causes and this is never more evident than in the moments just before one fails on behalf of a cause. The political drama underlying international competition enhances the physical contest underway and the world witnessed a triangulation of national ambitions in the fraught race for high diving medals at the London 2012 Olympics. Alongside the old adversaries of China and America, each vying for Olympic dominance over the other as an expression of ultimate global superpower status, a cherished British media personality sought to satisfy the home crowd's desire for medals and achieve a long-standing ambition of Olympic success.

On 11 August 2012, in the 10 meter dive competition at the London Aquatics Centre, China's Qiu Bo, the American David Boudia and the British teenager Tom Daley competed for medals. Chinese crowds were hoping that Bo, generally acknowledged as the favourite and the most consistent diver in competition, would be able to win gold and by so doing reassert Chinese dominance over America in athletic competitions. The American audience had less reason to suspect that David Boudia, a successful and respected diver in international competition but generally regarded as being less consistent than Bo, would achieve a top podium finish and yet, in the overall competition between national teams Boudia might be able to ensure that American competitors took home more medals than their Chinese counterparts, and by so doing win the Olympics, in effect beating China in the process.

Daley, the reigning European Champion and former World Number 1 ranked diver, had been the subject of intense media coverage ever since competing for Britain in the 10 meter platform final at the 2008 Olympic Games before turning 15. In 2012 he carried national hopes and heavy expectations despite being younger than both Bo and Boudia and performing less technically difficult dives.

Three elements of a dive are assessed in scoring, the approach, the flight and entry into the water, with subcomponents of height, rotation, extension and others contributing towards the evaluation of each phase of the dive. Each judge (of which there are seven in Olympic competition) scores the dive out of ten marks in relation to execution of the different components of the dive. These 'raw marks' are then multiplied by the Degree of Difficulty of the dive. The FINA, the international governing body of aquatic sports, publishes D.D., or Degree of Difficulty ratings as numbers to one decimal place, with most Olympic-level dives having a difficulty somewhere between 3 and 4.

The 10 meter dive competition at the Olympics consists of three rounds of six dives, with divers needing to progress through the preliminary and semi-final rounds before competing in the final six dive competition. In the London Olympic competition the score for each dive resulted from an aggregation of judges scores and multiplication of the total by the level of difficulty awarded to a dive.[1] This means that competitors performing dives with proportionally lower D.D., such as Daley, must execute their dives better than divers performing higher D.D. dives, such as Boudia and Bo in order to succeed.

Bo was characteristically excellent in the preliminary and semi-final stages progressing to the final in first place in both heats. After a shaky start, Daley emerged 15th in the preliminaries, with only the top 18 divers going through, while Boudia looked even less likely to contribute to America's Olympic cause, scraping through the preliminary heat as the 18th, and last diver into the semis.

By the time of the sixth and last dive of the final, Boudia, Bo and Daley were emerging as medal contenders, with China's Lin Yue also still in the podium race. Daley was the first of the four to dive and executed brilliantly, and was awarded full marks by one of the judges, and so with his final dive Daley moved into gold medal position.

Boudia, Yue and Bo were now under serious pressure to perform to their maximum if they wanted to displace the teenager from the podium. All three were diving more complex dives, and so there would be more points on offer should they execute well but there was also with a greater difficulty a greater potential for error. By consistently increasing his points tally Daley had been able to make the final, deciding dive very uncomfortable for his competitors.

Boudia dived next and gloriously, achieving a huge score and pushing Daley into silver. With Yue and Bo still to go Daley could still be knocked off the rostrum and the only competitive pressure he could still exert was through his points score.

The pressure told on Yue, who entered the water with a splash and dropped to fifth, meaning Daley was guaranteed a medal, but the international conflict between the two superpowers was still to be decided – could Bo triumph over Boudia and take gold or would the pressure prove too much?

Bo's dive was excellent. You could have heard a pin drop in the Aquatics Centre as the crowd waited for his scores to be announced. The dive was excellent but not quite excellent enough and the elated American was confirmed as gold medallist, with Bo in silver and Daley taking bronze, and in celebration the Britain's fellow teammates threw him into the pool while the partisan crowd cheered.

In the nights and days that followed, commentators and journalists told the story of Daley's fated medal triumph in the context of his possession of celebrated national characteristics of resilience, doggedness and determination: of how the younger diver, with less complex dives who struggled in the early rounds hung in to win a medal in front of a home crowd.

A key twist in this narrative will be the fortitude Daley showed after initial calamity. Daley's first dive of the final, a comparatively low difficulty of 3.6, did not go according to plan and resulted in a relatively poor score of 75.60. With such a low score for such a simple dive it looked as though Daley's medal quest would be over before it had even begun; with divers like Bo and Boudia, with high difficulty dives to come, Daley could not compete unless his execution was much, much better.

Olympic diving silver medallist Leon Taylor, commentating for the BBC on the 10 meter final said at the time of Daley's first dive, 'it's not so good. That's a very poor start for Daley', as a clearly frustrated Daley surfaced from the pool shaking his head. ' "The flashes", he's saying' continued Taylor, 'well if it's the [camera] flashes you can ask for a redive.'

It transpired that Daley asked for a second attempt at the dive on the grounds that camera flash bulbs going off in the crowd distracted him during the dive. Daley's request was granted and standing on the edge of the 10 meter platform to dive again Daley stood over a precipice of national disappointment – would 'Beijing's most photographed

14-year-old'[2] fail to fulfil his apparent destiny in London, ironically because of the distraction of a camera flash?

At his second attempt at the dive Daley scored an impressive 91.80, restoring him in the medal race and putting pressure on Bo, Boudia and the other divers in the field from the outset, pressure that, by the final dives, would help to win Daley a medal.

The 'remarkable' occurrence of the re-dive was later stressed by sports journalists, as well as the fact that the 'dramatic' manner in which he won bronze was 'utterly in keeping with Daley's life',[3] which had been lived publically ever since Daley went to the Beijing Olympics as a fourteen-year-old. Daley's shouldering of the expectations of the enormous home crowd, and his resilience to dive again after such a bad start to the final competition, became a central thread in the heroic accounts of Daley's medal triumph across the British press.

Exploiting Daley's media presence and the intimate knowledge of Daley's life shared publicly as a result, commentators and journalists made implicit links between Daley's stoicism in contending with the death of his father the previous year and his heroism in responding to adversity in the first dive of the final.

Daley's statements about dedicating the medal to the memory of his father were much reported throughout the national press, which re-drew the precocious wunderkind Daley in the light of his success as a hardened competitor and mature young man: 'because of all the hard work I've put in over the past 18 months, after losing my dad, all the tough times, it was about time my family had some good news' ITV reported Daley saying, and 'today was the day that I've got something to show for all the hard work and all the effort I've put in'.[4]

The triangulation of national expectations on the medal podium was also reported in the British media to emphasize the perceived national characteristics possessed by the three divers. With infamous tact, the *Daily Mail* wrote that 'Bo looked like a man who understood that silver was not going to placate the diving commissars back in China',[5] while the press stressed the excellence required from David Boudia in order to overcome Qiu Bo, producing an image of Boudia resonating with imagery of American cinematic sporting heroes who, by personal brilliance overcome their superior (and often communist) adversaries.[6]

Against the backdrop of elite conflict between the world's superpowers, Daley's achievement was characterized in terms of the

British self-perceived sense of sportsmanship wherein taking part properly and playing honourably is more important than beating rivals. 'Although it's a bronze medal, for me it's a gold medal. The support from the British public has just been incredible', Daley was reported as saying by a number of British media outlets, while Duncan White of the *Telegraph* suggested wistfully that the manner and context in which Daley won bronze 'burnished it to gold'.[7] Daley's ability to overcome adversity, personal and professional, and to demonstrate resilience under pressure was celebrated nationally. His ability to 'hold it together' was celebrated more so than his achievement in winning bronze.

Speaking to the BBC after the competition was over, Daley said, 'it's tough when you are spinning around looking for the water and you see extra lights, it's very disorienting'. 'It was an important re-dive', he said, because 'I would not have got the bronze without it'. 'The environment has to be right', concluded Daley.[8]

Daley's comments about the environment in the aquatics centre give space to contemplate not only the politics and pressures of performing in front of a home crowd but also the pragmatics of optimal performance conditions and just what 'holding it together' might mean in this context. 'The home advantage cannot become a disadvantage because of all the photographers and fans trying to take pictures', commented Daley. Ensuring optimal performance conditions amidst the pressure of expectation and the inevitable distractions of an enthusiastic crowd of spectators was a challenge for Daley's training team, and one that would be met through considered exploitation of the rules and protocols of competition as well as by the personal fortitude that would be required from Daley to maintain focus in such a distracting environment.

One set of training strategies used to enable Daley to 'hold it together' have a very particular relationship to the ear, and to the development of dance technique in the twentieth century through experimentations in the sensorial space enveloping the body, centred on the inner ear.

Relaxation, focus and spatial awareness, all aiming to ground the body in its environment were aspects of the training offered to Tom Daley and Tonya Couch by choreographer Ben Dunks in the run-up to the 2012 Olympics.[9] Dunks, who trained with the Australian Ballet, had been appointed Artistic Director of Attik Dance, an Arts Council funded community dance company in the South West, the year before the Olympics and, for fifty weeks in 2012 the TEAM GB Junior Elite

Team worked weekly with Dunks to develop techniques for body relaxation and body awareness – for sensing their body's position in space accurately and for relaxing into this position to control the physical effects of performance anxiety and for improved biomechanical control during diving. GB Swimming Head Coach, Andy Banks, and Head of Youth Development, Julian Bellan, also asked Dunks to spend four one hour sessions with Olympic divers Daley and Couch on their Wednesday 'relax' day (in effect, their day off from more formal training activities) on physical release and relaxation techniques.

Dunks is a specialist in contemporary dance, which is a broad paradigm of techniques in dance, including release and contact-based work originating movement from breathing, gravity and momentum as opposed to from set moves or choreography.[10] Training in these techniques involves attentiveness to skeletal alignment and joint articulation and tends to foreground subjective internal experiences of the body over objective and analytical perspectives and data. In one sense, this approach is antithetical to the movement criteria of competitive diving, which calls for movement precision and close attention to objective standards. Much of the training of an Olympic diver, from strength and conditioning and ballistic technique to psychological preparation and relaxation, deemphasizes internal experiences of movement and focuses instead on controlling the outward appearance of body positioning, rotation and articulation.

There are precedents for the use of ballet training in the preparation of contemporary divers and there has been scholarly research into the role of Ballet in the training of high-diving athletes competing at national and international levels for at least 30 years: Diane Pruett's 1981 article, 'Ballet for Divers' in *The Journal of Physical Health and Recreation*[11], describes how the 'diving team at the University of Miami, under coach Steve McFarlane, began taking ballet classes…as a method of building agility, flexibility and motor skills'[12]. Practical application of ballet training techniques to competitive diving appears to have been underway long before scholarly interest developed. According to Greg Kehm's brief history of iconic moments in Olympic swimming and diving, Aileen Riggin, one of the first women to qualify for the American Olympic team, studied ballet to 'build up her strength' for diving at the 1920 Olympics in Antwerp[13] and, according to Dunks, ballet still forms a core aspect of Russian, Mexican and Chinese diving training and has, at times, been incorporated in the British training programme.[14] The practical application of ballet training techniques in strength building, flexibility and agility are evidently well known to diving trainers and the comparison between the outward focus of both ballet and high diving, towards the analytical observation of a critical audience, is self-evident. However, Banks and Bellan were trying something a little bit different in asking a contemporary dancer to teach release and relaxation to Daley, Couch and a group of the most promising 11–16 divers in the country.

Part of the training Dunks offered was concerned with take-off technique, which involved analysing and modelling the contact between foot and floor before jumping and during landing, and considering the body's alignment while mid-air. This involved technical exercises designed to remodel jumping technique, for example, jumping using the muscles of the foot for take-off and without bending from the knees.

Dunks encouraged dancers to make their own technical discoveries about the use of the foot muscles in jumping, and to avoid an over-reliance on strength and learned techniques, his overall aim being to enable them to incorporate new release-based principles in their jumping style, giving additional height and thus more time for the performance of mid-air manoeuvres. Some divers found it difficult to reconcile such an open-ended and autonomous approach with some of the more regimented aspects of their training in jumping technique, while others appeared able to incorporate the lessons of contemporary dance's somatic approach with their otherwise controlled technique.[15]

In addition to the technical focus on jumping technique, Dunks' release and relaxation training encouraged divers to attend to their dynamic position in space throughout the whole dive – from the moment before mounting the steps of the dive platform through to surfacing from the water after a dive. In this strand of work the intent was to draw to the attention of divers the range and complexity of perceptual information offered to them by their bodies; to foreground subtle sensorial data over extraneous distractions in the space and to promote an appreciation of the body's reliance on floor contact and skeletal balance to provide the basis for complex movement sequences.

Central to the foregrounding of the body's muscular–skeletal alignment and position in space was determining a sense of equilibrium:

the balance of forces within the body, and between the body and the environment to maintain the centre of mass over the base of support with least effort expended.

The body's sense of equilibrium arises in the inner ear vestibular complex. The utricle and saccule organs of the inner ear detect gravity and linear movement and help humans to maintain vertical orientation. The three semicircular canals of the vestibular complex, filled with a fluid called endolymph, detect rotational movement and are crucial to a high diver's sense of rotation in somersault positions. As the head rotates, the endolymph fluid lags behind the rotation because of inertia, exerting pressure on the sensory receptors within each canal. The sensors send impulses to the brain about the movement, enabling the correction or maintenance of proper movement in rotation.

When the inner ear is functioning properly, all three canals send signals consistent with one another, giving the brain a clear image of the body in space. Vestibular disorders, such as inner ear infections, can compromise the effectiveness of one or more canal and send to the brain confused or inconsistent information, making it difficult for the sufferer to maintain their balance, and often leading to nausea.

Disorientation can also result from inconsistency between data from the inner ear and proprioceptive information from the skin, muscles and joints. Sensory impulses from the ankles and the neck are particularly important in maintaining balance because these tell the brain about the position of the head and the contact between the body and the floor, through the foot.

Disorientation can also occur if proprioceptive information and vestibular impulses do not accord with data gathered by the eyes. The common phenomenon of sea sickness results from such inconsistency where individuals experience nausea especially when below deck because visual data, which presents to the brain a 'static' image of an interior room, does not map onto 'dynamic' data from proprioceptive sensors and the inner ear. It was this form of disorientation that led to Daley's first and nearly disastrous competition dive.

From a vestibular perspective, the human body is never completely still in space. Rather the body's equilibrium is characterized by perpetual reappraisal of body–space orientation and concomitant repositioning. Appreciating and working with this fact, rather than against it was a key aim of Dunk's training.

This biomechanical fact is well understood by competitive sports trainers (such as Head Coach Andy Banks, who has a degree in Human Movement with Biomechanics and Gymnastics) but the contemporary dance training and traditions informing Ben Dunks' work with Daley imagines the vestibular system in very particular, poetic and quotidian terms, which might facilitate a specific engagement with the biomechanical fact.

The magnitude, complexity and minutiae of body–space geometry in 'everyday life' became a focus for pedestrian movement in mid-twentieth-century dance and latterly for the calculus of Contact Improvisation and the associated somatic movement techniques Dunks teaches. Pedestrian movement in dance, often associated with the task-based 1960s choreographic works of Yvonne Rainer at the Judson Church memorial hall in Greenwich Village, New York, aimed to display 'the body as a simple object in motion'.[16] Through the early 1960s, Rainer came together with a number of now iconic figures in twentieth-century dance to form a collective of collaborators meeting weekly at the Judson Church to experiment with pedestrian approaches to producing choreography. Amongst her collaborators was Steve Paxton, whose experimentations with the biomechanics of everyday tasks and the role of gravity, skeletal geometry and spatial dynamics in producing movement gave rise to a new form, or protocol of dance called Contact Improvisation.

Paxton spoke about the constant choreography of simply being upright, about how, 'in the midst of standing still something else is occurring and the name for that is the small dance'.[17] He developed standing still into a training exercise wherein students concentrate on the detail of the 'small dance',[18] pushing subconscious proprioceptive and vestibular data into conscious thought to imaginative ends. Standing silently and still for long periods of time – twenty minutes or more – Paxton's students acquired a Zen-like calm and an appreciation of the innate dance of the body as at the level of small and subconscious movement bodies laboured to maintain balance and position, upright and bipedal against the environmental forces of gravity and resistance.

Dunks was drawing from this lineage of contemporary dance in the training that he offered to Daley, working with him upright and on the floor engaging his imagination in the information being offered to him by his vestibular system.

Historically, the 'small dance' and the instability of the body in physical space that preoccupied pedestrian dancers of the 1960s developed alongside an increasing critical and political preoccupation with the non-fixity of subjectivity, and the interrelation between non-fixed subjectivities and changing social and cultural spaces. Ramsay Burt has offered a succinct meta-analysis of the 'poststructuralist theorization of postmodern dance'[19] in scholarship, which looks retrospectively at pedestrian movement through the frame of Peggy Phelan's influential 'Ontology of Performance' (1993), foregrounding the influence of Barthes, Foucault, Derrida and Baudrillard's various theorizations of 'postmodern, media-saturated culture'.[20] Burt has shown that some categories in dance scholarship, for example 'postmodern', are disputed but that there is general agreement that techniques, such as in Contact Improvisation, developed in relation to the spirit of political activism of the 1960s as well as the circulation of philosophical and sociological ideas and concepts.[21]

Steve Paxton's 'seminal work' *Magnesium,* performed at Oberlin College in 1972 and generally regarded as the first Contact Improvisation performance, appeared to mark a new paradigm for dance in the twentieth century and was, in one sense, the culmination of the Judson Church experiments in a new form and protocol of dance.[22] The improvisatory structure of *Magnesium*, where 'men hurl themselves at each other, fall, roll about and get up again… collide deliberately and aggressively' before rising to Paxton's 'signature' subtle and almost imperceptible 'small dance',[23] appeared to signal not only a new dance paradigm but also a desire for new forms of sociality.

Magnesium and the small dance offered a metaphor for the situation of bodies and subjectivities within the postmodern world described by Derrida, Barthes, Foucault and others, such as Henri LeFebevre, whose *Critique of Everyday Life* had been so influential in the political activism of the 1960s.[24] The colliding bodies of *Magnesium,* and shifting momentum between falling and rising bodies, bodies catching and being caught might emblematize LeFebevre's definition of everyday life as an 'intersection of the sector man controls with the sector he does not control'.[25] LeFebevre's understanding of everyday life, which is really to say social life, was an understanding of life as rhythmical – as the transformative conflict occurring between the body's 'natural' physiological rhythms and the rhythms of social life.[26]

In Contact Improvisation the 'natural' task of simply standing up right and maintaining equilibrium might seem representative of the social and political challenges of maintaining a sense of identity amidst the various subjectivating forces (work, family, nation etc.) replayed through media culture. In this context, standing up right and being an upstanding citizen are re-presented as more complex and difficult than they might at first appear.

By the time Contact Improvisation had taken root in dance culture in the late 1970s, LeFebevre's[27] critiques of the post-structuralist thinking of Foucault and others was resulting in increased theorization of the social production of space, and the postmodern political geography of Edward Soja that followed accounted for subjectivity within environs now characterized by constant change in the directions of globalization, hybridity and hyper-reality. Soja, a professor of Urban Planning at UCLA and the London School of Economics, aimed to develop LeFebevre's theories to accommodate the changing practical realties of cities, and social spaces more generally. Soja uses Los Angeles to exemplify spaces undergoing deindustrialization, reindustrialization, globalization, centripetal decay, centrifugal expansion, social polarization, archipelagic growth and proliferation and the increasing emergence of embedded hyper realities within physical and social space. For Soja, there are possibilities for a 'thirdspace' to arise as we live, and must live, within the mutable environment described.[28]

Soja's thirdspace is to sociality more generally what Contact Improvisation is to dance more specifically – a new propositional basis for being physically in one's body and its environment, with new possibilities. Anna Furse, a contact dancer and correspondent of Paxton's, has suggested that the social, spatial and interpersonal structures of Contact Improvisation might help to 'free [practitioners] of the pressures that may be exerted on us in daily life, the domestic and professional roles we might occupy, the responsibilities, the stresses'[29] of living in society. Furse's hopes for Contact Improvisation are mirrored in Soja's ambitions for thirdspaces as 'an-Other way of understanding and acting to change the spatiality of human life'.[30]

The concept of thirdspace (or third place) arising in the late 1970s and 1980s in the thinking of sociologists such as Ray Oldenburg[31] saw possibilities for community building and cohesion in places in between the traditional dialectic of work and home. We might even see the Contact Improvisation 'jam' – informal, improvised communal performances – which tried to imagine new spatial and interpersonal modes for dance as a kind of thirdspace. Indeed, Oldenburg argued that, although all societies appear to possess informal meeting places, what is new in the mid-to-late twentieth century is the intentionality of seeking these places out as essential to the fulfilment of societal needs, for example political engagement.

Oldenburg defined eight characteristics of such spaces, which include accessibility, playfulness and conversation. Thirdspaces can be understood in relation to the conviviality of a public house but, in the late twentieth- and early twenty-first centuries, these spaces may only represent the appearance of conviviality while architecturally working to alienate individuals from each other within the space, as in, for example, an Internet café.

Robert Putnam described a twentieth-century trend of withdrawal from civic life in America in relation to the emergence of such spaces, which appear to offer communality while architecturally alienating individuals from one another and summed the phenomenon up beautifully in the title of his book *Bowling Alone*. The global phenomenon of social networking, through platforms such as Facebook, MySpace and Twitter, has produced a grotesquely large manifestation of such faulty, or false, thirdspace. Faulty in the sense that they offer only an appearance of sociality while manifestly alienating individuals from one another and from themselves, and perhaps also in the sense that this juxtaposition of the appearance of sociality and the experience of isolation, each alone in isolated bowling lanes or at home on a 'personal computer', has been thoroughly exploited to commercial ends. 'Social' data can be used to market and sell products to individuals; where the communal interest – real, apparent or imaged – in products is a key factor in selling products to individuals, as in the economy of the Facebook 'like' tool whereby individuals register a preference for a product or service, often in return for discounts on that product or service.[32]

The philosophizing of space and the practical explorations of movement possibilities within it undertaken in the 1970s and 1980s seemed to show that, all around, the body, its physical, its subject, object, social and private positions are in constant negotiation with its environment. The maintenance of any of these 'bodies' is determined by interaction with, and within environmental factors. Any coherence and integrity of the body that could be assumed prior to this thinking and practice now seemed anachronistic. Now the physical, social and political environments all seemed to pose a threat to the wholeness of bodies, subjectivities and identity itself.

Amidst the theorizing of the late twentieth-century state of identity flux Colette Conroy has seen 'a backlash against some rather abstract ideas of subjectivity and an attempt to get down to a discussion of something real [in performance theory]'.[33] One such attempt has come from theatre phenomenologist, Herbert Blau, who has suggested that 'the body, despite all subject (and sexual) positions, is not so transformable as our ideas about it'.[34]

However, recourse to the physical reality of the body does not provide for a stable basis either, as is apparent in the perilous implications of the perpetual small dance. Blau's assertion that some form of discrete body persists amidst the non-fixity of social, sexual and cultural positions is self-evidently true and yet the defining characteristic of this body, as it is with the environmental envelope engulfing it, would seem to be transformability.

The vestibular system situates the body within its physical environment and works constantly to rebalance that situation. The self-generation and maintenance accomplished through reimaging the body as a signifier of a unity that I discussed in *HEART* clearly also take place within an environmental – a social, cultural and political – context, as signs accumulate meaning relative to other signs. Undertaking to reimage what bodies might mean in such a context requires constant interaction between body and environment and this can perhaps best be understood through the metaphor of the vestibular system and its metabolic processes.

As a biomedical term, metabolism describes anabolic processes whereby matter is assimilated into an organism at a molecular level as well as catabolic ones by which complex molecules are broken down and excreted. This 'ecological' model provides a useful framework for conceptualizing the body-in-space as one part of a larger system wherein causality is circular, or möbius-like, without beginning or end; the environment enters the body through physical experience, manifested as sensory data and the body affects itself within this environment (and affects the environment) in response to that data. What enters the body through the vestibular system is not matter, as such, but data about matter and what exits the body is intentionality and movement in response to that data, affecting matter.

An ecological model has provided much impetus to phenomenologies of perception, such as J.J. Gibson's 'environmental affordances' that situate individuals as actors within their own particular 'lifeworld' of possibilities.[35] Individual perception is co-constitutive of the lifeworld, which yields or precludes possibilities to the actor within. Anthony Chemero has suggested that the relations between things in the environment 'are just as real as the things in the relationship'[36] and so, in thirdspaces the possibilities afforded to individuals are as likely to be affected by environmental things as by individual actors themselves.

Dunks taught the Team GB divers that the physical proposition of the body in space is not simple or fixed. Conscious attention is required from the body to the environment to maintain optimal positioning in space, and this could be done through a new attentiveness to subconscious, proprioceptive and vestibular information. What is more, optimal positioning does not result in a vacuum but rather as a consequence of balancing of many, often opposing forces acting to bring the body out of alignment. What is optimal in relation to this ecological model is only the complementary of everything pessimal. In the context of Dunks' training, the 'passive weight'[37] bearing that Cynthia Novak identified in Paxton's *Magnesium,* whereby dancers lift and balance each other easily by the opposition of gravitational forces across skeletal pivot points, as opposed to by great physical effort, might offer a good example of what I mean by the complementarity here: 'optimal' lifting, using least energy for greatest effect, is accomplished by rotating a body around a pivot, using 'pessimal' gravitational forces effecting lifting, pulling bodies downwards to the earth, to send them upwards into the air.

The biological problem proposed by being in the world – the requirement to work with or against forces of gravity and resistance, to interpret sensorial data, manage motor responses and regulate skeletal alignment not to mention to overcome specific instances of pain, hunger, injury, disease and all the other threats to tasks as seemingly simple as standing up, and the absolute necessity of dealing with this problem – put simply, the problem of being a body in competitive and everyday situations – is representative of the problems of managing subjectivity amidst the social and historical forces and rhythms of spatiality.

Thirdspace, imagined to recuperate communality and reinvigorate civic life, may have something remedial to offer to the unsettled body that we each inhabit by virtue of being both human and in the world. However, civic agency and social reproduction are not necessarily dependant upon the integrity of individual identity as the exponentiation and entrenchment of faulty thirdspaces would suggest.

Operational thirdspace – operational in the sense that it provides for, in practical terms at least as much sociality as it purports to provide – may offer something to the body politic, and may act to keep it whole against the fragmentary effects of globalization. The small dance might help the discrete physical body to cohere and persist against forces of atrophy, decay and collapse. Perhaps social techniques of the thirdspace will alleviate the pressures of having social identity in the media-saturated world, and centre individuals within the maelstrom of globalization and the proliferation of hyper realities in the same way that the Dunks' techniques of balance and release may have given Tom Daley resilience against the distractions and disruptions of the environment of the Olympic high diving competition. Let us hope so on both counts because, as I explained in *HEART*, the challenge of generating and maintaining ourselves is something that we are each increasingly charged to do at home, at work and in spaces between these places.

As well as the practical role of the ear in maintaining equilibrium, and the analogy between the physical and social requirement for equilibrium in recent times, the ear has a symbolic association with the concept of obedience in training.

Obedience would appear to be a fourteenth-century addition to the English language but it has its roots in the Latin *oboedire*, a compound of *ob*, 'to', and *audire*, 'to listen'.

Obedience may at first sound like a concept deriving from the paradigmatic activity of observational control associated with disciplined bodies (the bodies we had before thirdspace became a necessity[38]). Observation and control generated social subjects and shaped the physical envelope that they occupied and, according to some, these techniques still guide and characterize some training practices. The news agency Reuters reported disgust on Chinese blogging sites after a Shanghai newspaper described how the Chinese diver, Wu Minxia, who won gold in individual and 'synchro' 3 meter springboard diving at London 2012, had been shielded by coaches from news of her grandparents' deaths and her mother's long struggle with cancer for fear that the upsetting events would disrupt her training for the Olympics. 'We long ago realised that our daughter doesn't belong to us completely', said the diver's father.[39]

The story reignited a narrative that has been smouldering for a long time and that hinges on the suspicion and antagonism between the two Olympic superpowers. Since China's reincorporation into the international Olympic movement in the 1980s, following a three-decade-long hiatus induced by the Cultural Revolution and fragile international relations, the relative success of America and China has served as an indicator of the relative potency of American democratic government and the Chinese post-Soviet *juguo tizhi*, or 'whole nation system'.

The antagonism centres on a juxtaposition of the levels of personal autonomy enjoyed by international athletes (and by extension, national citizens) and the relative success of one group in international competition can serve as a powerful reinforcement to the sociopolitical system in which they have trained.

The assertion, frequently espoused by America and European commentators, is that the training of athletes in China's whole nation system is oppressive and perhaps even abusive and that results are obtained at great personal costs, and for the sake of national prestige. In another characteristically sensationalist *Daily Mail* article entitled 'Training or torture? Inside the brutal Chinese gymnasium where the country's future Olympic stars are beaten into shape', published during the London Olympics, Matt Blake made the unsubstantiated claim that '[Chinese] charges [in training centres] are often taught by rote that their mission in life is to beat the Americans and all-comers to the top of the podium'.[40]

Abuse claims couched in the somewhat limp journalistic technique of the disingenuous-question-headline also appeared in *The Week* during the controversy of Wu Minxia situation: 'China's Olympics training programme: abusive?' ran the banner, and then rather less ambiguously, 'the country has become a sports powerhouse, but at a great cost to its athletes, many of whom are whisked from their families at a young age and kept in a brutal bubble'.[41]

At one level of the competition between superpowers the results speak for themselves. For American interests, the success of athletes, such as Boudia, trained in a democratic system, proves the superiority of that system.

Even when these athletes are defeated by competitors allegedly oppressed by their trainers, the very success of such oppressed athletes might be used to confirm the toxicity of the system in which they train: at the risk of sounding like the fox disparaging the sour grapes out of reach, in an international PR double-whammy the success of China's athletes at the Olympics can also be used to underscore the oppressiveness of China's training regime, and by extension sociopolitical system: 'You wonder why the Chinese women [divers] are so successful?' asked American University diving coach Johannah Doecke, before answering; '[because] most of the men are coaches [sic]. The women are literally beaten into submission'.[42]

Doecke, who trained an émigré Chinese provincial champion, Chen Ni, in America, said that, following Ni's childhood training in China, 'if she [Ni] made a mistake she would instantly kowtow and apologise'. 'As I worked with Chen', said Doecke, 'I would hear from time to time, "if you want to get a good performance out of her, you'll have to beat her."' In China, 'if you said no to anything, you would be chastised, slapped around. It's a brutal system', according to Doecke.[43]

Chinese coaches and athletes, including Wu Minxia, are often incredulous at the accusations of their American counterparts. 'It's not only Chinese athletes who are like this [in training]', complained Wu.[44]

'You have to train hard. Why does the West think like this?', said Shi Zhihao, the male head of China's women's table tennis team in response to comments made to the Olympic news service by British Olympic table tennis players Joanna Parker and Kelly Sibley about Chinese training methods. 'It wouldn't be legal in Britain to train as hard as the Chinese', said Parker, while Sibley told a story of physical abuse witnessed at a Chinese training centre in Shanghai.[45] Responding to the insinuation that Chinese athletes are subject to stern physical discipline and perhaps even physical and psychological abuse by coaches in pursuit of Olympic success Shi Zhihao said, 'China is very free, if you want you can do it [train], and if you don't want to do it you don't have to.'[46]

On either side of the juxtaposition pejorative descriptions and stereotypes abound – American athletes and America, archetypal of 'the West', can appear as lacking the necessary grit to achieve perfection, while China and its athletes are depicted as brutal and irrational in pursuit of glory. Sometimes both sides reclaim their stereotyped image from the other, as Shi Zhihao attempts to do, not denying their characterization by the other but instead reading it as admission of inferiority by the opposition.

In the ongoing conflict between superpower nations, sublimated and conducted as sporting competition two different images of training emerge, the differentiation being between athletes listening to trainers and taking autonomous decisions to cooperate in the training being asked for and athletes being subjected to discipline, taking at best quasi-autonomous decisions about participation in training under personal and social pressures.

This is perhaps only the interpretation that American interests seek to represent but, at a conceptual level, the collective consciousness (even if only in 'the West') differentiates between training and discipline, or perhaps between *right* training and *wrong* training on the grounds of the forms of obedience evoked in each.

Today, Western democracies tend to think of obedience entailing a particular form of paternalistic compliance – a student obeys a teacher as a civilian obeys the law – and, following global conflicts and catastrophes of the early twentieth century, we remain uneasy about the consequences of one person obeying another – soldiers may obey generals but 'I was only following orders' will no longer stand as a justification for immoral action.

We might see obedience as a benign force when it acts on behalf of the best interests of the weaker party in an equation. A child's obedience to her mother might safeguard her from danger and form her character in socially advantageous ways but obedience was also the means by which social subjects were inculcated in oppressive systems of governance and political and ideological campaigns in the episteme of discipline.[47]

In relation to training specifically, thinking about obedience from an etymological, rather than socio-historical, perspective is helpful. Obedience might connote civic and filial subjection through compliant action but it also denotes an attitude of thought and imagination preceding or accompanying action. Listening to and appreciating the content of a parent's command is related to but different from carrying out that action which they are asking for and what is more, carrying out that action might be done autonomously or subserviently. Although the action may be the same in practical terms, the attitude of the actor may differ, and this has implications for responsibility.

A fundamental philosophical principle in the field of responsibility is establishing *intentional* action, and I referred to this in *FOOT* in relation to the juridical requirement for ascertaining a guilty mind (*mens rea*) in conjunction with guilty acts, (*actus reus*) because the act is not culpable unless the mind is guilty (*actus non facit reum nisi mens sit rea*). We also find a sliding scale here because full culpability for intending to commit an act will also require integrity, or sovereignty of intention – even if I intend to commit a particular act there would have to be other possible acts open to me, which I could freely choose to perform instead of this particular act in order for me to be truly culpable for a given act. 'I was only following orders' may not be a moral excuse but it serves as a partial defence and mitigation against some if not all of the guilt of a guilty act.

The nuance apparent in the concept of obedience helps to differentiate the experience of training from the experience of discipline and this was well illustrated in the public spat between Chinese coaches and athletes and American and British competitors at London 2012.

The controlling effects of observation are much discussed in social theory and theatre and performance scholarship and the theorizing of actor–audience dynamics and the subjections and objectifications entailed by these have been widely debated in the wake of Foucault's theorization of the 'panotican'[48] and the appropriation by theatre theory of Laura Mulvey's influential concept of 'the gaze', of a male cinematic audience.[49]

The prevalence of this thinking in theatre and performance philosophy and practice has tended to set itself to assail perceived binaries, between actor and audience, male and female stereotypes and 'mind' and 'body' concepts.[50] The gaze has afforded a means to contest and critique inequality in theatre and for performance practice and scholarship during the 1970s and 1980s this attack was equally political and ideological as it was intellectual and artistic.[51]

In the subsequent episteme wherein we live *between* work and home and oscillate between subject positions, the binary situations of 'one place or another' have been superseded by an ecology encompassing both, and all. The paradigmatic activity of bodies now is not observation or control but metabolism, and the requirement of training is towards obedience, to the *right* things in any given context, in order to keep oneself coherently whole, even if only transiently.[52]

In training, at one level we can witness obedience to seniors, institutionally, as trainees heed advice from trainers and undertake the exercises demanded but this is difficult if not impossible to differentiate from discipline. The ideological conflict between China and America suggests that there might not be a way to determine what is *right* training and what is *wrong* training, since definitions of what is right and proper in terms of obedience in training would appear to differ internationally.

However, if we look again to the propositional context for obedience, which is evoked by the experience of vocation that I described in *MOUTH* we see a form of obedience to things and activities, rather than individuals and institutions. For divers, there are the laws of gravity and resistance, rotational motion and aesthetics to obey, and perhaps to obey before, despite or as well as trainers and not just because of them. Wu Minxia, in response to criticism of her coaches, said, 'I chose to be a diver to pursue this [Olympic] goal.'[53] 'I always dive better in competition', said Daley in a promotional video on his website, 'and it's something that I love to do and that's why I do diving.'[54] 'There are some days when I don't want to go to training but it's just like anything; there are some days when you don't want to go to work, some days when you don't want to go to school', said Daley, 'if I wasn't to go to a training session I would miss going to training.'[55] There is, it would appear, in diving, and in training to dive, for Wu and Daley a summons to each of them, personally, from the activity of diving and the encounter with its things, its surfaces, it feelings and spaces.

Alphonso Lingis, in his book on the philosophical concept of *The Imperative* – the force that commands the mind to reason and individuals to right action – suggests that in our encounters with different things and experiences the imperative summons our intellects, imaginations and bodies differently: 'hang gliders learn from the wind and thermals and from materials the right way to make and fly a hang glider, as the composer learns from the symphony emerging before him which are not yet the right notes'.[56] As for performers, writes Lingis, 'there are the right feelings to find for every turn in the concerto and dance, and there are the right feelings to find for an ancient ritual in a sacred space'.[57]

Lingis argues that the more baffling the problem presented to us by the world – for example, the problem of attaining rotation mid air above water – 'the more there arise, exultant and proud, people who find in [the problem] a summons for their minds, their feelings and their skills'.[58]

Obedience to the imperative might occur within an institutional context and, of course, the obedience to people and to organizations rests upon the obedience to the particular imperative to a given activity or thing. This means that individuals remain open to abuse by institutions. Institutions can exploit an individual's fidelity to an imperative provided that the institution can capture a monopoly on encounters with that thing or activity, as may be the case in elite national training programmes, but equally the encounter with the imperative can be retained as a private experience, as Daley and Wu testify.

The experience of vocation that I described in *MOUTH* provides the propositional basis for interpersonal and institutional structures. Vocation posits the relational structure between expert and novice – which will ensure the continuation of disciplinary values through institutions and schools – but the technique by which the propositional becomes the performative in training is, metaphorically, in the domain of the ear. It is the practical obedience to the conditions posited, propositionally by vocation; in the performance of the roles stipulated by these conditions, that institutional and disciplinary values come to be embodied.

The dynamic between expert and novice described in *MOUTH* entailed, propositionally, a subjection of one party to the other; obedience is concerned with how the propositional shifts into the performative in training experiences. The 'listening to' denoted by obedience reminds us that training, unlike its recent epistemological forbear, discipline, entails *self-subjection* as a primary and definitive characteristic.

Where a calling to training might contain within it the basis for certain interpersonal conditions described by the language structure of vocation, obedience can be seen as a technique for mapping these interpersonal conditions within an institutional, communal and hierarchical structure providing the basis for tuition. Obedience can also be seen as the relation between individuals and their practice, unmediated, or rather irrespective of its mediation by encounters with others.

Training can be understood to differ from discipline to the degree to which the least powerful within these structures knowingly and willing participate in their maintenance and reproduction. We might also permit that in training individuals are not only subject to other individuals but are also, and perhaps, first, subject to the directives issued in their encounters with the world and its things. International sport will probably always maintain a political dimension, with athlete bodies co-opted to national causes but for an athlete with a vocation to diving, the experience of moving through the air towards the water's surface demands an obedience to that experience, which summons their feelings, their skills, their bodies and entire person, and which is met with at once in the encounter with the platform, the water and the space between. Standing atop the 10 meter platform and preparing to re-dive, Tom Daley may well have been supressing the anxiety associated with his national celebrity, managing the pressures of expectation placed on him by his coaches and organizing his body's response to the environment enveloping it. He may also have been attending to generating the *right* feelings towards the baffling problem facing him and meeting with the summons of the air and the water at once, privately and with sovereignty.

8
BODY OF WORK

Throughout this book I have been attempting to show how training derives from and is co-constitutive of the human condition, and how it produces and determines through the body a nascent ideology of training, which is asserting itself globally today. To this end, at the outset of the book I wrote that it would be making some challenging claims for and about training, and now at its end I want to consider again these claims in light of the findings of *EAR, HAND, MOUTH, FOOT* and *HEART*.

I claimed that training has always been a response to the problems experienced as a result of having a body and being in the world, and that training was not an exclusive activity but one in which we all participate in more or less organized and self-conscious way. Having, or being, a body-in-the-world today entails new and quite specific problems and because of this I suggested that training was an assurgent ideology and the paradigmatic activity of an incipient global culture.

In the preceding chapters, training emerges as a particular form of human work – as the work of being human. The picture of training emerging is of an activity that is definitive of each of us as humans, as well as of our sociological categories of human, and which is closely related to the physical bodies that we are as well as the concepts of body available to us.[1] Training is the work of being human, in the sense that training happens because of the human condition – because of our plurality, our potentiality, our capacity for signification and the social and biological requirements of 'keeping ourselves together' in a world of things that might cause each of us to fall apart. Training is also the work of being human in the sense that it reproduces and maintains some key determinants of humanness in the early twenty-first century: the idea of expertise and the social reproduction of disciplinary knowledge, representatively under the expert control of the hand; through the mouth, the notion of predetermined talent that predicates the global economic system; by the ear, the regulation of encounters with the imperative by the organization of contact with the world and its things; a sense of authenticity and coherence required to manage social identities and sustain a private sense of self, symbolized by the heart; and by foot, the very idea of our human nature as something shared and common to all.

Although my understanding of the human condition – which, being philosophical is different to the late-postmodern anthropological ideal of human nature – derives specifically from Hannah Arendt, the idea of the 'human condition' goes beyond the confines of her theorization. There is an historical dimension to this idea; as I explained in *FOOT*, the recent increasing globalization of experience has given rise to intensification of our understanding of the world as one whole and the human being as one distinct and definitive thing about it or within it. This increasing collective, global consciousness,[2] as Roland Robertson called it, searches ever more ardently for the shared and common grounds and traits of being human.[3] 'We are all the same, at some level', was what Hannah Arendt was saying when she described the human condition as plural – we recognize uniqueness in each other, in our abilities, our dispositions, our appearance and our actions, but we also recognize our own; that we are each human nonetheless. For Arendt, one of our shared traits was a moral responsibility to each other and I have utilized the educational philosophy of Aristotle and John Dewey to suggest that another aspect of the human condition is our potentiality – our capacity to get better at things – and our generation of a social life in which these technical accomplishments have continuity beyond the terminal limits of each human birth and death.[4] That we, as humans, signify is a fact well established through semiology[5] and, as Judith Butler and others have so compellingly shown, our significatory nature gives rise to the performativity of every aspect of our being.[6] The fact that we 'generate affects' is a cornerstone of performance theory and the realization that through so doing we might be able to correct or perfect a private or public sense of deficiency or inauthenticity has been a key theme in training discourse for as long as there has been a discourse on training.[7] In the two preceding chapters, *HEART* and *EAR,* I sought to show how the need to keep ourselves together is not only necessary for optimal performance[8] but is also a requirement for living as a human being, with a body, in the world.[9] In these chapters, I described how the metabolic nature of human existence – the need to incorporate and to excorporate the world and its things for biological survival[10] and for the coherence of our social being,[11] and our personal and private sense of integrity and sovereignty[12] – might also be constitutive of the human condition.

I have suggested that these aspects of the human condition are, through training, co-constitutive of being human. What I mean by this is that we possess these conditions – plurality, potentiality, significatory and metabolic capacity – because we are human and that we are, or become human because we do things – we train – with these conditions that we posses. This might seem like a tautology but what I am saying is not the same as simply suggesting that these conditions are definitive of being human because being human, so Aristotle,[13] Arendt,[14] Dewey[15] and Butler[16] have asserted, entails a culmination, a maturation, a realization of our human condition, and this involves training. In this sense training is ontological, and is the pragmatic process by which our human attributes give rise to our humanness.[17] The human condition gives the conditions for training and training allows for the fruition of the human condition.

More specifically, training is co-constitutive of the human condition because the plurality described by Hannah Arendt as definitive of the human condition is a fundamental condition of training, allowing for a form of communal action required to sustain practice over time.[18] It allows for the transfer of knowledge within communities and the preservation of communal values of practice, while also possessing the latent potential to revolutionize practice.[19]

The potentiality inherent in the human animal, the animal that can do less, gives the means for transformative capacity and also for the dynamic situation of novice and expert in relation to one another. The capacity for the latency of expertise enables the transformation of skills and the differentiation of individuals on this basis. She who possesses skills (in potentiality) becomes she who practises skills (in actuality) and, as Aristotle wrote, this does not involve an alteration because this is the gift of the self to itself, and to actuality.[20] The realization and culmination of expertise in turn permits for a more stable or completed sense of sense, and this was what I started out by saying as I wrote about Andy Park in *FIRST CUT,* the preface to the book.

Potentiality differentiates the human animal from other animals, and thus training relates to a fundamental principle of humans specifically – as Alan Read puts it, humans must *learn* and *choose* how to act unlike other creatures who *know* how to act.[21] Thus, humans are characterized as much by their transformability as by their deficiency, by their capacity to *not do* when *to do* would be preferable, performatively (either ethically, technically, aesthetically etc.).

Humans are also distinguished from other animals because of their capacity to signify and by the simple and profound fact that humans *necessarily* signify and thus must come to terms with their own deficiency through signification, and training meets this necessity. Animals, as Nicholas Ridout suggests, are 'presented as a raw mass from which no meaning, no history and no politics can be developed'[22] and animals only attain meaning when their ' "natural" behaviours, whether trained or untrained, are framed within human contexts in which they become meaningful'.[23] The theatre-maker Romeo Castellucci – the figurehead of the influential theatre company Societas Raffaello Sanzio – attacked by six trained Alsatians on stage for the dramatic opening of his production *Inferno* (2006), argued that 'on stage, the animal is comfortable (being not perfectible) in the confidence of its own body'.[24] For animals, Alsatians for example, 'training' refers to the techniques by which non-human agency is brought under human control and this is quite different to the human capacity to perfect the body through training, enabling individuals to recuperate an inherent deficiency or to reimagine what the body can signify – to complete or refine an individual's private sense of self and to augment the ways in which other people reflect on us. Training can heal the wound inherent in the body – the fact that unlike animals that *know* how to act, we humans can, and will, do less – by controlling the play of signification on the body such that rather than the representation of humans' inherent shortcomings, training can enable the body to stand in signification of the body's sufficiency.[25]

Controlling the play of signs on, through and by the body situates bodies within a semantic context. The challenge of controlling significations on the body in relation to significations in the environment requires the body to maintain a particular ecological relation to other bodies and things. Human plurality embroils us in others and our relations with others embroil us in the world and its things. It is my contention that this co-constitutive relation has always existed between training and the human condition but that from modern times it has been complicated, accelerated and its importance to life has been renewed, made more vital and pressing.

Maintaining stability – of social and cultural positions, of a sense of identity, or self – in the nascent global, mediatized culture puts renewed pressure on these inherently problematic aspects of our condition as humans.[26] Living through postmodernism, which as López and Potter note, 'seriously bruised the self confidence to which reason, objectivity and knowledge had become accustomed',[27] has not been easy on self-identity.[28] The predicates of constant, coherent or at least more-or-less stable identity were rocked to their epistemological foundations by a widespread recognition through the mid-to-late twentieth century of the sociological causes of knowledge.[29] Nonetheless, the concept of identity still seems to hang on an idea of continuity, even if not permanence, perhaps because of, as I wrote in *ANATOMY*, the problems of postmodernism's epistemological theorizing in general; that, as Harold Veeser claims, every act of unmasking uses the tools that it critiques, and risks falling prey to these.[30] Despite what Lopez and Potter somewhat provocatively call the 'ultimately intellectually incoherent challenge to [epistemological] foundations'[31] entailed in postmodernism, the pressures these challenges placed on the conceptual predicates of our concept of identity still make increasingly urgent demands of training, which has itself become implicated in the expansion of the global culture.

Today, being-in-the-world means living in an environment characterized by non-fixity and fragmentation. Constance Classen, in *The Book of Touch*, suggests that postmodernity was defined by a paradox between immediacy and remoteness and that the alienation felt by postmoderns may result from the dichotomy between the excitement felt because of a constant suggestion of tactility (through media) and the frustration resulting from the actual deprivation of physical touch. According to Classen, touch is the hungriest sense of postmodernity, and this may also be because of its need for contact with *real* things.[32] I suggested in *HEART* that, in the times that we live in today, after the critical and experiential framework of postmodernity has been embedded in our collective consciousness, the need for a sense of authenticity has not gone away. The metabolic relation including the body and the environment is newly charged in this moment and the perpetual interchange occurring between the physical body and its physical environment occurs alongside a freshly exigent interchange between identities, albeit nostalgically, seeking stasis and an environment in flux.

Here the relationship between training as a category and the human condition coincides with the relationship between training as an ideology and human life in an early twenty-first-century moment. Training not only corresponds to our human condition but also augments and reproduces some current values by which we understand the concept of 'human'.

While training may be predicated upon innate aspects of the human being, and body, it is also generative of body constructs and the ideologies, myths and sociality of these. As I suggested in *FOOT,* feet may connect bodies with the earth and ground humans in their bipedal history but the foot might also be used through training to stand for an illusory sense of a shared past. Although training is related to innateness, it is also implicated in the generation of originary myths about a thing called human nature. If participating in a shared, essential human nature was as simple as partaking together in cultural practices least altered over time, then the postmodern moment would not have been as restlessly in search of a sense of authenticity as it seemingly was, or is.[33]

I described in *HEART* how the sense of authenticity of human experience – of the conformity of the inside and the outside, of private feelings and their public representation and reception – has always been a consideration for theatre and performance. The heart has for centuries symbolized human emotion and has been seated at the heart of physiological discourse on passion and feeling.[34] In the contemporary moment the sense of authentic feeling is a concern for all, beyond the boundaries of the stage and auditorium.

As *The Managed Heart* showed, training in the organization and representation of human feelings has become typical of professional training per se in a global economy stimulated to capital through the expansion of the service sector. As this economy colonizes spaces beyond the traditional realm of work, its modus operandi infiltrates previously non-commercial human relations.[35] The requirement to play oneself at work, at home and everywhere between destabilizes the experience of self and makes relative all selves and associated behaviours.[36]

The instability of the constructs of self and identity is not a new phenomenon. Plato saw this danger as inherent in mimesis. The valency of mimesis, its potential for generating all possibilities and thereby undermining certainty in each and every course of action, has always been a threat but today awareness and anxiety about this problem is more widespread and the contexts in which this problem can be met have been multiplied.[37]

As Audrey Mestre and Pipín Ferreras discovered, in relation to human feeling, training's capacity to reimagine the play of the body as a signifier can enable the representation to others, and to the self, of authentic feeling, and of authenticity as such.[38] Connecting *HEART* to *FOOT* in a way that James Weldon Johnson would never do, I point to the findings of these chapters to suggest that this capacity now helps to inculcate the global Human Development ideology, by working operationally in practices as diverse as spirituality, employment, nutrition, daytime television and comic book publishing.[39]

The representation of authenticity that training can produce remains unstable, requiring work to be maintained and the sense of authenticity it can offer is transient and perhaps ultimately illusory. However, amidst the environmental climate of collapse where the concept of authenticity has become fragile to the point of failure, training's capacity for self-representation is urgent and potent and is colonizing new spaces and practices.[40]

One of the abiding appeals of training in relation to its capacity to generate a sense and experience of authenticity is, as I wrote in *MOUTH,* the myth of talent. The particular ideological structure of the talent equation – that talent is innate and only as generic potential; it will require subjection of the novice to the expert to turn this potential into actuality – is a distorted remnant of a particular theological project represented by the figure of John the Baptist.[41]

Our contemporary and secular understanding of the meaning of vocation, outlined in *MOUTH*, has entailed a mysterious and mystifying sense of talent to help to justify social inequalities and to facilitate the subjection of one individual or group to another. Vocation, in this sense, can also ensure the social reproduction of particular values in relation to talent. This might boil down to reproducing taste, as preference in the arts, or it might naturalize particular ethics or ideological principles.

The mouth, in its association with the voice of one crying in the wilderness, has now become the locus of a new global media franchise whose primary commentary may appear to be a discourse on talent – on who has *it* and who doesn't: the proliferation of the talent show format internationally, initially for singing but more latterly for everything from cookery and haircutting to needlework and farming reinforces this fact.[42]

In *EAR,* the equation between caller and listener inherent in vocation is seen to provide the base on which to establish the relationship between novice and expert in talent discourse, providing an institutional structure for training and a basis for obedience, as a framework of compliance. This form of obedience was definitive of a pre-twentieth-century episteme of discipline, which has received much critical attention and which provides now a well-worn paradigm through which to consider all human activity.[43]

However, obedience as it relates to the ear, etymologically, (as, *to listen to*) also provides a framework of private experience, unique to training. That we are each called to personally and immediately by the world and its things is a self-evident phenomenological fact. However, as Tom Daley and Wu Minxia showed, we each meet this summons differently and we are each called to privately by the things of the world and each respond to this summons differently.[44]

Training is predicated upon obedience, to the imperative. The imperative might be found in the physical world; in, for example, the challenge faced by humans to maintain equilibrium, which has been incorporated by Steve Paxton into the realm of dance as both a training task and an aesthetic. The imperative may also be found in the social world and in our relationships with others. Where this is the case, there exists the possibility for exploitation of one individual by another. Although there is a difference here, the encounters with the imperative in the physical world are not more authentic than encounters in the social one. What is more, all encounters represent a challenge to humans – this is in fact their definitive feature – and thus potential dangers varying from falling down to economic exploitation and social alienation. This understanding can help us to see training as an ontological principal and not only as a specific disciplinary activity.

The differential between a private obedience to practice – to the problems faced by being human and in the world – and a social obedience to institutional superiors also provides a basis for differentiating training from the activity of discipline that historically speaking preceded it.[45] Through discipline individuals subject to other individuals through means of observation, and for purposes of control. In training, individuals self-subject to the imperative as it is met with, at once in the different directives issued by the world and its things, although in practical terms the difference may only be discernible privately.[46]

Arlie Hochschild, Edward Soja and others described different aspects of the life after lives lived within what Alphonso Lingis called the 'grids of the modern disciplinary archipelago'[47] – of schools, factories, offices, hospitals and nursing homes. The blurring of the distinctions, and the opening up of terrains between these spaces by communications technology, global transport and new models of employment, sociality, leisure and health and well-being have begun to transform the disciplinary forces that once worked discretely within each. The infiltration of ideas and ideals of self-representation across all of these territories has produced a new context in and by which our public and private senses of self is concocted.

Amidst this new environment training emerges as a remedial ideology. Training has always offered rehabilitation of the body's innate insufficiency and a programmatic response to the problems of having to *act* and to *mean*. In the contemporary environs at the eroding edges of the disciplinary archipelago, these problems have lead to wounds in identity and to the concepts by which identities have been stabilized in the past, and in response, today training is reasserted as a curative facility.

This image of training that I have drawn throughout the chapters of this book has emerged from taking apart the body and its associated concepts and analysing the practical and symbolic uses of each body part in training. The anatomical method, which encompasses the human body as a physical and conceptual proposition, has yielded knowledge about this emergent ideology by looking at the ways in which body parts practically and symbolically manifest ideological values, and how these ideas resonate together.

The ear situates bodies in the world and represents the labours of keeping oneself together. Ears place the body in space, while hands, which as Heidegger argued, *are* human, represent the orientation of our instable embodiment situation in time. The history of the heart is the history of a truth organ, and centre of human feeling, while the mouth refers us to a lifelong engagement with the imperatives met with in the world. The foot binds humans to the earth and represents a connection to the past, through bipedal history. This grounding of the human condition in human history has provided techniques and mechanisms whereby the concept of human development enters human consciousness and discourse.

Training is not something that some of us do, it is something that we all do, although some of us do it, and talk about doing it in a particularly self-conscious and organized way. Training arises because of our human condition but training also exists to stabilize specific values about humans and humanness. The disciplinary grids that produced subjectivities, addressing some of the problems posed by being a body-in-the-world are now breaking down into new structures and training is achieving a new currency as a global ideology. Training is and always has been a response to the problems experienced as a result of having a body and being in the world.

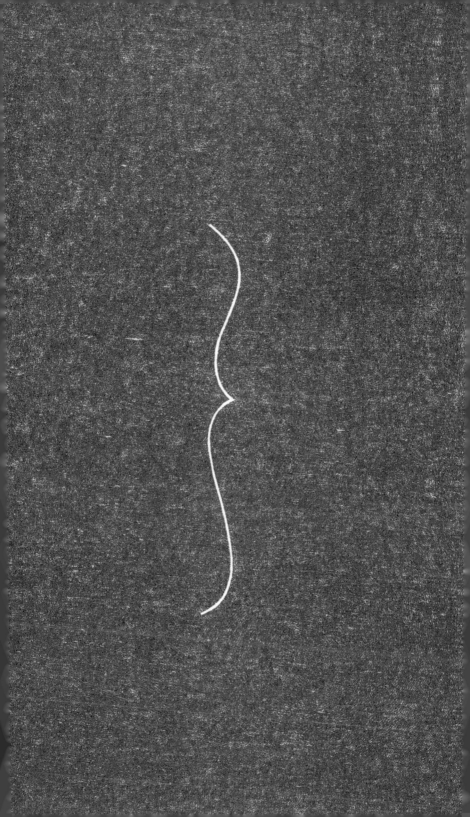

9
SECOND CUT

What of all those bits of bodies that didn't make the first cut? As I explained at the outset, there were specific reasons for choosing hands, feet, mouths, ears and hearts to open up my *Anatomy of Performance Training*, but perhaps now, in light of the findings summarized in the previous chapter, I will need to commission Andy Park to make some more prints.

The picture emerging of training's ontological relation to being human, and the particular practicalities of this relationship in the present moment, could be further enriched and clarified by analysis of more body parts, to exemplify and complexify the account of performance training herein. The elaboration might go on indefinitely with the addition of more and more body parts but the suite of parts that I envisage for a second cut would help specifically to deepen and extend the arguments about training contained here.

I suspect that Andy could do a nice woodcut of lungs and *LUNG* might be a good place to start another chapter not only because breath and breathing have a central place in discourses and practices of performance today but also because breathing is the basis for speaking, which, as I contended in *MOUTH*, is especially relevant to vocation. Breathing and speaking technique is still taught formally in universities and drama schools training actors in United Kingdom, Europe and America and Patsy Rodenburg's numerous books on the subjects suggest one touchstone to this work.[1] More broadly, these techniques form the basis of the vocal training that predominates in the current talent show phenomenon that I made reference to in *MOUTH*, and connecting the philosophy of training with practicalities here might consolidate the link between the ontological category of training and the ideology of training globally today. Mark Seton's account of the personal, social and institutional consequences of talent discourse, 'Recognising and mis-recognising the 'x' factor: the audition selection process in actor-training institutions revisited', points presciently towards the need to better understand and control this discourse, specifically in actor training but also institutional trainings more generally.[2]

Breathing techniques and symbolism are also implicated in rituals and rites and, as I started to explore in *HEART*, breath control has a practical function in the attainment and management of emotional and psychological states necessary for given performances. Further increasing the examples of training to incorporate more and more diverse case studies of training and performance, including in religious and social rituals, might enhance the sense of training's pervasiveness in all areas of social life. Furthermore, in relation to training, breathing and breath stand symbolically for the animation of practical techniques and their embodiment by living, breathing beings. Breath offers another approach to questions about training's relationship to humanness, both in the philosophical sense of the human condition and in the political sense of 'human nature', which I described in *FOOT* and which is bound historically to the rise of the training ideology in the present moment.

Another chapter could be *EYE*, not only because so much has been written about spectating in theatre scholarship in the wake of the theorization of the disciplinary episteme, but also because in the cultural context of today's training ideology we are each more watched and more watchful than ever before. In the globalized context of social life, which I have described throughout this book as reliant on and resultant from the assurgency of the training ideology, new technologies increasingly mediatize our image and confront us with the imagery of ourselves and others for our critical evaluation and intervention. In his article for *Philosophy Now,* 'The Death of Postmodernism and Beyond', Alan Kirby has suggested that the global culture after the decline of postmodernity is typified by modes of production where 'action is the necessary condition of the cultural product'.[3] In the contemporary moment, 'by definition' he goes on, 'cultural products cannot and do not exist unless the individual intervenes physically in them'.[4] The eye could be the basis of further investigations into the management of self-identity through training because of its relation to the means of cultural production right now. According to Kirby, today's 'cultural phenomenon *par excellence* is the internet', and hardware such as the computer screen and the webcam, software like Skype, Facebook and FaceTime are the means by which we come eye-to-eye with ourselves and each other in this paradigm. The interventions into identity elicited by the Internet might be normalizing and conservative in representing and reproducing the kinds of values found in particular talent discourses, as I suggested in *FOOT* and *HEART* but following Arendt's thinking about the human capacity for 'action', the sociality of such intervention might also help to dismantle unhelpful systems of thought and provide new ones.

Watching is central to the global talent show format that predicates the training ideology internationally but we are also each in our own lives required to be more vigilant of our own actions. As many scholars, notably Nicholas Ridout, have shown, this gives our actions a newly urgent ethical dimension but it also reasserts the need to prepare our actions and to be prepared for the consequences of them and this is a matter of training. Ridout describes a lineage of ethical philosophy from Socrates through Kant to Levinas that emphasizes the significance of the 'unexamined life' to good conduct. 'To act ethically' for Kant, for instance, 'is to act entirely disinterestedly, without regard whatsoever for the attention of others',[5] and yet in the globalized media culture to act without being seen, or without making one's actions visible is, as Kirby suggests, an increasingly problematic prospect. The potential for human beings to get better, ethically, individually and as a group, as Aristotle wanted them to do, and as I discussed in *FOOT*, requires a form of training and considering how this training might occur in our historical moment could be accomplished through a chapter on the *EYE*.

In this context, *SKIN* also matters. As Constance Classen suggested in *The Book of Touch*, the postmodern moment was, or is, hungry for physical contact and unfulfilled by the continuing suggestion and frustration of the possibility for it. Skin, the largest organ of the body, is representative of a global phenomenon whereby we are, through technology, brought closer together while being held, physically, apart. The need to manage this situation and to attain and maintain a sense of self within it puts further pressure on training.

Skin is an organ but also a part of the integumentary system, which includes nails and hair, both of which seem to warrant inclusion with an anatomy of performance training. Hairs, standing on ends and tingling, might move what I have written about emotion into the allied realms of sensation and nails, scratching at something and clawing forward might be representative of the experimental efforts of trainees to feel their way into practice. NAILS and HAIR, those dead ends, could perhaps go well together as a chapter on the dying limits of the body and the terminal decay of competencies and expertise hard-worn through training. This might provide, if nothing else, a counterpoint to Arendt's, albeit cautious optimism about the prospects of the human condition in the times of what Alan Read has called the 'last human venue'; at the moment – our moment – when 'extinction is available in (at least) three relatively accessible and well-documented contemporary modes': nuclear accident or endeavour, ecological disrepair and 'by the ratcheting up of mass exterminations common to genocides of the last century',[6] probably the most notorious of which, the Holocaust, prompted Hannah Arendt to start thinking about the problems of animal laborans and homo faber in the first place.[7]

SPINE is another topic now demanding attention. Spines are of special interest in certain performance training practices, such as the Alexander Technique and Meyerhold's Biomechanical training, but they also function anatomically and architecturally as load bearers, structures from which to hang other lesser structures. In this way the spine allows a consideration of practice as a corpus, which I pointed towards in relation to asana in MOUTH, and as a doctrine. Symbolically, the spine of a particular training discipline encompasses practical techniques, ideas and individuals and provides an anchor point for technical and theoretical ideals moving outwards away from this fulcrum. An essay on spine would allow an analysis of the institutional politics of disciplinary regimes, the authority of ideas and the policing of ownership of these, and this seems worthy of comment before the opened spine of this book closes finally, for now.

I also now need to write a chapter titled TONGUE, because tongues are sensory organs but are also euphemistically representative of tastes, preferences of one kind or another, whose values are maintained by the valorization of specific talent formulations. The idea of taste as a useful formulation is oft maligned by science and yet it operates everywhere in our daily lives. As I have shown in MOUTH, individual preferences reproduce talent formations which help to ensure the social reproduction of training values and techniques. *TONGUE* would allow for further consideration of the social life of disciplinary practice, and perhaps also the social death of 'lost arts', such as the etiquette skills of deportment, elocution and domestic conduct. In this way an abridged history of the lives and deaths of values in society might be traced through the internal operations of training disciplines and institutions, a reversal of the tendency in theory to see social institutions as organs of propositional and ideological ideas.[8]

Perhaps it is parochial, or overly-Judeo-Christian, of me to see a way into gender relations in training through the rib. If my consideration of Salome and John the Baptist in *MOUTH* was too male, or too Christian for some readers, then the pre-lapsarian imagery of Eden, and Eve fashioned from Adam's rib, might also dissatisfy. This imagery suggests, at least to me, *one* narrative by which to consider the ingraining of gender values within training practices and institutions. Symbolically, the rib cage suggests protectiveness and more specifically a protection of the inside against that which is outside. Disciplinary training is exclusive but the training category, and increasingly its incumbent ideology, is all-inclusive. Maybe there is a way into the politics of gender and of training's exclusivity more generally through a chapter called *RIB*, or perhaps I am reaching the limitations of my imagination for now.

NOTES

Chapter 2

1   Jean-François Lyotard's 1979 book *The Postmodern Condition* can be seen to have properly introduced the term (postmodernism) to the philosophical lexicon.

2   To be clear, I am suggesting here that 'we' are moving through and have perhaps moved out from a postmodern epoch in the sense that cultural production (theatre being one example) and theory now find the frameworks of postmodernism proposed by Lyotard to be, as José López and Garry Potter have put it, 'in decline' or simply, 'out of fashion' (López, J. and Potter, G. (eds), *After Postmodernism: An Introduction to Critical Realism*, London & New York, NY: The Athlone Press, 2005, p. 4).

3   See Robertson, R., *Globalization: Social Theory and Global Culture*, London: Sage, 2000 (first published, 1992), p. 183.

4   Robertson, 2000, pp. 1–4.

5   *After Postmodernism* is the title of López and Potter's edited book (2005).

6   In López and Potter (eds), 2005, pp. 193, 194, 292 & 296.

7   López and Potter, 2005, pp. 193, 194, 292 & 296.

8   This is, as López, Potter and the twenty-three contributors to their book recognize, a contestable claim. One basis for the claim is simply the fact that many of the radical propositions of works such as *The Postmodern Condition,* 'no longer seem outrageous; most now have a clichéd ring to them' (López and Potter, 2005, p. 4). Taken in totality, the perspectives of this group of twenty-five suggests not only that postmodernism may be something of an exhausted concept, intellectually, but also that it may not be the most suitable paradigm through which to analyse cultural productions anymore. This latter claim is the basis of Alan Kirby's article in *Philosophy Now*, 'The Death of Postmodernism and Beyond' (issue 58, November/December, 2006) because while 'the sense of superannuation, of the impotence and the irrelevance of so much Theory among academics, also bears testimony to the passing of postmodernism ... the people who produce the cultural material which academics and non-academics read, watch and listen to, have simply given up on postmodernism'. For Kirby, the evidence of a move away from the postmodern paradigm in aesthetic production is typified by a shift from authors to recipients: 'postmodernism, like modernism and romanticism before it, fetishized ... the author, even when the author chose to indict or pretended to abolish him or herself. But the culture we have now fetishizes the *recipient* of the text to the degree that they become a partial or whole author of it.' Kirby suggests that this has been seen as a 'democratization of culture' but also points out accounts of the 'excruciating banality and vacuity of the cultural products thereby generated'.

9 Sharon Marie Carnicke has written at length about the influence on yoga on Stanislavski's practice and the history of the censorship and subsequent re-inclusion of this interest in his published works (*Stanislavsky in Focus*, 1998).

10 See Lisa Wolford's *Grotowski's Objective Drama Research* (1996, p. 23) for a brief summary of Grotowski's interest in, and use of hatha yoga in actor training.

11 For summary of the history of apnea see *Manual of Freediving: Underwater on a Single Breath* by Umberto Pelizzari and Stefano Tovagalieri (Naples, Italy: Idelson Gnochi, 2004, pp. 1–18).

12 Dewey, J. *Democracy and Education*, (first print 1916) Los Angeles: Indo-European Publishing, 2012, p. 2.

13 Dewey, 2012.

14 Grotowski's famous formulation, expressed, for example, within the hugely influential *Towards a Poor Theatre,* 1968.

15 See Foucault's *Discipline and Punish: The Birth of the Prison* (1977) for the originator of the disciplinary analytical paradigm. See also Jon McKenzie's *Perform or Else: From Discipline to Performance* (2001) for brief history of the epistemological context.

16 Lingis, A., *The Imperative*, Bloomington, IN: University of Indiana Press, 1998, p. 179.

17 Lingis, 1998.

18 Lingis, 1998, pp. 179–180.

19 Kan't position is, of course, more wide reaching than this folk maxim; our actions should exemplify universal moral laws without any sense of personal expediency or relativity.

20 The thinking that takes places within different cultural or ideological paradigms represents differences, meaning that perhaps the content of all thought is arbitrary. However, thinking is a part of all paradigms, and given that it is different in each paradigm it is not an operation of any one paradigm. Thus, the content of thinking may be ideologically and culturally determined but the faculty of thinking is indifferent to these determinates. Moreover, the occurrence of thought within all cultural and ideological paradigms indicates that the principle guiding thought and giving rise to it is not ideological and cultural in its nature. This principle is the imperative.

21 Carver, R., *All of Us*, London: Harvill, 1996, pp. 55–56.

22 Mckenzie, 2001.

23 Clearly, this is hypothesis but contention would entail a fairly radical perspective on infant development and evolutionary biology. To say that even our earliest experiences of our own bodies are mediated through social constructs would be to take a fairly radical position. This may or may not be the case, and besides I am not trying to make that case here. I am suggesting that, while even our tactile experiences of our own bodies may be mediated, the urgency of physical sensation - be it hunger, pain or ecstasy - tends to supplant the rigours of decorum in our experiences of selfhood.

24 Shepherd, S., *Theatre, Body, Pleasure*, Oxford & New York, NY: Routledge, 2006, p. 6.

25 Shepherd, 2006, p. 4.

26 See Maxwell in St. John, ed., *Victor Turner and Contemporary Cultural Performance,* 2008.

27 Poetics, 4, 1448 b 4–9 (quoted in Somville, P., *Essai sur la Poétique d'Aristote et sur quelques aspects de son posterité*, Paris: J. Vrin, 1975, p. 44).

28 See Kear, A. 'Troublesome amateurs: theatre, ethics and the labour of mimesis', in Matthews, J. and Torevell, D. (eds) *A Life of Ethics and Performance*, Newcastle Upon Tyne: Cambridge Scholars, 2001, pp. 85–114.

29 The sweeping and generalized 'theatre history' is intended to show how generalized and sweeping the very idea of one theatre history actually is.

30 See Plato's *The Republic* and Aristotle's *Poetics*.

31 Shepherd, 2006, p. 1.

32 Book I, Chapter IX.

33 Book II, Chapter II.

34 Book X.

35 Shepherd, 2006, p. 1.

36 Part 1, Book 1, The Metaphysics.

37 Shepherd, 2006, p. 3.

38 In my first book, *Training for Performance,* I suggested that the predominance of 'mind–body' or 'psychophysicality' discourse in performance training scholarship was arresting the development of research within this field (London: Methuen Drama, 2011, pp. 42–56). Frank Camilleri, who has reviewed my book (*International Journal of Performance Arts & Digital Media*, 8(2), 2012, pp. 263–268), has responded to this proposition and suggested that 'a shift beyond the prevalence of psychophysicality discourse' might also be 'rooted in the practice of exercises' as well as the theorization of these (Camilleri, F. 'Habitational action: beyond inner and outer action', in *Theatre, Dance &*

Performance Training, 4(1), 2003, p. 30). I demur aspects of Camilleri's reading of my work but I welcome his willingness to take my position seriously and to respond to my proposition.

39 See chapter 2 of *Training for Performance*, London: Methuen Drama, 2011.

40 Politics, VII, 17, 1337 a 2.

41 Furse, A., 'Being touched', in Matthews, J. and Torevell, D. (eds) *A Life of Ethics and Performance*, Newcastle Upon Tyne: Cambridge Scholars, 2011, p. 49.

42 Furse, 2011, p. 49.

43 This has been occasioned by 'the spread of Capitalism, Western imperialism, and the development of a global media system' (Robertson, 2000, p. 55), which has, as Robertson writes, 'been addressed at great length' (p. 29) in critical discourse on globalization.

44 Heelas, P., *The New Age Movement*, Oxford: Blackwell Publishing, 1996, p. 169.

45 Bruce, S., *Religion in the Modern World: From Cathedrals to Cults*, Oxford: Oxford University Press, 1996, p. 197.

46 See Andrew Ross', *Strange Weather: Culture, Science and Technology in the Age of Limits*, London & New York, NY: Verso, 1991, p. 21, and Wendy Parkins', 'Oprah Winfrey's change your life TV and the spiritual everyday' in *Journal of Media and Cultural Studies*, London: Taylor & Francis, 15(2), 2001, pp. 145–157.

47 Heelas, P., 'The new age in cultural context: the premodern, the modern and the postmodern', in *Religion* 23,1993, pp. 103–116, and Heelas, P.L.F., 'Prosperity and the new age movement. The efficacy of spiritual economics', in Wilson, B., and Cressell, J. (eds) New *Religious Movements: Challenges and Response*, London: Routledge, 1999, pp. 49–77.

48 Roberts, R., 'Power and empowerment: new age managers and the dialectics of modernity/postmodernity' in *Religion Today*, 9(3), 1994, pp. 3–13.

49 Van Hove, H., 'L'emergence d'un 'marche spirituel' religieux' in *Social Compass*, 46(2), 1999, pp. 161–172.

50 Possamai, A., *In Search of New Age Spiritualties*, Aldershot, Hampshire: Ashgate, 2005, notably pp. 131–133.

51 Furse, 2011.

52 See Laura Mulveys influential essay 'Visual pleasure and narrative cinema', originally Published in *Screen*, 16(3), Autumn 1975, pp. 6–18, thoroughly appropriated by performance theory. For examples, see Shepherd (2006) and Schneider, R., *The Explicit Body in Performance*,London & New York, NY: Routledge, 2013 (e.g., pp. 60, 62, 74, 90, 97).

53 This will be discussed more fully in *FOOT.*

54 See Veeser, H., *The New Historicism*, London & New York, NY: Routledge, 1989.

55 See Ajzenstat, O., 'Levinas vs Levinas: Hebrew, Greek and Linguistic justice', in *Philosophy and Rhetoric*, 38(2), 2005, pp. 145–158.

56 See Vanhoozer, K.J., *The Drama of Doctrine: A Canonical-Linguistic Approach to Christian Theology*, Westminster: John Knox Press, 2005, p. 269.

57 See Ajzenstat (2005).

58 Kohn, T., 'The Aikido body: expressions of group identities and self discoveries in Martial Arts Training', in Dyck, N., and Archetti, E.P. (eds) *Sport, Dance and Embodied Identities*, Oxford: Berg, 2003, p. 142.

59 For examples, see, Loukes, R., 'Tracing bodies: researching psychophysical training for performance through practice', in *Performance Research*, 8(4), 2003, pp. 54–60.

60 Read, A., *Theatre, Intimacy and Engagement: The Last Human Venue*, Basingstoke Hamps: Palgrave MacMillan, 2008, p. 283.

61 John Law, 'Making a Mess with Method', published by the Centre for Science Studies, Lancaster University, Lancaster LA1 4YN, UK, at http://www.comp.lancs.ac.uk/sociology/papers/Law-Making-a-Mess-with-Method.pdf.

62 In Matthews, J. and Torevell, D. (eds) *A Life of Ethics and Performance*, Newcastle Upon Tyne: Cambridge Scholars, 2011, and Paul Allain and Alison Hodge's books with and about Gardzienice (1998 and 2003 respectively).

63 Personal correspondence, 13th November, 2013.

64 Myers, D.G. 1989, *The New Historicism in Literary Study*, viewed 27 April 2006.

65 As Veeser points out, such theorizing often exhibits a blindspot, or perhaps a mutespot is a better term of phrase; the theory emerging within an epistemological context must also be of the epistemological context, and therefore shaped by it, and yet it may not explicitly acknowledge this fact.

66 Paglia, Camille. 'Junk Bonds and Corporate Raiders: Academe in the Hour of the Wolf', reprinted in *Sex, Art and American Culture: New Essays* (1992).

67 Classen, C., *The Book of Touch*, Oxford: Berg, 2005, p. 3.

68 See Benedetti, J., *The Art of the Actor*, London: Methuen Drama, 2005, pp. 26–28 for a history encompassing Quintillian's writings on the hand.

69 See Benedetti, 2005, pp. 7–31 and *Sandford Meisner On Acting*, New York, NY: Random House, 1987, pp. 16–40.

70 Welton, M., *Feeling Theatre*, Basingstoke, Hamps: Palgrave MacMillan, 2011.

71 Some wag might suggest that we might instead talk about 'getting to the bottom' of a matter but it seems clear that this is not a body metaphor!.

72 Butler, J., *Gender Trouble*, Abingdon, Oxford & New York, NY: Routledge, 1990, p. 196.

73 See Ridout, N., *Stage Fright: Animals and Other Theatrical Problems*, Cambridge, MA: Cambridge University Press, 2006.

74 See Alan Read on 'The early animal', in Matthews, J. and Torevell, D. (eds) *A Life of Ethics and Performance*, Newcastle Upon Tyne: Cambridge Scholars, 2011, pp. 142–144.

75 I will pick up this line of thought specifically in *FOOT*.

76 The supposition that I follow throughout this book is influenced by the increasingly widespread sense that postmodernism has ceased to be the most influential or helpful paradigm through which to understand the current moment. Many, including López and Potter (2005) and Alan Kirby (2006), whom I cite in this book, have suggested new emergent paradigms of thinking, such as 'critical realism' and 'pseudo-modernism', respectively, arising after postmodernity and with the dawning of the twenty-first century. My own sense of these currents of thinking is that no general consensus has yet appeared in society about the paradigm replacing postmodernism but that postmodernism is if not obsolete then at least exhausted. Accordingly, I make efforts throughout this book to connect the modernist thinking of people like Arendt with the postmodernist ideas of Judith Butler, Peggy Phelan, Michel Foucault and others because these would seem to be the theories reposited and recirculating in our contemporary moment, whatever this moment may ultimately show itself to have been. I also endeavour to be historical in this book about the decline of postmodernism and, following López, Potter and Kirby I see this beginning towards the end of the twentieth century and continuing into the present.

Chapter 3

1 The account of Viviani and Galileo that follows is pieced together from several sources, including Michael Hunter's edited book *Archives of the Scientific Revolution: The Formation and Exchange of Ideas in Seventeenth-Century Europe,* Woodbridge: Boydell Press, 1998, *Retrying Galileo* by Maurice Finocchiaro, Berkeley, LA and London: University of California Press, 2005 and Dava Sobel's *Galileo's Daughter,* London: Fourth Estate, 1999.

2 See Dava Sobel's, *Galileo's Daughter* London: Fourth Estate, 1999, pp. 374–384.

3 In total, three fingers of the right hand, a single vertebra and one tooth were removed from Galileo's remains by his followers.

4 Quoted in Tallis, R., *The Hand: A Philosophical Inquiry in Human Being*, Edinburgh: Edinburgh University Press, 2003, p. 4.

5 This is a simplistic but generally accurate distillation of the central theme running through the Western philosophical tradition of philosophy of education, as expressed in numerous works on the subject, including, Winch, C., and Gingell, J., *Key Concepts in the Philosophy of Education*,

London: Routledge, 1999, Ulich, R., *Three Thousand Years of Educational Wisdom*, Cambridge, MA: Harvard University Press, 1954, Snook, I., *Indoctrination and Education*, London: Routledge, 1972, O'Connor, D., *An Introduction to Philosophy of Education*, London: Routledge, 1957, Peters, R., *The Philosophy of Education*, Oxford: Oxford University Press, 1973, Murphy, M., *The History and Philosophy of Education: Voices of Educational Pioneers*, Upper Saddle River, NJ: Pearson, 2006, and countless others on the topic.

6   For fuller discussion of the necessarily cursory history, see, Curren, R.R., *Aristotle on the Necessity of Public Education*, Lanham, MD: Rowman and Littlefield, 2000, Scheffler, I., *Reason and Teaching*, Indianapolis, IN: Hackett, 1973 and 1989, Siegel, H., *Educating Reason: Rationality, Critical Thinking, and Education*, London: Routledge, 1988, *Rationality Redeemed?: Further Dialogues on an Educational Ideal*, New York, NY: Routledge, 1997 and 'Philosophy of education', in *Britannica Online Encyclopaedia*, 2007.

7   *Process and Reality*, New York, NY : The Free Press, distributed by Simon and Schuster, 1979, p. 39.

8   Clearly, these are all English language examples. This is a convention that I follow throughout this chapter because these proverbial/psycho-linguistic examples of associations between hands and expertise are a comparatively minor point about the ontological and ideological relationships between hands and training.

9   *Aristotle* in 23 Volumes, trans. Hugh Tredennick, Cambridge, MA: Harvard University Press (London: William Heinemann Ltd. 1933, *1989*) Volume 1, Book 1, Chapter 1, p. 3.

10 Diderot attributes these words to the mathematician Nicholas Saunderson in his *Letter on the Blind*. According to Diderot, these are Saunderson's dying words to a priest attending his deathbed (see Sam Stark's, *Diderot: French Philosopher and Father of the Encyclopedia*, New York, NY: Rosen Publishing Group, 2006, p. 54).

11 See Aristotle, trans. William Ogle, *On the Parts of Animals*, Whitefish, MT: Kessinger Publishing, 2004, p. 21.

12 See Benedetti, J., *The Art of the Actor*, London: Methuen Drama, 2005, p. 20.

13 Benedetti, 2005, p. 80.

14 Benedetti, 2005.

15 See, Max Black's classic text, *Metaphors and Models*, Ithaca, NY: Cornell University Press, 1962.

16 See Jonathon Pitches', *Vsevolod Meyerhold*, London & New York: Routledge, 2003 for a fulsome appreciation of the centrality of these exercises to Meyerhold's training approach.

17 See Macgowan, K. and Melnitz, W., *The Living Stage*, Englewood Cliffs, NJ: Prentice-Hall, 1955.

18 Krasner, D., in Hodge, A. (ed.) *Twentieth-Century Actor Training*, London & New York, NY: Routledge, 2000, p. 144.

19 Spolin, V., *Theatre Games for Rehearsal*, Evanston, IL: Northwestern University Press, 2011, p. 59.

20 See Clive Barker's, *Theatre Games*, London: Methuen Drama, (first published 1977) 2010, p. 73.

21 See Pitches, 2003, p. 67.

22 Pitches, 2003, p. 72.

23 In Hodge, A., (ed.) *Actor Training, 2nd Edition*, Oxford & New York, NY: Routledge, 2010, p. 191.

24 Hodge, 2010.

25 For discussion of this discourse within twentieth- and twenty-first-century actor training see my article, 'Acting freely' in *Performance Research*, 14(2), 2009, pp.103–112.

26 Oida, Y. and Marhsall, L., *The Invisible Actor*, London: Methuen, 1997, pp. 75–76.

27 Martin, Heidegger, *Parmenides*, trans. Andre Schuwer and Richard Rojcewicz, Bloomington, IN: Indiana University Press, 1992, pp. 80–81.

28 Heidegger, 1992.

29 See Hinchman, L.P. and Hinchman, S. (eds) *Hannah Arendt: Critical Essays*, Albany, NY: State University of New York Press, pp. 233–235.

30 Sennet, R., *The Craftsman*, London: Penguin, 2008, p. 153.

31 Philosophically speaking, we might see the body and the world as co-constitutive. The distinction that I am drawing here is between the phenomenological encounter with the world through the senses, producing a 'sense' of the world and the self, and the instrumental, material encounter, through the body, with things.

32 Darwin, C., *The Descent of Man and Selection in Relation to Sex*, London: J Murray, 1871, p. 164.

33 One of eight philosophical treatises on the early Victorian scientific orthodoxy, funded posthumously by the Earl of Bridgewater and published by the Royal Society of London.

34 Bell, C., *The Hand: Its Mechanism and Vital Endowments as Evincing Design*, London: William Clowes and Sons, 1833, p. 157.

35 Bell, 1833.

36 Kidd, J., *On the Adaptation of External Nature to the Physical Condition of Man*, London: William Pickering, 1834, p. 33.

37 For a fuller discussion of this conclusion see 'Acting freely' in *Performance Research*, 14(2), 2009, pp. 103–112.

38 See Needham, P., *Galileo Makes a Book. The First Edition of Sidereus Nuncius, Venice 1610*, Berlin: Akademie Verlag, 2011, pp. 192, 249.

39 Duchenne, G.-B., *The Mechanism of Human Facial Expression*, trans. R.A., Cuthbertson, Cambridge, MA: Cambridge University Press, 1990, p. 19.

40 See Adam Kendon's, *Gesture: Visible Action as Utterance*, Cambridge, MA: Cambridge University Press, 2004 for further discussion, and Book XI, III., 87.

41 For a fulsome historical account, see Joseph Roach's *The Player's Passion: Studies in the Science of Acting*, Ontario, Canada: Associated University Press, 1985.

42 Book XI.

43 Act III, Scene II.

44 In Benedetti 2005, p. 49.

45 Benedetti 2005, p. 70.

46 Dina Rickman, in *Huffington Post*, 28th May 2012.

47 See Charles de Tolnay, *The Youth of Michelangelo*, Princeton, NJ: Princeton University Press, 1947, p. 11.

Chapter 4

1 Allain, P., *Gardzienice: Polish Theatre in Transition*, Amsterdam: Harwood, 1997, p. 66.

2 Kear, A., 'Troublesome amateurs: theatre, ethics and the Labour of Mimesis,' in Matthews, J. and Torevell, D. (eds) *A Life of Ethics and Performance*, Newcastle Upon Tyne: Cambridge Scholars, 2011, p. 102.

3 Kear, 2011, p. 90.

4 Ridout, N., *Stage Fright: Animals and Other Theatrical Problems*, Cambridge, MA: Cambridge University Press, 2006, p. 5.

5 Lehmann, H.-T., *Postdramatic Theatre* (1999, in English, Routledge, 2006) p. 23.

6 Lehmann, 1999.

7 Kear, 2011, p. 99.

8 Kear, 2011, pp. 105–106.

9 Hodge, A., 'Gardzienice's influence in the West', in *Contemporary Theatre Review*, 15(1), 2005, p. 59.

10 Hodge, 2005.

11 Hodge, 2005.

12 Hodge, 2005.

13 Hodge, 2005.

14 Hodge, 2005.

15 Romnaska, M., *The Post-traumatic Theatre of Grotowski and Kantor*, London: Anthem Press, 2012, p. 280.

16 Slowiak, J. and Cuesta, J., *Jerzy Grotowski*, London & New York, NY: Routledge, 2007, p. 25.

17 Allain, 1997, p. 64.

18 Allain, 1997.

19 Allain, 1997.

20 Allain, 1997, p. 65.

21 Allain, 1997.
22 Alison Hodge described Staniewski's 'Ethnographic ambition', in *Hidden Territories: The Theatre of Gardzienice*, London & New York, NY: Routledge, 2004, p. 9 and Staniewski stresses the research purpose of his 'Expeditions to indigenous cultures' (p. 24), but perhaps these activities could be described as cultural tourism, rather than ethnographic research.
23 Staniewski and Hodge, 2004, p. 21.
24 Staniewski and Hodge, 2004.
25 Staniewski and Hodge, 2004.
26 Staniewski and Hodge, 2004, p. 24.
27 Staniewski and Hodge, 2004.
28 I have summarized this controversy in *Training for Performance* (2011, pp. 49–52).
29 I have summarized this controversy in *Training for Performance* (2011, p. 50).
30 London & New York: Routledge, 2002, p. 75.
31 In Staniewski and Hodge, 2004, p. 21.
32 Staniewski and Hodge 2004.
33 Staniewski and Hodge 2004.
34 Staniewski and Hodge 2004, p. 24.
35 Book 1 Chapter 9.
36 Book 1 Chapter 9.
37 Book 9, Chapter 9, lines 9–11.
38 Book 5, Chapter 11, lines 29–31.
39 Book 6, Chapter 6.
40 Book 2, Chapter 2, lines 18–21.
41 See Bartlett, and Collins's, 'Interpretive essay' at the conclusion of their translation of *Aristotle's Nichomanchean Ethics*, London: University of Chicago Press, 2011, p. 254.
42 *Nichomanchean Ethics,* Book 6, Chapter 12, lines 9–10.
43 Amato, J., *On Foot: A History of Walking*, New York, NY & London: University of New York Press, 2005, p. 258.
44 See Bert Mordle's archived history at http://archiveshub.ac.uk/features/brwsa.html.
45 See National Parks webpages at http://www.nationalparks.gov.uk/learningabout/whatisanationalpark/history.
46 Staniewski and Hodge, 2004, p. 21.
47 Staniewski and Hodge, 2004.
48 Robertson, R., *Globalization: Social Theory and Culture*, London: Sage, 1992, p. 1.
49 This is Robertson's reading of Marshall McLuhan's influential idea of the 'Global village', expressed in his 1960 book *Explorations in Communication* (see Robertson, 1992, p. 9).
50 This is Robertson's reading of Marshall McLuhan's influential idea of the 'Global village', expressed in his 1960 book *Explorations in Communication* (see Robertson, 1992, p. 9).

51 Robertson, 1992, pp. 8–32.

52 Agemben, G., 'On potentiality,' in *Potentialities: Collected Essays in Philosophy*, Stanford, CA: Stanford University Press, 1999, pp.177–185.

53 See McDougall, C., *Born to Run*, London: Profile Books & New York, NY: Random House, 2009.

54 Part of a lesser-used sub-title to McDougall's book.

55 McDougall, 2009, p. 4.

56 Ibid.

57 From Taranienko, Z., *Gardzienice: Praktyki Teatralne Wolzimierza Staniewskiego*, Lublin Wydanicto test (unpublished trans. Zubryzcka, A.), 1997, p. 143, also in Alison Hodge's article, 'Wlodzimierz Staniewski' in her *Twentieth-Century Actor Training*, London & New York, NY: Routledge, 2000, p. 238.

58 *Nichomanchean Ethics*, Book 2, Chapter 2, lines 18–21.

59 Shepherd, S., *Theatre, Body, Pleasure*, New York, NY & London: Routledge, 2006, p. 3.

60 Grotowski, J., *Towards a Poor Theatre*, New York, NY: Routledge, 1968, p. 16.

61 P. 35.

62 Donnellan, D., *The Actor and the Target*, London: Nick Hern Books, 2002, p. 2, emphasis in original.

63 See Hodge, 2005.

64 See Hodge's writings on and with Staniewski (Hidden Territories, 2004) as well as her edited collection *Twentieth-Century Actor Training* (2000).

65 Robertson, 1992, p. 9.

66 Robertson, 1992, p. 8.

67 'Globalization as a concept' refers to 'the compression of the world', as well as our increasing awareness of the world as one whole (Robertson, 1992, p. 8).

68 Heelas, P., *The New Age Movement*, Oxford: Blackwell Publishing, 1996, p. 169.

69 I offer this as a cursory, introductory summary of Possamai and Heelas's research that is to follow, and to be unpacked in more detail.

70 Possamai, A., *In Search of New Age Spiritualties*, Aldershot, Hampshire: Ashgate Publishing, 2005, p. 12.

71 See Baumann, Z., 'Postmodern Religion?' in Heelas, P., (ed.) *Religion, Modernity and Postmodernity*, Oxford: Blackwell, 1998, pp. 55–78.

72 Possamai, A., in Hulme, L. and McPhillips, K. (eds) *Popular Spiritualties: The Politics of Contemporary Enchantment*, Aldershot, Hampshire: Ashgate Publishing, 2006, p. 54.

73 Possamai, 2006.

74 In Possamai, 2005, p. 132.

75 Possamai, 2005.

76 Possamai, 2005.

77 In Hulme and McPhillips (eds), 2006, p. 58.

78 Grixti, J., 'Consumer identities: heroic fantasies and the trivialisation of selfhood' in *Journal of Popular Culture*, 28, 1994, p. 214.

79 See Straczynski, J. Michael, with Robinson, James, and Jurgens, *Superman* issues 701–714, DC Comics, June 2010 onwards. My thanks to Lee Miller and Alan Butler – who know a lot more about *Superman* than me! – for your helpful advice on this section of the book.

80 Kear, 2011, p. 89.

Chapter 5

1 All quotes from *Salome* are taken from the 1996 edition, illustrated by Audrey Beardsley, Boston, MA: Brandon Publishing Company.

2 See Benkovitz, M.J., *Aubrey Beardsley: An Account of His Life*, New York, NY: Putnam, 1981, p. 84.

3 See Gottleib's, R., *Lives and Letters*, New York, NY: Farrar, Straus & Giroux, 2001, p. 14.

4 KJV Mark 6: 14–29.

5 Whitson, W.A.M., trans *The Works of Flavius Josephus*, Baltimore, MD: Armstrong and Berry, 1839, Book XVIII, Chapter V, no. 2, p. 267.

6 KJV Matthew 14: 1–12.

7 Our sociality, or perhaps better, our politicality, for Arendt results from our 'human condition of plurality'; from the fact that we are all the same (which is to say, we are all human) and all unique (which is to say, we are each human) and 'this plurality is specifically the condition – not only the *conditio sine qua non*, but the *conditio per quam* – of all political life' (Arendt, H., *The Human Condition*, Chicago, IL: University of Chicago Press, 1958, p. 7).

8 Dana Villa sums up Arendt's position pithily in her writings on the subject when she says that, for Arendt, 'the late modern consciousness is irreducibly instrumentalist' (Villa, D., *Arendt and Heidegger: The Fate of the Political*, Princeton, NJ: University of Princeton Press, 1996, p. 200)

9 This is the same theme preoccupying Heidegger – the problem or, 'question concerning technology'. For both Heidegger and Arendt the question arises as a problem because of faulty thinking on the subject, which frames the question as either primarily instrumental – *how well do things (machines; technology) serve needs?* – and/or anthropocentric (*how well do man-made things serve Man?).* For Arendt specifically the 'problem' exists in the 'automatic motion' of technology which has no recourse to morality, rationality or social realities and thus threatens to 'rule and even destroy the world and things' (Arendt, 1958, p. 151).

10 In contradistinction from labour and work, embroiled in and with things and matter, 'action [is] the only activity that goes on directly between men without the intermediary of things or matter' (Arendt, 1958, p. 7).

11 This is, Arendt claims, in the very nature of beginnings, which is represented by and representative of our human birth: 'the new beginning inherent in birth can make itself felt in the world only because the newcomer possesses the capacity of beginning something anew, that is, of acting' (Arendt, 1958, p. 9); 'that something new is started', Arendt tells her reader, 'which cannot be expected from whatever may have happened before' (pp. 177–8). This 'startling unexpectedness is inherent in all beginnings' and the fact that 'man is capable of action means that the unexpected can be expected from him' and 'that he is able to perform what is infinitely improbable' (pp. 177–8). This is 'only because each man is unique, so that with each birth something uniquely new comes into the world' (pp. 177–8).

12 The idea of community is essential to Arendt's philosophy. Man is an actor in a social world but the community is an audience to action, its judge and a repository for information about its outcome. Sheldon Wolin has suggested that, in Arendt's thought, 'audience is a metaphor for the political community whose nature is to be a community of remembrance' (Wolin, S., 'Hannah Arendt and the ordinance of time' in *Social Research*, 44 (1), 1977, p. 97).

13 Established in 1965, the British Wheel of Yoga is the Sport England recognized national governing body for yoga. It is the largest membership Yoga organization in the United Kingdom with a national network with over 4,000 qualified teachers, running a range of qualifications and courses for personal and professional development, from beginner to In-Service Training for teachers.

14 Singleton, M., *Yoga Body: The Origins of Modern Posture Practice*, Oxford: Oxford University Press, 2010, p. 4.

15 Singleton, 2010, p. 3.

16 See Arendt, in Benhabib, S., *The Reluctant Modernism of Hannah Arendt*, Lanham, MD: Rowman & Littlefield, 2003, p. 199.

17 'In its most elementary form, the human condition of action is implicit even in Genesis ("Male and female created He *them*") if we understand that this story of man's creation is distinguished in principle from the one according to which God originally created Man (adam), "him" and not "them"' (Arendt, 1958, p. 8).

18 KJV Luke I, John I: 6.

19 KJV Luke I: 20.

20 KJV John I: 23.

21 See Weber, M., trans. Parsons, T., *The Protestant Ethic and the Spirit of Capitalism*, Chelmsford, MA: Courier Dover, 2003, p. 181. Although Weber's history of vocation and my assertion here relate primarily to the economies of Europe, United Kingdom and United States, this Protestant doctrine has been widely exported as a consequence of its own functions, playing a considerable part in what we tend to refer to as globalization.

22 *Catechism of the Catholic Church* 2392.

23 Cochran, L., *The Sense of Vocation: A Study of Career and Life Development*, Albany, NY: SUNY Press, 1990, p. vii.

24 Mill, J.S., in Cochran, L., 1990, p. 2.

25 See David, L.J., *A Dictionary of Biblical Tradition in English Literature*, Grand Rapids, MI: Wm. B Eerdmans Publishing, 1992, p. 4. See also Max Weber's, 2003, trans, Alcott Parsons, chapter 3, p. 19, note 1.

26 This is clearly a simplification of the central thesis. See Weber for complete discussion.

27 Ryken, L., *Redeeming the Time: A Christian Approach to Work and Leisure*, Grand Rapids, MI: Baker Books, 1995, p. 200.

28 Owen, D., and Strong, T.B., (eds) *Max Weber: The Vocation Lectures*, Indianapolis, IN: Hackett Publishing Company, 2004, p. xiii.

29 Owen and Strong, 2004.

30 Owen and Strong, 2004.

31 Owen and Strong, 2004.

32 KJV Matthew X.

33 KJV Luke 1:13–15.

34 It seems that Mark emphasizes this observation to reinforce the interpretation that John is Elijah, or that as Luke puts it, John came in 'the spirit and power of Elijah' (1:16–17), who is described in the Old Testament books of Kings as wearing a garment of hair secured with a leather belt (2 Kings 1:8).

35 Gospels of Matthew, Mark and Luke, which are so called because they are largely synchronous in content.

36 Weber, 1958, p. 181.

37 See Knowles, D., *From Pachomius to Ignatius: A Study in the Constitutional History of the Religious Orders*, Oxford: Clarendon Press, 1966 for a detailed history of the development and formalization of monastic rules.

38 Weber, 1958, p. 181.

39 See Foucault, M., *Discipline and Punish: The Birth of the Prison*, New York: Vintage Books (Random House), 1977.

40 Lingis, A., *The Imperative*, Bloomington, IN: University of Indiana Press, p. 166.

41 See González, J.L., *The Story of Christianity, Volume 1: The Early Church to the Dawn of the Reformation*, New York, NY: Harper Collins, 2010, pp. 91–93.

42 For a fuller history and discussion see Weber, or *Training for Performance*, 2011, p. 94.

43 I have written in greater depth and detail about the significance of vocation to performance training in *Training for Performance* (2011, pp. 67–104).

44 See Book of Numbers, 6, lines 1–21.

45 Iconically, by Marx, whose theory of alienation (*Entfremdung*) sees alienation as a systemic result of living in a socially stratified society. Social strata arising from capitalist production, in which workers are unable to determine their own actions (see *Economic and Philosophical Manuscripts*, 1844). Also, specifically in relation to Arendt's critique of the 'rise of the social' in *The Human Condition* which refers to the expansion of the market economy from the early modern period and the increasing accumulation of capital and social wealth. With the rise of the social everything has become an object of production and consumption, of acquisition and exchange; and the distinction between the private and the public blurs – a theme I shall return to in *HEART*.

46 This is not to say that the possibility for alienation and oppression does not exist with the Christian religious paradigm.

47 See Weber 1958.

48 There are, of course, numerous partial safeguards against alienation, some of which come under the auspices of the rather alienated-sounding 'human resources' bureaucratic structure/culture.

49 Davies, J., 'The transformative conditions of psychoanalytic training: an anthropological perspective', in *The British Journal of Psychotherapy*, 24(1), 2008, p. 54.

50 Davies, 2008.

51 Davies, 2008.

52 Davies, 2008, p. 63.

53 See Valentine, M., 'The abuse of power in the analytical setting', in *British Journal of Psychotherapy* 19(2), 1996, pp. 174–181 and Hinshelwood, R.D. 'Questions of training' in *Free Associations* 2, 1985, pp. 7–18.

54 See Davies, 2008.

55 Davies, 2008 p. 56.

56 Davies, 2008.

57 Davies, 2008.

58 Wallace, A., *Culture and Personality*, New York, NY: Random House, 1961.

59 Frank, D. and Frank, J.B., *Persuasion and Healing*. Baltimore, MD: Johns Hopkins Press, (first published 1961), 1993, p. 195.

60 Bandura, A., *Social Learning Theory*. Engelwood Cliffs, NJ: Prentice-Hall, 1977.

61 See Wilson, F.R., *The Hand: How Its Uses Shapes the Brain, Language and Culture*, New York, NY: Pantheon, 1998, pp. 204–207.

62 See Sennett, R., *The Craftsman*, London: Penguin, 2008, p. 190.

63 Specifically, in what follows I address instructional language and do not analyse demonstration that may accompany instruction. Demonstration in relation to corrective touch is addressed in *HAND*.

64 Sennett, 2008, p. 183.

65 Whether or not dead denotation is suitable for practising existing skills as part of a deepening process of training is moot.

66 In Matthews, J. and Torevell, D. (eds) *A Life of Ethics and Performance*, Newcastle Upon Tyne: Cambridge Scholars, 2011, p. 21.

67 Eagleton, T., *Reason, Faith and Revolution: Reflections on the God Debate*, New Haven, CT: Yale University Press, 2009, p. 111.

68 Sennet, 2008, p. 186.
69 See Casement, P., *Further Learning from the Patient*. London: Routledge, 1990, Gellner, E., *The Psychoanalytic Movement*. London: Paladin, 1985, and Valentine (1996) and Hinshelwood (1985).
70 Davies, 2008, p. 51.
71 Sennet, 2008, p. 188.
72 P. 189.
73 Davies, 2008, p. 51.
74 See Singleton, 2010, p. 3. This claim is contested on philological grounds by James Mallinson in 'A Response to Mark Singleton's *Yoga Body*', a paper given at The Academy of Religions conference, San Francisco, 19th November, 2011.
75 Sennet, 2008, p. 191.
76 Vergeer, I., and Roberts, J. 'Movement and stretching imagery during flexibility training', in *Journal of Sports Sciences*, 24(2), February 2006, pp. 197–208.
77 Vegeer and Roberts, 2006, p. 199.
78 Vegeer and Roberts, 2006.
79 Vegeer and Roberts, 2006.
80 Vegeer and Roberts, 2006.
81 P. 197.
82 Vegeer and Roberts, 2006.
83 See Rider, M.S., and Achterberg, J. 'Effect of music-assisted imagery on neutrophils and lymphocytes', in *Biofeedback and Self Regulation*, 14, 1989, pp. 247–257 and Rider, M.S., Achterberg, J., Lawlis, G.F., Goven, A., Toledo, R., & Butler, J.R. 'Effect of immune system imagery on secretory IgA', in *Biofeedback and Self Regulation*, 15, 1990, 317–333.
84 See Vergeer and Roberts for meta-analysis of research in the field.
85 See Mallinson, 2011, p. 3.
86 See Singleton, 2010, p. 3.
87 This is a central argument of Singleton's book *Yoga Body* (2010).
88 Connor, S., 'Beside Himself: Glen Gould and the prospects of performance', a talk broadcast on BBC Radio 3 on Thursday 4 November 1999 as part of an evening exploring the life and work of Glenn Gould. It was produced by Tim Dee and a text of the talk is available at http://www.stevenconnor.com/gould.htm.
89 Arendt, 1958, p. 246.
90 Arendt, 1958, pp. 237, 241.

Chapter 6

1 Pelizzari, U., and Tovagalieri, S., *Manual of Freediving: Underwater on a Single Breath*, Naples, Italy: Idelson Gnochi, 2004, p. 49e.

2   'No limits' freediving involves a weighted sledge suspended on a dive wire
    that carries the diver to the required depth. Other disciplines of freediving
    include 'constant weight' and 'variable weight' freediving, which use a dive
    wire but no weighted sledge in order to travel downwards under water.
    'No limits' freediving allows divers to reach deeper than other disciplines.
3   See Francisco 'Pipín' Ferreras, with Robertson, L., *The Dive: A Story of
    Love and Obsession*, New York, NY: Harper Collins, 2004, p. 1.
4   Francisco, 2004, p. 4.
5   Francisco, 2004.
6   *No Limits,* written and directed by Alison Ellwood, video documentary for
    ESPN Films & ESPNW, 2013.
7   See Serra, C., *The Last Attempt*, Philadelphia, PA: Xlibris Corporation,
    2006.
8   A peculiarity of the Dominican Republic legal system means that events
    such as this are not automatically investigated but rather a family member
    of the deceased must request an investigation. No such request has been
    made.
9   Ferraras with Robertson, 2004, p. 1.
10 Ferraras with Robertson, 2004, p. 1.
11 A 1970s tourism ad campaign for the State of New York, featuring the
    now iconic logo, designed by graphic artist Milton Glasser.
12 Shields, S., *Speaking from the Heart: Gender and the Social Meaning of
    Emotion*, Cambridge, MA: Cambridge University Press, 2002, p. 3.
13 Shields, 2002, p. 1.
14 Shields, 2002.
15 Shields, 2002, p. 2.
16 In Shields, 2002, p. 3.
17 This is a necessarily simplified history of biomedical understanding of
    the heart. For a fuller account see Ole Martin Høystad's, *A History of the
    Heart*, London: Reaktion, 2007.
18 Galen, trans., Tallmadge-May, M., Ithaca, NY: Cornell University Press,
    1968, p. 292.
19 In Keele K.D., 'Leonardo da Vinci, and the movement of the heart', in
    Proceedings of the Royal Society of Medicine, 44, 1951, pp. 209–213.
20 Roach, J., *The Player's Passion: Studies in the Science of Acting*,
    Cranbury, NJ, London & Ontario: Associated University Press, 1985,
    p. 39.
21 Roach, 1985.
22 Burton, R., *The Anatomy of Melancholy*, New York, NY: W.J., Widdleton,
    1870 Volume 1, Part 1, Section 2, p. 346.
23 Act IV Scene V.
24 Wright in Roach, 1985, p. 39.
25 Roach, 1985.
26 Garrick himself refers to 'electrical fire', or a lack thereof, in his famous
    letter to Sturz (1769) on the acting of Mlle. Clarion, picking up on new

language and terminology in circulation and foreshadowing the publication of Galvani's theories (1780). For more, see Roach 1985, especially the chapter, 'Nature Still, but Nature Mechanized', pp. 58–99.

27 Dixon argues that emotions came into being only during the nineteenth century, emerging as a distinct psychological category displacing other categories such as appetites, passions, sentiments and affections. 'The emotions' is now an over-inclusive category undermining subtle discourse on the wide range of mental states humans are capable of (See Dixon, T., *Passions to Emotions: The Creation of a Secular Psychological Category*, Cambridge, MA: Cambridge University Press, 2003).

28 In Shields, 2002, p. 5.

29 Shields, 2002.

30 Shields, 2002.

31 This is a generalized, summary definition, leaning towards the more commonly accepted 'folk' theory of emotion offered by Cannon and Bard. The also popular James-Lange theory see things slightly differently in contending that emotional shifts arise after agitation of the heart muscle rather than before (see Cannon, Walter, December 1927, "The James-Lange Theory of Emotions: A Critical Examination and an Alternative Theory". *The American Journal of Psychology 39:* 106–124).

32 Pelizzari and Tovagalieri, 2004, p. 46.

33 Pelizzari & Tovagalieri, 2004, p. 75.

34 Pelizzari & Tovagalieri, 2004, p. 49.

35 Pelizzari & Tovagalieri, 2004, p. 131–132.

36 Pelizzari & Tovagalieri, 2004, p. 75.

37 Pelizzari & Tovagalieri, 2004, p. 95.

38 Joseph Roach also uses the barometer metaphor (Roach, 1985, as does Fay Alberti in her book *Matters of the Heart: History, Medicine and Emotion*, Oxford: Oxford University Press, 2010, p. 3.

39 See Jean Benedetti on Diderot in his book *The Art of Acting*, London: Methuen Drama, 2005, pp. 79–92.

40 See Hochschild, A.R., *The Managed Heart: Commercialization of Human Feeling*, Berkeley, CA, Los Angeles, CA, & London: University of California Press, (First published 1983), 2012, p. ix.

41 Hochschild is more preoccupied by those aspects of Stanislavski's theories association with his earlier interests in Ribot's 'affective memory', and his techniques of what is often called 'emotion memory' than by his later interests in 'the method of physical actions', or working from the 'outside in' as well as the 'inside out' (for history of Stanislavski's thought see Carnicke, S., *Stanislavsky in Focus: An Acting Master for the Twenty-First Century*, London & New York, NY: Routledge Theatre Classics, 2008, especially p. 153).

42 Hochschild, 2012, p. 229.

43 In Matthews, J. and Torevell, D. (eds), *A Life of Ethics and Performance*, Newcastle Upon Tyne: Cambridge Scholars, 2011, pp. 85–115.

44 In Hochschild, 2012, p. 203.
45 Hochschild, 2012, p. 205.
46 Ibid.
47 Hochschild, 2012, p. 192.
48 In Matthews and Torevell (eds), 2011, p. 37.
49 Matthews and Torevell (eds), 2011.
50 Pp. 38–39.
51 Hochschild, 2012, p. 245.
52 I use Hosein's essay here rather than the numerous works on gender control specifically (DeBeauvoir, Irigaray, Butler etc.) because of his meta-analytical perspective on these accounts and schematic summary of their models.
53 Hosein in Matthews and Torevell (eds), 2011, p. 43.
54 Matthews and Torevell (eds), 2011.
55 Hochschild, 2012, p. 205.
56 In Matthews, J., *Training for Performance*, London: Methuen Drama, 2011, p. 201.
57 In Matthews, J., *Training for Performance*, London: Methuen Drama, 2011, pp. 201, 202.
58 In *No Limits*, 2013.
59 *No Limits*, 2013.
60 Pelizzari and Tovagalieri, 2004, p. 24.
61 P. 23.
62 P. 23.
63 P. 24.
64 Ferraras with Robertson, 2004, p. 4.
65 P. 5.
66 P. 4.
67 In *No Limits,* 2013.
68 Ferraras with Robertson, 2004, p. 4.
69 P. 5.
70 P. 5.
71 See Ferraras with Robertson, 2004, back cover.
72 In *No Limits*, 2013.
73 *No Limits*, 2013.

Chapter 7

1 At London 2012 Olympics new protocol was introduced such that the two highest and the two lowest scores were disregarded from the aggregate total. This was done to mitigate the effect any one judge can have on an overall dive score.
2 Williams, R., writing in *The Guardian,* August 11th 2008.

3 Slater, M., writing for *BBC Sport Online*, Sunday 12th August, 2012.
4 *Ellie Barker*, writing for ITV West Country, Sunday, 12th August, 2012.
5 Folley, M., writing for *Daily Mail,* Saturday 11th August, 2012.
6 For examples see the 'Rocky' film series, especially *Rocky IV*, in which the eponymous fighter tackles an opponent from the USSR.
7 White, D., writing for *Telegraph*, Sunday 12th August, 2012.
8 In Slater, 2012.
9 I thank Ben Dunks for his willingness to meet me and to discuss this training and for permitting me to draw from our conversations and ongoing correspondence in composing this chapter.
10 Skinner Releasing Technique, originated by Joan Skinner, emerged around the same time as pedestrian movement in America in the 1960s, sharing some concerns with pedestrian dance's task-based efficiency. According to Cynthia Novak, in the 1970s 'Contact Improvisation was joined with release to a large degree' in England, where Mary Fulkerston, one of Steve Paxton's early contact collaborators, began teaching at Dartington College, in Devon (see *Sharing the Dance: Contact Improvisation and American Culture,* Madison, WI & London: University of Wisconsin Press, 1990, p. 170). Perhaps accordingly, in the United Kingdom, the term 'Contemporary Dance' is often used to encompass this paradigm of techniques.
11 Volume 52, issue 5.
12 Ibid., p. 35.
13 *Great Moments in Olympic History: Swimming and Diving,* New York: Rosen Publishing Group, 2007, p. 16.
14 In interview with the author, September 2013.
15 Dunks told me about watching the young divers he had been working with practise diving from a board into a poll after his class. For some, trying to practise the lessons of release confused their jumping technique and had negative effects on their performance, while others achieved more height, finding a new rhythm in their take-off.
16 Cooper-Albright, A., *Choreographing Difference: The Body and Identity in Contemporary Dance*, Middleton, CT: Wesleyan University Press, 1997, p. 20.
17 *Theatre Papers (1977–78)*, No. 4, 'Steve Paxton in interview with Peter Hulton', Director: Peter Hulton, DVD-ROM produced by Dartington College of Arts, Theatre Dept. and archived at Exeter University at http://spa.exeter.ac.uk/drama/research/exeterdigitalarchives.
18 *Theatre Papers (1977–78)*, No. 4, 'Steve Paxton in interview with Peter Hulton', Director: Peter Hulton, DVD-ROM produced by Dartington College of Arts, Theatre Dept. and archived at Exeter University at http://spa.exeter.ac.uk/drama/research/exeterdigitalarchives.
19 Burt, R., *Judson Dance Theatre: Performative Traces*, Abingdon, Oxon & New York, NY: Routledge, 2006, p. 7.
20 Burt, 2006.

21 Burt, 2006, pp. 116–118.

22 According to Cynthia Novak, *Magnesium* is generally cited as the first
work of Contact Improvisation (Novak, C., *Sharing the Dance: Contact
Improvisation and American Culture*, Madison, WI & London: University of
Wisconsin Press, 1990, p. 61).

23 Goldman, D., *I want to be Ready: Improvised Dance as a Practice of
Freedom*, Ann Arbor, MI : University of Michigan Press, p. 105.

24 Lefebvre had been a 'powerful influence' during the student revolts
in Paris in May 1968 and has been depicted as 'the "father" of that
movement' (see Middleton's, S., *Henri Lefebvre and Education: Space,
History, Theory*, Abingdon, Oxon & New York, NY: Routledge, 2014,
p. 5). Lefebvre influence in America, and specifically on the 1960s politics
of Greenwich village, is less direct but rather he might be seen as one
figure within a generalized increased interest in, and politics of 'the
everyday' in the 1960s.

25 LeFebevre, H., *Critique of Everyday Life*, London: Verso, 1991, p. 21.

26 Lefebvre, H., trans. Regular, Catherine *Rhythmanalysis*, Continuum, 2004.

27 See *La Production de l'espace* 1974.

28 Homi K. Bhabha offers a postcolonial perspective on thirdspace in *The
Location of Culture* (1994) but have chosen to trace Oldenburg's ideas
through to Soja because of Soja's efforts to synthesize and incorporate
the thinking from Lefebvre and Foucault with postcolonial theorization from
Bhabha, and Spivak, Hooks and Said.

29 In Matthews, J. and Torevell, D. (eds) *A Life of Ethics and Performance*,
Newcastle Upon Tyne: Cambridge Scholars, 2011, p. 62.

30 See Soja, E., *ThirdSpace: Journeys to Los Angeles and Other Real-and-
Imagined Places*, Oxford: Blackwell, 1996, p. 57.

31 See Oldenburg, R., *The Great Good Place*, New York, NY: Paragon
Books, 1989.

32 Some twentieth-century public art practice has also sought to become
a practical example of such a thirdspace, with varying degrees of
success. Turner Prize–winner Jeremy Deller re-enacted a moment of civil
upheaval – commissioning historic battle re-enactors to recreate the clash
between police and striking miners at Orgeave in the 1980s – in an effort
to allow participants to reappraise the historic events and reconsider their
future position in relation. However, the social capital assumed by such
a play methodology is as apt to alienate as it is to include, or to channel
grievances and residual tensions (see Mike Figgis's video for ArtAngel
Media and Channel 4, 2001).

33 See Conroy, C., *Theatre and the Body*, Basingstoke, Hampshire: Palgrave
MacMillan, 2009.

34 Blau, H., *Nothing in Itself: Complexions of Fashion*, Bloomington, IN:
Indiana University Press, 1999, p. 9.

35 In Matthews, J., *Training for Performance*, London: Methuen Drama,
2001, p. 60.

36 Chemero, A., 'Radical Empiricism through the ages', review of Harry Heft's *Ecological Psychology in Contexts: James Gibson, Roger Barker, and the Legacy of William James' Radical Empiricism*, in *Contemporary Psychology*, 48, 2003, pp. 18–20.

37 Novak, 1990, p. 66.

38 See Foucault's *Discipline and Punish* and Jon Mckenzie's *Perform or Else.* McKenzie convincingly suggests that in the late twentieth-century 'performance' supplanted 'discipline' as the predominant onto-historical category for understanding our social existence. He proposed, 'performance will be to the twentieth and twenty first centuries what discipline was to the eighteenth and nineteenth: an onto-historical formation of power and knowledge' (New York, NY & London: Routledge, 2000, p. 174).

39 In Tom Harper, writing in *Independent,* 3rd August 2012.

40 Matt Blake, 'torture or training', for *Mail Online,* 1st August 2012.

41 'The Week Staff' writing for *The Week,* 2nd August 2012.

42 In Ian Ransom and Ryan McNeil's 'Medals obscure cost of China's State-run sports programme' for *Reuters,* Thursday 9th August 2012.

43 In Ransom and McNeil, 2012.

44 In Ransom and McNeil, 2012.

45 In Ransom and McNeil, 2012.

46 In Ransom and McNeil, 2012.

47 I should be clear that, in reading Jon McKenzie, I am not suggesting that discipline, in the Foucauldian sense, does not exist anymore but rather that performance may have supplanted discipline from its predominant position in systems of social control.

48 The image of Bentham's panotican prison was evoked by Foucault as a metaphor for modern 'disciplinary' societies and the all-pervasive inclination to observe and normalize: 'On the whole, therefore, one can speak of the formation of a disciplinary society in this movement that stretches from the enclosed disciplines, a sort of social "quarantine", to an indefinitely generalizable mechanism of "panopticism"' (Foucault, M., *Discipline and Punish: The Birth of the Prison*, London: Penguin, 1991 reprint, p. 216).

49 See Mulvey, L., 'Visual pleasure and narrative cinema', originally published in *Screen*, 16(3), Autumn 1975, pp. 6–18.

50 See Shepherd's *Theatre, Body and Pleasure* for discussion of the phenomenon in relation to binaries of male/female, active/passive and mind/body.

51 Matthews, J., *Training for Performance*, London: Methuen Drama, 2011, pp. 40–66.

52 The requirement for obedience in training is ontological; it is in the nature of the category of training itself, but, in the historical moment described throughout this chapter, the metabolic nature of the challenge to remain whole entails contending with a range of 'new' problems (proposed by hybridity, globalization, hyper-reality etc.).

53 In Ransom and McNeil, 2012.

54 Published online at Tomdaley.tv, 31st May 2012.

55 Published online at Tomdaley.tv, 31st May 2012.

56 Lingis, A., *The Imperative*, Bloomington, IN: Indian University Press, 1998, p. 1.

57 Lingis, 1998.

58 Lingis, 1998, p. 2.

Chapter 8

1 I am referring here to the difference between the discrete body, defined by Herbert Blau, persisting throughout different body concepts (see p. 143 of *EAR*) and the various social and cultural 'bodies' that form the basis of Simon Shepherd's work, *Theatre, Body, Pleasure*, discussed in *ANATOMY* (see pp. 14–15).

2 Robertson, R., *Globalization: Social Theory and Culture*, London: Sage, 1992, pp. 8, 183.

3 This is one of the theses I develop in *FOOT* with reference to Gardzienice and the Tarahumara.

4 See *FOOT*, p. 66, and *ANATOMY* p. 9.

5 In fact, for the preeminent semiologist De Saussure, there is no encounter with the world except through signification. This is one of the central claims of his *Course in General Linguistics* (trans. Wade Baskin, London: Fontana, 1974).

6 See *ANATOMY*, pp. 28–29.

7 See *ANATOMY*, pp. 16–18 and *FOOT* pp. 67–68. See also, *HEART* pp. 123–125 for one history of this discourse.

8 See *EAR*, pp. 143–144.

9 See Herbert Blau and discussion thereof in *EAR*, p. 143.

10 This is the meaning of 'work', and for *animal laborans* (see *MOUTH*, pp. 80–82).

11 See *HEART*, p. 123.

12 See *HEART*, pp. 125–127.

13 In the transformation of generic to existing potential (see *FOOT*, pp. 66–67).

14 By the displacement of *animal laborans* by *homo faber* (see *MOUTH*, pp. 80–81.

15 In the realization and perpetuation through time of social values (see *ANATOMY*, p. 9).

16 Following de Beauvoir ('one is not born but rather becomes a woman') to show that identity comes into being only through its necessary social performance (Butler, *Gender Trouble,* 1990 1990, p. 8).

17 I am referring here to our social (Dewey and Butler) lives and our private selves (Aristotle), and to our qualities as *homo faber* and *animal laborans*.

18 This is the social life that Dewey refers to (see *ANATOMY*, p. 9).

19 See Arendt on 'action' in *MOUTH*, pp. 81, 88, 104.

20 Aristotle translated by Agamben in *Potentialities,* Stanford, CA: Stanford University Press, 1999, p. 18.

21 In Matthews, J. and Torevell, D. (eds) *A Life of Ethics and Performance*, Newcastle Upon Tyne: Cambridge Scholars, 2011, p. 138.

22 Ridout, N., *Stage Fright: Animals and Other Theatrical Problems*, Cambridge, MA: Cambridge University Press, 2004, p. 60.

23 Ridout, 2004.

24 Castellucci, R., 'The animal being on stage', in *Performance Research*, 5(2), p. 25.

25 See *HEART*, pp. 124–126.

26 Problematic in the sense that they require more or less voluntary and conscious attention; they are given but not static conditions, or rather they are given conditions of instability and flux.

27 López, J. and Potter, G. (eds), *After Postmodernism*, London: Athlone Press, 2005, p. 3.

28 One good example of this is the 'gender trouble' defined by Judith Butler, prompted by these challenges to epistemology itself, that I described in *ANATOMY* (pp. 28–29).

29 Lopez and Potter see this as one of the, if not the principal, achievements of postmodernism (2005, p. 4).

30 See Veeser, H., *The New Historicism*, London & New York, NY: Routledge, 1989.

31 Lopez and Potter, 2005, p. 3.

32 See Classen, C., *The Book of Touch*, Oxford: Berg, 2005.

33 This might depend on whether or not the postmodern moment is passed or merely passing and, since there seems to be no good consensus on what times after postmodern times might be, or be called, this seems the most suitable way to pose this thought.

34 See *HEART*, pp. 113–116.

35 Some cultural materialists may choose to adopt a radical position and say that there are no relations that are outside of commerce, and there never have been. This position looks on at the world as a structural proposition and contradicts or dismisses individuals' sense of their own imbrication with commercial forces; as Kear has written (in *A Life of Ethics and Performance*, 2011, pp. 85–114) maybe even free time is commodified. However, the point I am making is that increasingly commercial imperatives are self-evident, and must consciously be dealt with by individuals in this developed global culture in ways that they did not previously require to be dealt with.

36 This is a key theme in Butler's *Gender Trouble* (1990).

37 This may be in part due to the wide spread of theories, such as Butler's.
38 See *HEART*, pp. 125–128.
39 See *FOOT*, pp. 70–73.
40 See Ross, Heelas and Possami in *FOOT*, pp. 70–71.
41 See *MOUTH*, pp. 83–87.
42 For examples see BBC3's annual *Young Talent of Year*, which has
    included competitions for beauticians, gardeners, tailors, plumbers,
    butchers and farmers.
43 See Lingis on the 'disciplinary archipelago' in *MOUTH* (p. 87).
44 See *EAR*, pp. 150–152.
45 I am now suggesting that discipline does not exist anymore but rather,
    following McKenzie, Butler and others, that it has been supplanted by
    performance as the key epistemological and ontological paradigm of
    social existence.
46 See *EAR*, pp. 147–150.
47 Lingis, A., *The Imperative*, Bloomington IN: University of Indiana Press,
    1998, p. 166.

Chapter 9

1   Examples include *The Right to Speak* (Routledge, 1992), *The Actor
    Speaks* (Palgrave MacMillan, 2000) and *Speaking Shakespeare* (Palgrave
    MacMillan, 2002).
2   *Australasian Drama Studies*, No. 50, April 2007, pp. 170–182.
3   Kirby, A., *Philosophy Now* (58), November/December, 2006.
4   Kirby, 2006.
5   Ridout in Matthews, J. and Torevell, D. (eds), *A Life of Ethics and
    Performance*, Newcastle Upon Tyne: Cambridge Scholars, 2011, p. 9.
6   Read, A., *Theatre, Intimacy and Engagement: The Last Human Venue*,
    Basingstoke, Hampshire & New York, NY: Palgrave MacMillan, 2008,
    p. 273.
7   Arendt first dealt with this in her first major book *The Origins of
    Totalitarianism* (1951), before *The Human Condition* (1958) and her serial
    reporting for *The New Yorker* on the trial of Adolf Eichmann in 1961.
8   This represents at least one possible way of accounting for life after the
    disciplinary episteme, as described by Jon McKenzie and referenced
    throughout this book.

BIBLIOGRAPHY

Ajzenstat, O., 'Levinas vs Levinas: Hebrew, Greek and Linguistic justice', in *Philosophy and Rhetoric*, 38(2), 2005, pp.145–158.

Alberti, F.B., *Matters of the Heart: History, Medicine and Emotion*, Oxford: Oxford University Press, 2010.

Allain, P., *Gardzienice: Polish Theatre in Transition*, Amsterdam, The Netherlands: Harwood Publishing Press, 1997.

Amato, J., *On Foot: A History of Walking*, New York, NY & London: New York University Press, 2005.

Arendt, H., *Human Condition*, Chicago: University of Chicago Press, 1958.

Aristotle, trans. Tredennick, H. *The Metaphysics I-IV*, Cambridge, MA: Harvard University Press, 1933, reprinted 1989.

Aristotle, trans. Ogle, W., *On the Parts of Animals*, Whitefish, MT: Kessinger Publishing Co., 2004.

Bartlett, R.C. and Collins, S.D. (trans.) *Aristotle's Nichomanchean Ethics*, Chicago, IL: University of Chicago Press, 2011.

Baumann, Z., 'Postmodern Religion?', in Heelas, P. (ed.) *Religion, Modernity and Post-Modernity*, Oxford: Blackwell Publishing, 1998, pp. 55–78.

Bell, C., *Bridgewater Treatise IV: The Hand: Its Mechanism and Vital Endowments as Evincing Design*, Philadelphia, PA: Carey, Lea & Blanchard, 1833.

Benedetti, J., *The Art of the Actor*, London: Methuen Drama, 2005.

Benhabib, S., *The Reluctant Modernism of Hannah Arendt*, Lanham, MD: Rowman & Littlefield, 2003.

Benkovitz, M.J., *Aubrey Beardsley: An Account of His Life*, New York, NY: Putnam, 1981.

Blau, H., *Nothing in Itself: Complexions of Fashion*, Bloomington, IN: Indiana University Press, 1999.

Bruce, S., *Religion in the Modern World: From Cathedrals to Cults*, Oxford: Oxford University Press, 1996.

Burton, R., *The Anatomy of Melancholy*, New York, NY: W.J. Widdleton, 1870.

Carnicke, S.M., *Stanislavsky in Focus: An Acting Master for the Twenty First Century*, Abingdon, Oxon & New York, NY: Routledge, 1998.

Carver, R., *All of Us*, London: Harvill, 1996.

Casement, P., *Further Learning from the Patient*, London: Routledge, 1990.

Castellucci, R., 'The animal being on stage', in *Performance Research*, 5(2), 1991, pp. 23–28.

Chemero, A., 'Radical empiricism through the ages', review of Harry Heft's Ecological Psychology in Contexts: James Gibson, Roger Barker, and the Legacy of William James' radical empiricism, in *Contemporary Psychology*, 48, 2003, pp. 18–20.

Classen, C., *The Book of Touch*, Oxford: Berg, 2005.

Cochran, L., *The Sense of Vocation: A Study of Career and Life Development*, Albany, NY: SUNY Press, 1990.

Darwin, C., *The Descent of Man and Selection in Relation to Sex*, London: J. Murray, 1871.

Davies, J., 'The transformative conditions of psychoanalytic training: an anthropological perspective', in *The British Journal of Psychotherapy*, 24(1), 2008, pp. 50–64.

de Tolnay, C., *The Youth of Michelangelo*, Princeton, NJ: Princeton University Press, 1947.

Dewey, J., *Democracy and Education*, Los Angeles, CA: Indo-European Publishing (first published 1916), 2012.

Dixon, T., *Passions to Emotions: The Creation of a Secular Psychological Category*, Cambridge, MA: Cambridge University Press, 2003.

Duchenne, Guillaume de Boulogne, trans. Cuthbertson, R.A., *The Mechanism of Human Facial Expression*, Cambridge, MA: Cambridge University Press, 1990.

Eagleton, T., *Reason, Faith and Revolution: Reflections on the God Debate*, New Haven, CT: Yale University Press, 2009.

Foucault, M., *Discipline and Punish: The Birth of the Prison*, New York, NY: Vintage Books (Random House), 1977.

Francisco 'Pipín' Ferreras, with Robertson, L., *The Dive: A Story of Love and Obsession*, New York, NY: Harper Collins, 2004.

Furse, A., 'Being touched', in Matthews, J. and Torevell, D. (eds) *A Life of Ethics and Performance*, Newcastle Upon Tyne: Cambridge Scholars Publishing, 2011.

Galen, *On the Usefulness of Body Parts*, Ithaca, NY: Cornell University Press, 1968.

Gellner, E., *The Psychoanalytic Movement*, London: Paladin, 1985.

González, J.L., *The Story of Christianity, Volume 1: The Early Church to the Dawn of the Reformation*, New York, NY: Harper Collins, 2010.

Gottleib, R., *Lives and Letters*, New York, NY: Farrar, Straus & Giroux, 2001.

Grixti, J., 'Consumer identities: heroic fantasies and the trivialisation of selfhood', in *Journal of Popular Culture*, 28, 1994, pp. 207–228.

Heelas, P., 'The new age in cultural context: the premodern, the modern and the postmodern', in *Religion*, 23, 1993, pp. 103–116.

——, *The New Age Movement*, Oxford: Blackwell Publishing, 1996.

——, 'Prosperity and the new age movement. The efficacy of spiritual economics', in Wilson, B., and Cressell, J. (eds). *New Religious Movements: Challenges and Response*, London: Routledge, 1999, pp. 49–77.

Heidegger, M., trans. Schuwer, A. and Rojcewicz. R., *Parmenides*, Bloomington, IN: Indiana University Press, 1992.

Hinshelwood, R.D., Questions of training, in *Free Associations*, 2, 1985, pp. 7–18.

Hochschild, A.R., *The Managed Heart: Commercialization of Human Feeling*, Berkeley, CA, Los Angeles, CA & London: University of California Press (First published 1983), 2012.

Høystad, O.M., *A History of the Heart*, London: Reaktion, 2007.

Hulme, L. and McPhillips, K. (eds) *Popular Spiritualties: The Politics of Contemporary Enchantment*, Aldershot, Hampshire: Ashgate Publishing, 2006.

Jeffrey, D.L., *A Dictionary of Biblical Tradition in English Literature*, Grand Rapids, MI: Wm. B. Eerdmans Publishing, 1992.

Kear, A., 'Troublesome amateurs: theatre, ethics and the labour of mimesis', in Matthews, J. and Torevell, D. (eds) *A Life of Ethics and Performance*, Newcastle Upon Tyne: Cambridge Scholars Publishing, 2001.

Keele, K.D., 'Leonardo da Vinci, and the movement of the heart', in *Proceedings of the Royal Society of Medicine*, 44, 1951, pp. 209–213.

Kidd, J., *Bridgewater Treatise II: On the Adaptation of External Nature to the Physical Condition of Man*, Philadelphia, PA: Carey, Lea & Blanchard, 1836.

Knowles, D., *From Pachomius to Ignatius: A Study in the Constitutional History of the Religious Orders*, Oxford: Clarendon Press, 1966.

Kohn, T., 'The Aikido Body: expressions of group identities and self discoveries in martial arts training', in Dyck, N. and Archetti, E.P. (eds) *Sport, Dance and Embodied Identities*, Oxford: Berg, 2003.

Krasner, D., 'Starsberg, Adler, Meisner: method acting', in Hodge, A. (ed.) *Twentieth Century Actor Training*, New York, NY & London: Routledge, 2000, pp.129–150.

Lingis, A., *The Imperative*, Bloomington, IN: University of Indiana Press, 1998.

Loukes, R., 'Tracing bodies: researching psychophysical training for performance through practice', in *Performance Research*, 8(4), 2003, pp. 54–60.

Matthews, J., *Training for Performance*, London: Methuen Drama, 2011.

McKenzie, J., *Perform or Else: From Discipline to Performance*, London & New York, NY: Routledge, 2001.

Meisner, S., *Sandford Meisner on Acting*, New York, NY: Random House, 1987.

Mulvey, L., 'Visual pleasure and narrative cinema', originally Published in *Screen*, 16(3), Autumn 1975, pp. 6–18.

Myers, D.G., 'The New Historicism in literary study', in *Academic Questions*, 2(1), Winter 1988/89, pp. 27–36.

Oida, Y. and Marhsall, L., *The Invisible Actor*, London: Taylor & Francis, 1997.

Owen, D. and Strong, T.B. (eds) *Max Weber: The Vocation Lectures*, Indianapolis, IN: Hackett Publishing Company, 2004.

Paglia, C., 'Junk bonds and Corporate Raiders: Academe in the Hour of the Wolf', reprinted in *Sex, Art and American Culture: New Essays*, New York, NY: Vintage (Random House), 1992.

Parkins, W., 'Oprah Winfrey's change your life TV and the spiritual everyday', in *Journal of Media and Cultural Studies*, 15(2), 2001, pp. 145–157. London: Taylor & Francis.

Pelizzari, U. and Tovagalieri, S., *Manual of Freediving: Underwater on a Single Breath*, Naples, Italy: Idelson Gnochi, 2004.

Pitches, J., *Vesevold Meyerhold*, New York, NY & London: Routledge, 2003.

Possamai, A., *In Search of New Age Spiritualties*, Aldershot, Hampshire: Ashgate Publishing, 2005.

Rickman, D., 'Tony Blair at Leveson: pictures of the Prime Minister Pointing' in *Huffington Post*, posted 28 May 2012, accessible at http://www .huffingtonpost.co.uk/2012/05/28/tony-blair-at-leveson-pictures-blair -pointing_n_1549932.html, accessed on 19 September 2012.

Rider, M.S. and Achterberg, J., 'Effect of music-assisted imagery on neutrophils and lymphocytes', in *Biofeedback and Self Regulation*, 14, 1989, pp. 247–257.

Rider, M.S., Achterberg, J., Lawlis, G.F., Goven, A., Toledo, R., and Butler, J.R., 'Effect of immune system imagery on secretory IgA', in *Biofeedback and Self Regulation*, 15, 1990, pp. 317–333.

Ridout, N., *Stage Fright: Animals and Other Theatrical Problems*, Cambridge, MA: Cambridge University Press, 2006.

Roach, J., *The Player's Passion: Studies in the Science of Acting*, Cranbury, NJ, London & Ontario: Associated Universities Press, 1985.

——, *The Player's Passion: Studies in the Science of Acting*, New York, NY & London: Routledge (first published 1983), 2001.

Roberts, R., 'Power and empowerment: new age managers and the dialectics of modernity/postmodernity', in *Religion Today*, 9(3), 1994, pp. 3–13.

Romnaska, M., *The Post-Traumatic Theatre of Grotowski and Kantor*, London: Anthem Press, 2012.

Ross, A., *Strange Weather: Culture, Science and Technology in the Age of Limits*, London & New York, NY: Verso, 1991.

Ryken, L., *Redeeming the Time: A Christian Approach to Work and Leisure*, Grand Rapids, MI: Baker Books, 1995.

Serra, C., *The Last Attempt*, Bloomington, IN: Xlibris Corporation, 2006.

Sennett, R., *The Craftsman*, London: Penguin Books, 2008.

Shepherd, S., *Theatre, Body, Pleasure*, Oxford & New York, NY: Routledge, 2006.

Shields, S., *Speaking from the Heart: Gender and the Social Meaning of Emotion*, Cambridge, MA: Cambridge University Press, 2002.

Singleton, M., *Yoga Body: The Origins of Modern Posture Practice*, Oxford: Oxford University Press, 2010.

Slowiak, J. and Cuesta, J., *Jerzy Grotowski*, London & New York, NY: Routledge, 2007.

Sobel, D., *Galileo's Daughter*, London: Fourth Estate, 1999.

Soja, E., *ThirdSpace: Journeys to Los Angeles and Other Real-and-Imagined Places*, Oxford: Blackwell, 1996. University Press, 1985.

Spolin, V., *Theatre Games for Rehearsal*, Evanston, IL: Northwestern, 1985.

St. John, G. (ed.) *Victor Turner and Contemporary Cultural Performance*, New York, NY & Oxford: Berghahn Books, 2008.

Staniewski, W. and Hodge, A., *Hidden Territories: The Theatre of Gardzienice*, New York, NY & London: Routledge, 2004.

Stark, S., *Diderot*, New York, NY: The Rosen Publishing Group, 2006.

Tallis, R., *The Hand: A Philosophical Inquiry in Human Being*, Edinburgh: Edinburgh University Press, 2003.

Valentine, M., 'The abuse of power in the analytical setting', in *British Journal of Psychotherapy*, 19(2), 1996, pp. 174–181.

Van Hove, H., *'L'emergence d'un 'marche spirituel' religieux'*, in *Social Compass*, 46(2), 1999, pp. 161–172.

Vanhoozer, K.J., *The Drama of Doctrine: A Canonical-Linguistic Approach to Christian Theology*, Westminster, Greater London: John Knox Press, 2005.

Veeser, H., *The New Historicism*, London & New York, NY: Routledge, 1989.

Vergeer, I. and Roberts, J., 'Movement and stretching imagery during flexibility training', in *Journal of Sports Sciences*, 24(2), February 2006, pp. 197–208.

Weber, M., trans. Parsons, T., *The Protestant Ethic and the Spirit of Capitalism*, Chelmsford, MA: Courier Dover 2003.

Welton, M., *Feeling Theatre*, Basingstoke, Hampshire: Palgrave MacMillan, 2011.

Whitson, W.A.M., trans. *The Works of Flavius Josephus*, Baltimore, MD: Armstrong and Berry, 1839.

Wilson, F.R., *The Hand: How Its Uses Shapes the Brain, Language and Culture*, New York, NY: Pantheon, 1998.

Wolford, L., *Grotowski's Objective Drama Research*, Jackson, MS: University Press of Mississippi, 1996.

INDEX

Note: Locators followed by the letter 'n' refer to notes.